The Translator

DAVID FRYE teaches anthropology of Latin America at the University of Michigan. His translations include *First New Chronicle and Good Government* by Guaman Poma de Ayala and *The Mangy Parrot* by José Joaquín Fernández de Lizardi.

The Editor

ILAN STAVANS is Lewis-Sebring Professor in Latin American and Latino Culture at Amherst College. He is the author of many books, among them *Spanglish: The Making of a New American Language*. He is also general editor of *The Norton Anthology of Latino Literature*.

A NORTON CRITICAL EDITION

Álvar Núñez Cabeza de Vaca
CHRONICLE OF THE NARVÁEZ EXPEDITION

A NEW TRANSLATION

CONTEXT

CRITICISM

Translated by David Frye
UNIVERSITY OF MICHIGAN

Edited by Ilan Stavans
AMHERST COLLEGE

W • W • NORTON & COMPANY • *New York* • *London*

W. W. Norton & Company has been independent since its founding in 1923, when William Warder Norton and Mary D. Herter Norton first published lectures delivered at the People's Institute, the adult education division of New York City's Cooper Union. The firm soon expanded its program beyond the Institute, publishing books by celebrated academics from America and abroad. By mid-century, the two major pillars of Norton's publishing program—trade books and college texts—were firmly established. In the 1950s, the Norton family transferred control of the company to its employees, and today—with a staff of four hundred and a comparable number of trade, college, and professional titles published each year—W. W. Norton & Company stands as the largest and oldest publishing house owned wholly by its employees.

Production Manager: Sean Mintus

Library of Congress Cataloging-in-Publication Data

Nuñez Cabeza de Vaca, Alvar, 16th cent.
   [Relación y comentarios. English]
   Chronicle of the Narváez expedition : a new translation :
contexts, criticism / translated by David Frye ; edited by Ilan
Stavans. — 1st ed.
      p. cm. — (Norton critical edition)
   Includes bibliographical references.
   ISBN 978-0-393-91815-1 (pbk.)
   1. Nuñez Cabeza de Vaca, Alvar, 16th cent.   2. Explorers—
America—Biography.   3. Explorers—Spain—
Biography.   4. America—Discovery and exploration—
Spanish.   5. America—Early accounts to 1600.   6. Indians of
North America—Southwestern States.   I. Frye, David
L.   II. Stavans, Ilan.   III. Title.
   E125.N9A3 2012
   910.92—dc23
   [B]
                                                      2012026947

W. W. Norton & Company, Inc., 500 Fifth Avenue, New York, NY
10110
wwnorton.com

W. W. Norton & Company Ltd., Castle House, 75/76 Wells Street,
London W1T 3QT

1 2 3 4 5 6 7 8 9 0

Contents

Introduction

La relación, known in English as the *Chronicle of the Narváez Expedition*, Álvar Núñez Cabeza de Vaca's riveting account of his journey across North America, from Florida to Louisiana, Texas, and California, is at least two books in one. It is a record of a sixteenth-century soldier turned explorer who, along with three other survivors of a shipwreck, made his way across an unknown landscape—unknown not only in the geographical but in the cultural sense. Thus the material offers valuable ethnographic and meteorological information about the so-called New World as the region was forced into modernity. But Cabeza de Vaca wrote the account years after the events happened, basing it on memory and hoping that the writing would get him a position from the Spanish monarchs as *Adelantado* in the region of the River Plate. He recast those events as a spiritual test, enhancing his own heroic skills as a healer, his capacity to subdue the Indian population, and, ultimately, his commitment to the Catholic faith. Thus the record is also read as fiction, bringing into question the role of the firsthand observer who witnessed that encounter between Europeans and the indigenous population of the Americas.

Unlike other similar accounts of exploration, Cabeza de Vaca is mercifully brief and to the point, although in my view he is also an uninspired stylist. He is—or appears to be—knowledgeable of how an introspective journal ought to work in order to make its message come across. The descriptions of the geographical landscape are concrete, if also florid. And he pays attention to the human landscape in even more detail, almost making the thirty-eight brief chapters that constitute the *Chronicle of the Narváez Expedition* deliver the feel of a novel. He is not satisfied with explaining what happened to him and his colleagues (the Moroccan slave, Estevanico, and the Spanish shipmates, Andrés Dorentes and Alonso de Castillo Maldonado); he also wants to offer an emotional picture of their trek. In any case, this twofold approach is rather recent. After its first version circulated in 1537, generating interest especially among explorers, it went through two published editions in 1542 and 1555, but then it underwent a period of obscurity that lasted roughly until the end of the nineteenth century.

Its rediscovery took place in the second half of the nineteenth century. First came the appropriation by the United States, after the Mexican-American War of 1846–48 and with the signing of the Treaty of Guadalupe Hidalgo, of large portions of Mexican territory that now constitute what is known as the American Southwest. This imperialist expansion, almost fifty years after the Louisiana Purchase, put the country on track to become a regional—and, eventually, a global—power. The first English translation of Cabeza de Vaca's chronicle appeared three years after the war ended. Then, at the end of the century, the Spanish-American War made it possible for the United States to take control of strategic positions in the Caribbean and the Philippine archipelago. David Frye, in his "Translator's Preface" to this volume, alludes to this sequence of events, referring to an aesthetic that might be described as "imperialist nostalgia." After the four hundredth anniversary of 1492, a less euphoric, more contested view of events was in store, and Cabeza de Vaca's chronicle was a useful document to that effect. It painted a picture of the Iberian conquistadors as outright abusive, not to say criminal, and offered a revisionist history of how the newly acquired territories had lived in a barbaric state and now were part of the civilized world. Since then the *Chronicle of the Narváez Expedition* has never been out of print.

Indeed, not only in Spanish has the chronicle enjoyed a long shelf life. The number of translations into English has multiplied rather vertiginously in recent years. The reason is obvious: *Chronicle of the Narváez Expedition* is seen these days as a cornerstone not only in understanding the endeavor of Spanish colonization of the Americas but also in shaping the United States as a nation. The encounters between Europeans and the indigenous populations in Florida, Louisiana, and Texas that Cabeza de Vaca showcases set a pattern. Its repercussions on the racial, social, political, cultural, and religious spheres are still hotly debated. From Thomas Buckingham Smith's version in 1851 and Fanny Bandelier's in 1904, there are more than half a dozen available, the most scholarly of which is Rolena Adorno and Patrick Charles Pautz's three-volume *Álvar Núñez Cabeza de Vaca: His Account, His Life, and the Expedition of Narváez*. David Frye's careful rendition benefited from a comparative approach.

Fortunately, Cabeza de Vaca's account of his own wanderings has competition, three examples of which are included in this Norton Critical Edition. Alternative narratives of the Pánfilo de Narváez expedition circulated as well. They are presented in Gonzalo Fernández de Oviedo y Valdéz's *General and Natural History of the Indies* (1535), book 35, chapters I and II. There are also sequels of sorts about what happened to Andrés Dorentes and Estevanico in a letter written in 1539 by the viceroy of New Spain Antonio de Mendoza and in chapters I–V of Fray Marcos de Niza's *Relación on the Discovery of the Kingdom of Cíbola* (1539). This abundance is valuable in testing Cabeza de Vaca on two fronts: the trickiness of his memory as well as his honesty and even truthfulness. It is also important to appreciate Cabeza de Vaca's travel style in the context of the conquest and colonization of North America, not only in what is today Florida, Louisiana, and Texas but also in Mexico and even the Caribbean Basin. In the eyes of Spanish explorers, soldiers, and missionaries, these territories were virginal, at once enchanting to the eye and a potential target for looting.

To register that voracious spirit, I have included in this volume a letter from 1493 by Christopher Columbus, a biased traveler's account addressing a particular benefactor in the hopes that the funding for this and subsequent voyages will be covered. Although Columbus writes of his impressions of the Hispaniola, his rationale is similar to Cabeza de Vaca's in that he wants simultaneously to persuade and enchant his reader. What he describes should also not be taken as straightforward facts because Columbus was trying to sell the Spanish Crown on the value of his discoveries, so he concentrated on pointing out things of value, including docile future vassals, just as Cabeza de Vaca was writing in the hopes of getting a new commission—that is, he wanted to emphasize that none of the disaster was his fault, that he was a good commander when given a chance, and that the exploration of the coast was not a total loss, to the degree that he could point to anything—anything at all—that might be of some future value to the Spanish venture.

Also included in Contexts is a view from the vanquished as anthologized by Miguel León-Portilla in The *Broken Spears*. It is paired with a fragment of Hernán Cortés's first letter of *Relación*, dated 1520, about the arrival and conquest of Mexico. The section ends with an excerpt from *A Brief Account of the Destruction of the Indies* (1542), by Fray Bartolomé de Las Casas, known for disseminating the so-called *leyenda negra*, the Black Legend, about Spanish excesses in the New World. His objective was to denounce Spanish settler society for destroying the people of the Caribbean. To that effect, he used Columbus's descriptions of docile natives. It is important to add that the Indians described by Columbus and Las Casas are quite distinct from the groups Cabeza de Vaca lived with on the coast of Texas. The Caribbean Indians were intensive agriculturalists who lived in large villages organized into chiefdoms or kingdoms, whereas the Texas Indians were mainly hunter-gatherers, with some small-scale gardening, who lived in small bands with no overall political organization.

This section is followed by another called Criticism. What makes Cabeza de Vaca's narrative fascinating isn't only its contested contents but precisely the layers of reading it has accumulated over time. The narrative is a kind of collective mirror: people of different epochs find in it what they are looking for. In American literature, it is a forerunner of the "road narrative" that is also a journey of self-discovery. This tradition is best represented by Mark Twain's *Adventures of Huckleberry Finn* and Jack Kerouac's *On the Road*. The three shipwrecked protagonists in *Chronicle of the Narváez Expedition* not only traverse an alien natural world—sometimes by water—in which they are constantly at the mercy of the elements but also navigate a social landscape foreign to them where their improvisational cultural skills are called to play. Cabeza de Vaca's exposure to aboriginal tribes opens for the reader a window through which, like an anthropologist, it is possible to get a glimpse of military, linguistic, religious, financial, and hygienic aspects of early American life. This window is also a mirror whereby to appreciate the overall attitude, not to say the cultural mores, of the Spanish explorers in the New World. As the narrator and Estevanico, Dorentes, and Maldonado wander around, they are turned into allegories of displacement, inhabiting a no-man's land that is neither Spanish nor American, at least not yet.

Indeed, the durability of *Chronicle of the Narváez Expedition* is to be found in the way it inaugurated, along with other important texts of the period, an aesthetic view of the Americas as lands of self-invention. For is not Cabeza de Vaca an explorer as well as an immigrant *avant la lettre*? Granted he doesn't come to the New World with the intention of settling. That is, he isn't a settler the way the pilgrims of the *Mayflower* are. But he is surely not only a colonizer but a colonist, eager and ready to adapt to the customs of the land to take advantage of them. His attitude isn't that of a sheer observer, maybe even a tourist: he doesn't simply look; rather, he wants to take possession, to make himself comfortable in the fresh environment, just as "immigrants" like Richard Frethorne, Thomas Tillam, James Revel, Ayuba Suleiman Diallo, and Gottlieb Mittelberger would do in the decades to come. Perhaps he should also be considered one of the first immigrants to what more than two hundred years later would become the United States, for while he doesn't actually immigrate in the strict sense of the term, as a proto-immigrant he surveys, identifies, and catalogs the environment for future immigrants to follow suit and settle the place.

Thus far I have talked of two literary traditions in which *Chronicle of the Narváez Expedition* fits: the narrative of self-discovery and immigrant writing. There is a third important tradition of equal significance. Cabeza de Vaca's penchant for wonder, magic, and exoticism make him a forerunner of magic realism, a literary form practiced by twentieth-century Latin American authors such as Alejo

Carpentier, Gabriel García Márquez, and Jorge Amado. Like them, he isn't satisfied with simply describing what he sees; he emphasizes it, he exacerbates it, he makes events implausible by juxtaposing the real and the dreamlike. In his eyes a hurricane isn't a natural event but a sign of divine intervention. And his interaction with the natives is infused with a dose of fantasy impossible to ignore.

All this to say that Cabeza de Vaca is a favorite not only with history buffs but with artists of all kinds, from novelists to painters, from dancers to filmmakers. His work is often interpreted in multifarious formats, from short stories to movies to creative nonfiction. European historians like Salvador de Madariaga (*The Rise of the Spanish-American Empire*, 1949) and Samuel Eliot Morison (*The European Discovery of America*, 1974) use his chronicle as tableaux against which to appreciate the Spanish entrepreneurial quest. I have included some samples of narrative recreations by Morris Bishop (*The Odyssey of Cabeza de Vaca*, 1933), Paul Schneider (*Brutal Journey*, 2006), and Andrés Reséndez (*A Land So Strange*, 2007) in the hope that readers will appreciate that quest as a forerunner in the shaping of the United States as a nation. Literary scholars such as Rolena Adorno and Patrick Charles Pautz delve into the motifs in Cabeza de Vaca's text, and Beatríz Rivera-Barnes studies Cabeza de Vaca's overall approach to the environment.

Acknowledgments

I want to thank Carol Bemis for inviting me to prepare this Norton Critical Edition of *Chronicle of the Narváez Expedition*, and especially my friend David Frye, for joining me in this venture with a lucid, revealing new rendition of the text. To retranslate a classic is the duty of every generation, for to translate is to interpret. The past is never static. It is always in need of reconsideration. Gracias also to Rivka Genesen at Norton.

My full engagement with the text took place a decade before, when I wrote the introduction to the revamping of Fanny Bandelier's translation brought out by Penguin Classics. The odyssey by Álvar Núñez Cabeza de Vaca has remained in me since then. I have written about it and included a generous excerpt in the *Norton Anthology of Latino Literature* (chapters 1–4 and 19–26).

I am also grateful to Harold Augenbraum at the National Book Foundation, Werner Sollors at Harvard University, and Kirsten Silva Gruesz at the University of California–Santa Cruz for encouraging me to articulate succinctly my views on Cabeza de Vaca as a forerunner of American literary journeys of self-discovery.

Translator's Preface

Cabeza de Vaca's *La relación* was twice published in his lifetime, first in a small 1542 edition, apparently aimed mainly at influencing court opinion in the author's favor, and again in a larger and more widely distributed edition in 1555. By then, however, the central drama of the Spanish Empire had moved south to the struggles over the fabulous wealth of the Incas in Peru, and the northern lands through which Cabeza de Vaca and his companions had trekked in the 1520s were left almost completely alone by Europeans for the better part of the next two centuries. Indeed, it was not until the Spanish had begun to colonize Texas—more to keep the province out of French and British hands than for any interest in the seemingly impoverished land for its own sake—that they returned their attention to earlier explorations, and Cabeza de Vaca's chronicle was reprinted for the third time in 1731.

The first English translation followed more than a century later, after Texas and Florida had been wrested from Spanish and Mexican control and incorporated into the growing republic of the United States and the invention of steel plows, cotton gins, and the institution of plantation slavery on an industrial scale had transformed the setting of his book beyond all recognition. The newly awakened interest of 1850s North America in the vanished past represented by Cabeza de Vaca's narrative strikes me as a possible case of what Renato Rosaldo has called "imperialist nostalgia," a peculiar kind of longing "often found under imperialism, where people mourn the passing of what they themselves have transformed." The nostalgic draw of the text has remained strong. Since Buckingham Smith's 1851 translation, *La relación* has been translated and retranslated into English at least ten times.

In this translation, I have done my best to provide the feel of Cabeza de Vaca's admirably spare prose style and to make the English as open to the modern reader as his Spanish was for his early-sixteenth-century contemporaries. I have tried to steer a path between updating the vocabulary (I was tempted, for example, to translate Cabeza de Vaca's obsolete term *physico* by the equally obsolete English word *leech*, but opted instead for the more intelligible *physician*) on the one hand and avoiding blatant anachronisms on the other.

Above all, my thirty-year experience as an anthropologist and historian of northern Mexico and colonial New Spain has given me a different viewpoint on the text than that enjoyed by some translators, who have come at it more from a United States- (or even Texas-) centered approach, as witnessed by debates in the translations and their footnotes over the precise course of the survivors' trek through Texas and northern Mexico. I have been more interested, instead, in the social and cultural significance of the narrative, an interest I hope comes through in the translation and will be shared by the reader.

I have based this translation primarily on the 1542 Zamora edition, as transcribed in the remarkable scholarly edition by Adorno and Pautz (1999) with notes, additions, and emendations based on the 1555 Valladolid edition. I have also checked the text against Juan Francisco Maura's text of *La relación*, which he based on the Valladolid edition (Madrid, Cátedra, 1989). I have compared my translation against the most recent English versions and, in the few places where we have disagreed about interpretations, have noted the reason for my decisions in the notes; for the most part, however, the differences between us are a matter of style, not substance. Finally, I have included the chapter titles, which were introduced in the 1555 edition, and, with the help of Adorno and Pautz (1999), have marked the relatively few important discrepancies between the two early editions either in the text itself or in the footnotes.

The Text of
CHRONICLE OF THE NARVÁEZ EXPEDITION

The Report Presented by Álvar Núñez Cabeza de Vaca on What Happened in the Indies to the Fleet Carrying Governor Pánfilo de Narváez from 1527 to 1536, When He Returned to Seville with Three Men of His Company[†]

Prologue

Sacred, Imperial, and Catholic Majesty:

Among all the many princes that we know have existed in the world, none could be found, I think, whom men have endeavored to serve so willingly, so diligently and eagerly, as those we see serving Your Majesty today. Quite clearly this is not without good cause and reason, nor are men so blind that all follow this path blindly and without foundation; for we see that not only do natives of Spain, obliged by faith and obedience, do this, but even foreigners labor to outpace them. But since all are equal in their desire and willingness to serve, though some might outpace others to some degree, the great differences that arise are not caused by their own fault, but only by Fortune; more properly said, they are not anyone's fault, but caused only by the will and judgment of God. As a result, one man may end up performing more distinguished services than he had ever imagined, while for another everything may turn out backward, and he will have no witness to vouch for his intentions other than his diligence—and even that might remain so obscure that he will never be able to restore his good reputation.

As for myself, I can say that, on the expedition to the Mainland that I carried out by order of Your Majesty, I truly thought that my deeds and services were as clear and evident as those of my ancestors, and that I would not have to speak up to be counted among those who administer Your Majesty's offices with complete faithfulness and great care, and whom you reward. But insofar as neither my counsel nor my diligence managed to accomplish what we set out to do in Your Majesty's service, and for our sins God placed our fleet in greater peril and led us to a more wretched and unhappy end than any of all the others that have sailed to those lands, I had no opportunity to perform any other service than this: which is, to bring Your Majesty a report of what I was able to see and learn during the nine years when I wandered, lost and naked, through many and strange lands, regarding the situation of the lands and the provinces thereof, as well as the food supplies and animals raised there,

---

[†] All notes and bracketed interpolations are by the translator David Frye.

3

and the diverse customs of the many and barbarous nations with whom I dwelled and lived, and all the other details that I was able to learn and comprehend, so that Your Majesty may to some degree be served thereby. For even though I never had much hope of escaping from them, I always took great care and diligence to retain a detailed memory of everything, so that, should God be pleased at some time to bring me here where I am today, I might give testimony of my good will and serve Your Majesty, since this report provides advice—of some weight, in my opinion—to those who might go to conquer those lands in your name and at the same time bring them to the knowledge of the true faith and the true Lord and the service of Your Majesty.

I have written this report with such certain knowledge that, even though some readers may find the great novelties it contains very difficult to believe, they may believe them without any doubt, and may fully believe that I have shortened rather than enlarged upon everything, proof of which is the fact that I have offered it to Your Majesty as such. For which I entreat you to receive it by way of service: for this and only this is what a man who escaped naked was able to bring away with him.

Chapter 1. In Which He Recounts When the Fleet Set Sail, and the Officers and Men Who Went in It

On June 17, 1527, Governor Pánfilo de Narváez set sail from the port of Sanlúcar de Barrameda with Your Majesty's authorization and orders to conquer and govern the provinces on the mainland from the Río de las Palmas to the cape of La Florida.[1] There were five ships in his fleet, carrying six hundred men, more or less. The officers he brought (for they deserve mention) were these: Cabeza de Vaca, as treasurer and chief judicial officer; Alonso Enriquez, as purser; Alonso de Solis, as factor for Your Majesty and inspector; there was also a friar of the Order of Saint Francis, as commissary,

---

1. What we now call south Florida; the colonial Spanish term for all the land north and northeast of New Spain (i.e., colonial Mexico). It included, in a rather undefined way, not only modern Florida but most of what is now the United States as well as the modern Mexican state of Tamaulipas. Pánfilo de Narváez (1478–1528), a relative of Diego de Velázquez and the first Spanish governor of Cuba, who took part in the conquests of Jamaica (1509) and Cuba (1511) as well as the ill-fated attempt to wrest control of Mexico from Hernán Cortés on behalf of Velázquez (1520). In the typical fashion of the time, after this first allusion to his full name Cabeza de Vaca refers to Narváez only by his most important title, "the Governor." Sanlúcar de Barrameda is a seaport fifty miles south of Seville, the Spanish administrative and trade center for the Americas at the time. The Río de las Palmas, known today as the Río Soto la Marina, flows into the Gulf of Mexico about 100 miles north of Tampico and 150 miles south of the modern Texas–Mexico border. This region of Mexico formed the ephemeral province of Pánuco in the early 1500s. The Spanish abandoned Pánuco after its early failure as a colonial venture and did not return to bring it under their rule until the late 1740s.

named Fray Juan Suárez, along with four more monks of the same order. We arrived at the island of Santo Domingo,[2] where we stayed for nearly forty-five days, equipping ourselves with necessary things, notably horses. Here our fleet lost more than 140 men, who decided to stay there because of the proposals and promises that the locals made them.

We set sail from there and arrived at Santiago,[3] a port town on the island of Cuba, where, during the few days we stayed there, the Governor reinforced the fleet with men, arms, and horses. It happened there that a gentleman named Vasco Porcallo, a citizen of the town of Trinidad, on the same island, offered to give the Governor certain supplies he had in Trinidad, which lies one hundred leagues[4] from the port of Santiago. The Governor set sail with the whole fleet for that town, but upon arriving at a port named Cabo de Santa Cruz, which is halfway to Trinidad, he thought it best to wait there and send a single ship to bring back those supplies. So he ordered a certain Captain Pantoja to go there with his ship; and he told me to go with him, for greater security, while he stayed behind with four ships, because he had bought another ship on the island of Santo Domingo.

After we arrived at the port of Trinidad with these two ships, Captain Pantoja went with Vasco Porcallo to the town, which is one league from there, to get the supplies; I stayed at sea with the pilots, who told us that we should leave there with all possible speed, because that was a very unsafe port and many ships had been lost in it. And because what happened to us there was very noteworthy, it seemed to me that it would not be off the subject or contrary to the aim for which I chose to write this journey to tell it here.

The next morning the weather began to give bad signals, for it began to rain, and the sea grew so rough that, although I let the men go ashore, when they saw the weather and saw the town was a

2. The name of both the island (known in English as Hispaniola) and its largest city, the first permanent Spanish settlement in the Americas and still the capital of the Indies in 1527, though the balance was already beginning to shift then to the much newer but larger settlement of Mexico City.
3. On the mountainous eastern coast of Cuba (the closest region of the island to Santo Domingo), it was the first Spanish city on the island and its first colonial capital, founded in 1514.
4. A league was the amount of ground a traveler covered in one hour. Its length varied by terrain, means of transportation, and the traveler's best guess at the length of an hour. Cabeza de Vaca's leagues tend to be 3 to 3.5 miles long. In fact, Trinidad lies about 340 miles west, whether overland or by sea. It was founded as a Spanish town a few months after Santiago. "Citizen" (vecino): In the Spanish social world, having the status of vecino in a city, town, or village meant being entitled to the full range of rights and privileges that we now associate with citizenship, such as the right to vote in municipal elections, hold office, and share in the benefits of common property. Such rights were not automatically extended to all the legal residents (residentes) of a place. In early colonial Spanish America, vecino status was restricted to the most prominent Spanish colonizers and connoted relatively high rank and respectability.

league away, many came back to the ship to avoid the wet and cold. Just then a canoe[5] came from the town carrying a letter from a citizen of the town who begged me to go there, where they would give me the supplies that were on hand that might be necessary; but I declined the offer, saying that I could not leave the ships.

At midday the canoe returned with another letter that repeated the same request with great insistence, and they brought a horse for me to ride; I gave the same reply I had given the first time, saying that I would not leave the ships. But the pilots and the men begged me to go so that I might press them to bring the supplies as quickly as possible, so we might set sail right away from there, where they were in great fear that the ships would be lost if they stayed there long. For that reason, I decided to go to the town, though I left the pilots with instructions and orders before I went, that if the south wind that often wrecks the ships over there should begin to blow, and if they found themselves in great danger, they should beach the ships someplace where the men and horses might be saved. And with that I left, though I tried to get some of them to come with me; but they refused to leave, saying it was too wet and cold and the town was too far away, and that the next day, which was Sunday, they would go, with God's help, to hear mass.

One hour after I left, the sea became very wild, and the north wind was so intense that the ships' skiffs did not dare to make for land, nor could the men find any way to beach the ships, since the wind was against them; so it was only with great difficulty, facing doubly foul weather and much rain, that they stayed there all that day and all Sunday until nightfall. At that hour, the rain and the storm began to grow so strong that it was just as bad in the pueblo as well it was out at sea, for all the houses and the churches collapsed, and we had to hold tight to each other in groups of seven or eight men to keep the wind from carrying us off; and when we walked through the trees we feared them as much as we had the houses, for they were also falling and we did not want to be killed underneath them. We spent all night outside in this storm and danger, unable to find any spot or place where we might be safe for half an hour.

As we were doing this, we heard all night long, and especially after midnight, a tremendous clamor, and shouting voices, and many bells and flutes and tambourines and other instruments playing loudly,

5. *Canoa*; this is the first of a handful of exotic terms that Cabeza de Vaca uses, perhaps to give some local color to his narrative or to increase the sense of authenticity. The word is originally Taino and refers to the large dugouts that the Spanish first encountered in the Caribbean. We are left to assume that this canoe was rowed by one of the Spanish colonist's Taino servants or slaves. It is also important to notice that the word *canoa* was the first ever to travel back from the Americas to Spain. Appearing in the 1496 edition to Antonio de Nebrija's *Gramática*, it is assumed to be the first *americanismo* to be featured in a Spanish-language lexicon.

which lasted until morning, when the storm ceased. Never had such a terrifying thing been seen in those parts; I took sworn evidence about it, and sent the testimony to Your Majesty.

Monday morning we went down to the harbor and did not find the ships. We saw their buoys in the water, from which we recognized that they had been lost, and we walked along the shore to see if we could find any part of them. And since we found nothing we entered the woods and, after walking through them for a quarter league from the shore, we found one of the ships' rowboats resting in the treetops, and ten leagues farther down the coast two men of my crew were found, and lids from some boxes, and the bodies were so disfigured from hitting the rocks that they were unrecognizable. A cape and some tattered rigging were also found, and nothing else appeared. Sixty men perished on the ships, and twenty horses. Those who had gone ashore the day the ships arrived, perhaps thirty men, remained of all those who had come in both ships.

Thus we were left in great need and distress for several days, because all the supplies and stores in the pueblo had also been lost, and some cattle. The country was left in such a state that it was piteous to see: trees fallen, woods blighted, all without leaves or grass. Thus we stayed until November 5, when the Governor arrived with his four ships, which had also weathered a great storm and had also escaped by finding a safe place in time. The men he had on board, and those he found in Trinidad, were so terrified by what had happened that they were too afraid to board the ship again in winter, and they begged the Governor to spend it there; and he, seeing their will and the will of the town's citizens, wintered there. He put me in charge of the ships and the men, telling me to take them to winter at the port of Jagua,[6] which lies twelve leagues from there, where I stayed until February 20.

Chapter 2. How the Governor Came to the Port of Jagua and Brought a Pilot with Him

At that time the Governor came with a brigantine he had bought at Trinidad, and he brought with him a pilot named Miruelo; he had taken that man because they said he knew and had been on the Río de las Palmas and was a very good pilot for the whole North coast.[7]

---

6. I.e., Jagua Bay (Bahía de Jagua), a large natural harbor on the south coast of Cuba, about thirty-six miles west of Trinidad. In the 1520s, it was the center of an indigenous chiefdom (cacicazgo) under Spanish overlordship. The region was more or less abandoned from the collapse of the indigenous population in the 1500s until 1819, when the city of Cienfuegos was founded on the bay.

7. La costa norte; the coast of the "North Sea"; i.e., the western Atlantic system, including the Caribbean and the Gulf of Mexico; as opposed to the "South Sea" or Pacific Ocean, so-called because the Pacific lies south of the Atlantic across the Panama Isthmus.

He also left another ship he had bought on the coast of Lixarte,[8] which had Álvaro de la Cerda as captain, with forty foot soldiers and twelve horsemen. Two days after arriving, the Governor went aboard, and the men he took were four hundred foot soldiers and eighty horsemen on four ships and one brigantine.

The pilot we had recently taken on headed the ships into the shoals that they call the Canarreo Shoals, in such a way that the next day we ran aground. And we remained grounded for two weeks, the keels often touching bottom, until a storm from the south drove so much water into the shoals that we could set sail, though not without great danger.

After leaving there and arriving at Guaniguanico, we were caught by another storm and we very nearly perished. At Cabo Corrientes we had another, which lasted three days. After that, we rounded Cabo San Antonio and continued against contrary winds until we reached twelve leagues from Havana. While we were waiting until the next day to enter Havana, a storm from the south caught us and drove us from the shore. And we crossed to the coast of La Florida and we reached land on Tuesday, April 12, and we sailed along the coast in the Florida way.[9] And on Holy Thursday we cast anchor at the mouth of a bay,[1] at the head of which we saw some houses and habitations of Indians.

Chapter 3. How We Reached La Florida

On that same day the purser, Alonso Enríquez, left and landed on an island in the bay. And he called the Indians, who came and stayed with him for a good space of time, and through trade they gave him fish and a few pieces of venison. The next day, which was Good Friday, the Governor disembarked with as many men as he could take in the skiffs he had brought. And as we reached the *bohíos*[2] or houses we had seen of the Indians, we found them abandoned and deserted, for the people had gone away that night in their canoes. There was one of those *bohíos* so large that it could hold more than three hun-

---

8. An unknown site, presumably on the coast of the western half of Cuba. The 1555 Valladolid edition (hereafter noted as **V**) changes the phrase to "the coast of Havana," on the northern side of the island near its western end.
9. *La vía de la Florida*; i.e., in the direction of the southern tip of Florida. For travelers in the vicinity of Tampa, where they were, this meant going south.
1. Thought to be Tampa Bay.
2. Or *buhíos*; the second exotic word in the narrative, adopted in Caribbean Spanish from the Taino word for houses or lodges. The indigenous people of Florida did not speak Taino; Cabeza de Vaca is following colonial practice in treating indigenous groups and cultures as in some way interchangeable. He uses the word *bohío* to refer to thatched dwellings of indigenous people from Florida to Sinaloa. The large *bohío* mentioned in the next sentence was probably a village lodge or longhouse.

dred people. The others were smaller, and there we found a gold jingle³ among the fishnets.

The next day the Governor hoisted standards for Your Majesty and took possession of the land in your royal name, presented his titles of appointment, and was obeyed as Governor, as Your Majesty ordered done. We likewise presented ours to him, and he complied with them according to their contents.⁴ Then he ordered the rest of the men to disembark, as well as the horses, of which there were only forty-two, for between the great storms and the long time they had been at sea, the others had died. And these few that remained were so thin and distressed that for the time being we could get little use from them.

The next day the Indians of that pueblo came to us. And although they spoke to us, since we had no interpreter we did not understand them. But they made us many gestures and threats, and it seemed to us as if they were telling us to leave the country, and with that they left us, without putting up obstacles in our path, and they went away.

Chapter 4. How We Marched Inland

The day after, the Governor resolved to march inland to discover the land and see what there was in it. We—the commissary, the inspector, and I—went with him, with forty men, and among them six horsemen, whom we could not count on to be of much use. We went in a northerly direction until, late in the afternoon, we reached a very large bay, which seemed to us to enter far inland. We remained there that night, and the next day we went back to where the ships and the men were. The Governor ordered the brigantine to continue sailing along the coast on the Florida way and to search for the port that Miruelo, the pilot, had said he knew. But he had lost his way and did not know where we were, nor where the port was. And the brigantine was given the order that, if the port were not found, it was to cross over to Havana and seek the ship belonging to Álvaro de la Cerda, and after taking on some supplies, to come seek us.

---

3. *Sonaja de oro*; a pair of small disks like those set around the frame of a tambourine. Cabeza de Vaca is careful to mention every potentially precious item found along the way, no matter how small, because it may hint at larger stores of gold to be found elsewhere in the area.

4. This curious ceremony was the crucial ritual for taking possession of territory in the Spanish system. By raising the royal standard and presenting his official documents, the Governor is legally founding a new settlement at this spot. It is this act that makes him "the Governor" and gives him the authority to make decisions of justice and war from this point forth. As we will later see, he has a notary (*escribano*) along to record just such official business. This settlement does not last for even a day, as it turns out, but a similar act on the part of Hernán Cortés gave him the legal authority, within the Spanish system, to carry out the conquest of Mexico.

After the brigantine set off, we went back to marching inland—
the same men as before, and a few more—and we followed the shore
of the bay that we had found, and after walking four leagues we took
four Indians. And we showed them maize to see whether they recognized it, for until then we had seen no trace of it. They told us they
would take us to where there was some. And so they led us to their
pueblo, which lies at the end of the bay, near where we were, and
there they showed us a little maize that was not yet ready to be
picked. There we found many Castilian traders' boxes, and in each
one of them was the body of a dead man, and the bodies were covered with painted deer hides. It seemed to the commissary that this
was some sort of idolatry, and he burned the boxes with the bodies.
We also found pieces of linen cloth, and feather headdresses that
seemed to be from New Spain. We also found samples of gold. Using
signs, we asked the Indians where those things had come from. They
signaled to us that, very far from there, there was a province called
Apalachen[5] where there was a lot of gold, and they made signs that
there was a great deal of everything we held in esteem. They said
that in Apalachen there was plenty. And, taking those Indians as
guides, we set off from there. And after walking ten or twelve leagues,
we found another pueblo of fifteen houses, where there was a large
patch of corn planted that was already good for picking, and we also
found some that was already dried. And after staying there two days,
we returned to where the purser, the men, and the ships were, and
we told the purser and pilots what we had seen and the news that the
Indians had given us.

And the next day, which was May 1, the Governor took aside the
commissary, the purser, the inspector, and me, and a sailor named
Bartolomé Fernández, and a notary called Jerónimo de Alaniz. And
with all of us together, he told us that it was his will to march inland,
leaving the ships to follow the coast until they reached the port; and
that the pilots said and believed that if they went in the Palmas way[6]

5. The area around Apalachee Bay and Tallahassee in the northwest corner of the Florida
peninsula. Years later this name was applied to the Appalachian Mountains, several
hundred miles north. In two early published versions of the text the name of this province is variously spelled Apalachen, Apalache, Palache, and Palachen.
6. I.e., north from Tampa Bay and west across the entire Gulf Coast in the direction of
their goal, the port of Río de las Palmas. Hugging the coastline, this would be a voyage
of at least fourteen hundred miles. Two facts seem to explain Narváez's disastrous decision here: the pilots' conviction that they were already within walking distance of their
final goal, and the governor's desire to conquer the "rich" (i.e., gold-bearing) province of
Apalachen. To these we might also add a third consideration: the traditional Castilian
disdain and suspicion of all things maritime; the Portuguese were great sailors, but the
Castilians generally hired other people—Portuguese, Basques, Catalans, Italians—to
do the sailing for them. The alacrity with which the others agree to the governor's mod-
est proposal seems to indicate that they all preferred to walk rather than spend one
more day on a boat. Later generations romanticized these "voyages of exploration," but
for the participants, leaders, and financers of such ventures, exploration was at most a
means to an end, the end being the conquest of a province rich enough in gold or silver

they would reach it soon. And on this he begged us to give him our opinions.

I replied that, as it seemed to me, he should by no means leave the ships until they were first in a safe and settled port, and he should note that the pilots were unsure of the way, could not agree on anything, and did not know where they were. And besides, the horses were not in fit condition to be of any use to us if need should arise. And on top of all this, we were mute without an interpreter,[7] so that we could hardly have dealings with the Indians or find out what we wanted to know about the land. And we were entering a land about which we had no information, nor did we know what kind of land it was, or what there might be there, or what kind of people inhabited it, or where we were within it. And on top of all this, we did not have supplies for marching into we knew not where; for, given what was on board the ships, we could give each man a ration of no more than one pound of hardtack and another pound of salt pork for marching inland. My opinion, then, was that we should embark and sail in search of a port and a land better suited to settlement, for the land we had seen was in itself as deserted and poor as any that had ever been found in those parts.

To the commissary it seemed quite the contrary; he said that we should not embark, but follow the coast in search of a harbor, for the pilots said that it could not be more than ten or fifteen leagues from there to Pánuco, and that if we always followed the coast there was no way we could miss it, because they said that the coast turned inland for twelve leagues there. The first ones who found it should wait there for the others. To embark would just be to tempt God, because after we set sail from Castile we had suffered so many tribulations, so many storms, so many lost ships and men, until we came to that place. For these reasons, he should follow along the coast until reaching the port, and the ships with the rest of the men would go in the same direction until they reached the same port.

To all the others who were there it seemed good to do just as he said, except to the notary, who said that, rather than abandon the ships, the Governor should leave them in a well known and safe port, and in a settled area; having done so, he might march inland and do as seemed best to him.

---

to repay their considerable financial investments. For the men of the company who did not put money into the venture, their investment was their time and their willingness to risk their lives on a potentially lucrative return.

7. I.e., *Lengua*; "tongue" (literal translation) and by extension "language" as well as "interpreter." Capturing a local indigenous person, typically a teenage boy or girl, and using him or her as an interpreter for negotiating with local leaders was standard conquest procedure from the earliest days—Columbus did it on his first voyage—and could often lead to capitulation or accommodation of demands for tribute without the risks of outright war.

The Governor followed his own opinion and what the others counseled him.

Seeing his decision, I demanded on Your Majesty's behalf that he not leave the ships until they were safe at port, and I asked the notary we had there to make a certified copy of my statement.

The Governor replied that, since he agreed with the opinions of the majority of other officers and the commissary, I had no standing to make such demands of him. And he asked the notary to give him a certified statement as to how, since that land did not have the means to support a settlement, nor a port for the ships, he was breaking up the pueblo he had founded, and was going off with it to search for a better port and land. And then he ordered the men who were to go with him to get ready, fitting themselves out with what was they would need for the journey. After doing that, in the presence of everyone there he told me that, since I was so opposed to and so fearful of the march inland, I should stay and take charge of the ships and the men who remained in them, and that I should form a settlement if I arrived before he did.

This I declined.

After we all left, that same evening he sent word to me that he felt he could not trust anybody else to take charge of the ships, and he begged me to do it. Seeing that in spite of his insistence I continued to decline, he asked me the reason why I refused to accept.

I replied that I refused to take on that duty because I felt certain that he would never see the ships again, nor would the ships see him, and that this was obvious, seeing how utterly unprepared they were for marching inland. I would rather risk the danger that he and the others were risking, and suffer what he and they would suffer, than take charge of the ships and give occasion for someone to say that I had opposed the march and had stayed behind out of fear, putting my honor in dispute; and I would rather risk my life than place my honor in such a circumstance.

Seeing that he was getting nowhere with me, he begged many others to talk to me about it and to beg me, but I gave them the same answer I gave him. And so he appointed a magistrate[8] he had brought named Caravallo to be his lieutenant and stay with the ships.

Chapter 5. How the Governor Left the Ships

On Saturday, May 1, the same day this had taken place, he ordered that each of those who were to go with him be given two pounds of hardtack and half a pound of salt pork. And like that, we set off to

---

8. *Alcalde*; a position in local government that combined judicial and executive functions. Presumably Caravallo had been an *alcalde* in some Spanish town or pueblo in the Caribbean or perhaps back in Spain.

march inland. The total of all the people we took along was three hundred men; among them went the commissary, Fray Juan Suárez, and another friar called Fray Juan de Palos, and three clerics, and the officers. We horsemen who accompanied them came to forty on horseback. And so we marched on the supplies we carried with us, for two weeks, finding nothing else to eat but palm hearts[9] like those of Andalusia. In all this time we did not meet a single Indian, nor did we see a house or a settlement. Finally we reached a river that we crossed with great difficulty, by swimming and on rafts. It took us a day to ford it because its current was so strong. After we had crossed to the other side, some two hundred Indians, more or less, came at us. The Governor went at them, and after he spoke to them by signs they gestured at us in such a way that we had to turn upon them. We seized five or six, and they took us to their houses, which lay some half a league from there, where we found a large quantity of corn ready for picking. And we gave infinite thanks to our Lord for having aided us in our great need, for it was certainly true that, as we were new to these difficulties, beyond the exhaustion we felt, we were very weakened by hunger.

And on our third day there, we got together—the purser, the inspector, the commissary, and I—and we begged the Governor to send someone out to search for the sea, because the Indians were telling us that the sea was not very far away.

He replied that we should not bother speaking of it, saying that it was very far away. And since I was the one who most insisted, he told me that I should go discover the sea and search for a port, and that I should go on foot with forty men. And so I set off the next day with Captain Alonso del Castillo and forty men of his company. And so we walked until midday, when we reached some sandy banks that seemed to stretch far inland. We walked along them for some one and a half leagues, with water up to our knees and stepping on oyster shells that cut our feet badly and caused us a great deal of trouble, until we reached the same river we had crossed before, which emptied into that very cove. And since we couldn't cross it because of our lack of equipment for such a thing, we returned to camp and told the Governor what we had found and that it was necessary to ford the river again at the same place we had crossed it the first time, so that we could fully explore that cove and find out if there was a harbor there.

The next day he ordered a captain named Valenzuela to go with sixty men on foot and six on horse, cross the river, follow it down

9. *Palmitos*; refers both to the small palm and to its edible "heart," the growing bud at its center. The Spanish *palmito* is *Chamaerops humilis*, or Mediterranean fan palm, the only palm native to Europe. There are several species of palm in Florida named palmetto (after Spanish *palmito*); this one is probably the dwarf palmetto, *Sabal minor*.

until he reached the sea, and find out whether there was a harbor there. After two days away, he came back and said that he had discovered the cove, and that the whole thing was a shallow, knee-deep bay, and there was no harbor to be found; and that he had seen five or six canoes full of Indians rowing from one place to another, and that they were wearing many feathered headdresses.

Having learned this, the next day we set off, always in quest of the province that the Indians had named for us, Apalachen, taking the ones we had captured from them as guides. And so we went on until June 17, and we found no Indians who would dare to wait for us.

And then a lord[1] came at us, whom an Indian carried on his back, wearing a painted deerskin. He was bringing many people with him, and they came before him playing reed flutes. And so he reached the place where the Governor was, and he stayed with him for an hour, and by signs we gave him to understand that we were going to Apalachen, and by the signs that he made it seemed to us that he was an enemy of the people of Apalachen and that he would go help us against them. We gave him beads and bells and other trade goods, and he gave the Governor the hide that he was wearing. And so he returned, and we began following him along the way he was going.

That night we reached a river,[2] which was very deep and very wide, and its current very strong. And because we did not dare to ford it with rafts, we made a canoe for the purpose, and it took us a whole day to ford it. And if the Indians had wished to attack us, they could have easily hindered our passage, and even with their helping us we had a great deal of trouble. One horseman called Juan Velázquez, a native of Cuellar, would not wait and rode his horse into the river, and the current was so strong that it threw him from his horse, and he grabbed the reins, and drowned himself and the horse. And those Indians of that lord, whose name was Dulchanchellin,[3] found the horse and told us where we could find him downstream. So they went after him. And his death caused us much grief, because until then we had not lost anyone. The horse made a supper for many that night.

Having crossed there, the next day we reached the pueblo of that lord, and he sent us corn there. That night, when they went for water, someone shot an arrow at a Christian,[4] and God willed it that they did not wound him. The next day we set off from there without any of the natives showing up, for they had all fled. But continuing on our trail, Indians appeared, and they were prepared for war. And

1. *Un señor*; an indigenous ruler or a member of the indigenous ruling or noble class.
2. Perhaps the Suwannee River.
3. The only personal name of a Native American that appears in the narrative.
4. In Castilian usage, no doubt conditioned by centuries of religious conflict in Iberia, the term was virtually synonymous with "Spanish" or "Castilian."

even though we called them, they would neither come back nor wait, but preferred to withdraw and follow us along the same trail we were taking. The Governor left a few horsemen in ambush near the trail. As the Indians passed, the horsemen set upon them and took three or four of them. And we kept them as guides after that, and they led us through a land that was very difficult to walk across and marvelous to see, for in it there are very great woodlands and trees that are wonderfully tall, and there are so many of them fallen to the ground that they obstructed our path, so that we could not get through without many detours and great trouble. Many of the trees that had not fallen were cleft from top to bottom by the lightning bolts that strike that land, where there always are huge storms and tempests.

With all this hardship, we walked until the day after St. John's,[5] when we came in sight of Apalachen, without being noticed by the local Indians. We gave many thanks to God for being so near it, for we believed that what we had been told about the country was true and this now would bring to an end the great hardships we had gone through, both from the long, bad trail we had walked and from the great hunger we had suffered. For although we sometimes found corn, most of the time we marched seven or eight leagues without running into any. And there were many among us who, besides suffering great fatigue and hunger, had their backs covered with wounds from carrying their armor, not to mention other things that presented themselves. But now we found that we had arrived where we wished to be and where we had been told there would be so much food and gold, and it seemed to us that much of our hardships and fatigue had fallen from us.

Chapter 6. How We Arrived at Apalachen

Once we were in sight of Apalachen, the Governor ordered me to take nine horsemen and fifty foot and enter the pueblo. So the inspector and I undertook this. After entering it, we found only women and boys, for the men were not in the pueblo on that occasion. But soon afterward, as we were walking through it, they came and began to fight, shooting arrows at us. They killed the inspector's horse, but in the end they fled and left us. There we found a large quantity of maize ready to be picked and a lot of dry maize that they already had stored. We also found many deerskins and among them a few woven blankets, small and of poor quality, with which the women cover up their bodies somewhat. They had many vessels for grinding maize. In the pueblo there were forty small houses, built low and in sheltered places out of fear of the great

5. St. John's Day is June 24.

storms that continuously occur in that land. The construction is of straw. And they are surrounded by very dense woodlands and tall groves and many pools of standing water, where there are so many and such huge fallen trees that they obstruct the way and are the reason why one cannot walk through there without great trouble and danger.

Chapter 7. On the Condition of the Land

The land, for the most part, from where we landed to the pueblo and land of Apalachen, is flat; the soil is sandy, hard-packed and firm. All throughout it there are very large trees and open woodlands where there are nut trees and laurels, and others called sweetgums, cedars, junipers and live oaks and pines and oaks, and low palmettos like those of Castile. All throughout it there are many lagoons, large and small, some very difficult to cross, partly because of their great depth, partly because so many trees have fallen around them. Their floors are sandy, and the ones we found in the province of Apalachen are much larger than what we saw up to then. There are many maize fields in this province. And the houses are scattered all over the countryside, much like those of Djerba.[6]

The animals we saw in those lands were: three types of deer, rabbits and hares, bears and lions, and other wild beasts, among which we saw one that carries its young in a pouch[7] that it has in its belly, and as long as they are small it carries them there, until they are able to look for food, and if they happen to be out looking for food and people approach, the mother does not flee until she has gathered them in her pouch. Over there, the land is very cold. It has good pasture for cattle. There are many types of birds: geese in large numbers, ducks, mallards, wigeons, flycatchers, night herons and herons, partridges; we saw many hawks, kites, sparrow hawks, kestrels, and many other birds.

Two days[8] after we arrived at Apalachen, the Indians that had fled from there came back to us in peace, asking us for their women and children. And we gave them to them, except that the Governor

6. An island off the coast of Tunisia (*los Gelves* in Spanish). Adorno and Pautz (p. 12:129) have explained this seemingly obscure reference by the fact that Cabeza de Vaca almost certainly knew veterans of the failed 1510 Spanish attempt to conquer the island. A second campaign in 1521 brought Djerba under Spanish rule until its recapture by the Ottoman Empire. A glance at satellite images of Djerba confirms its scattered settlement pattern, which contrasts strongly with the Castilian pattern of densely concentrated agricultural towns in rural provinces.
7. Clearly a Virginia opossum, the only marsupial in the Americas north of Mexico. There are no marsupials native to Europe.
8. In V this becomes "two hours."

kept one of their *caciques*[9] with him, which was the reason why they grew agitated. And then the next day they returned prepared for war. And they attacked us with such valor and alacrity that they managed to set fire to the houses where we were staying. But as soon as we sallied forth they fled, and they took refuge in the lagoons that they had very close by. Because of this, and because of the big maize fields, we could not do them any harm, except for one that we killed. The day after, other Indians from another pueblo that was on the other side came and attacked us in the same fashion as the first. And they escaped in the same way, and one of them also died.

We remained in this pueblo for twenty-five days, during which time we made three excursions through the land, and we found it to be very poorly populated and very bad for walking across because of the bad crossings and woodlands and lagoons there. We asked the cacique whom we had captured and the other Indians whom we were bringing with us who their neighbors and enemies were, and about the condition and settlements of the land, the quality of its people, and about supplies and everything else in it. They told us, each of them separately, that the largest pueblo in that whole land was Apalachen, and that farther along there were fewer people, who were much poorer than they were, and that the country was thinly settled and its inhabitants widely scattered, and that, going farther along, there were large lagoons and dense woodlands and great deserts and wastes.

Then we asked about the land to the south, what pueblos and resources it had. They said that, in that direction, nine days' march toward the sea, there was a pueblo named Aute, and the Indians there had a lot of corn, and they also had beans and squash, and since they were so near the sea they could get fish, and that those people were their friends.

We—seeing the poverty of the land, and the bad news they were giving us about its settlements and everything else, and the way the Indians were constantly making war on us, wounding our men and horses in the places we went to for water, and doing so from the lagoons, and from such safe positions that we could not attack them, for they hid in the lagoons and shot arrows at us, and they killed a lord of Tezcoco named Don Pedro whom the commissary had brought with him—we decided among ourselves to depart and go search for the sea and that pueblo of Aute, which they had told us about. And so we left, twenty-five days after we had arrived.

9. From the Taino word for "ruler," this was another colonial Spanish term (along with *senor*, "lord") for the indigenous rulers they encountered not only in the Caribbean but throughout the Americas. Cabeza de Vaca uses the two terms interchangeably.

The first day we crossed those lagoons and fords without seeing a single Indian. But on the second day, we reached a lagoon that was very hard to cross, because the water reached up to our chests and there were a many fallen trees in it. Once we were in the middle of the lagoon, we were attacked by many Indians who were hiding behind trees to keep us from seeing them; others stood on the fallen trees. And they began to shoot arrows at us, so that they wounded many men and horses, and they captured the guide we had brought with us before we could get out of the lagoon. And after we had got out of it, they went back to pursuing us, trying to block our way, in such a way that it did us no good to turn aside or to fortify our position and try to fight them, for they would hide in the lake right away, and from there they would wound our men and horses.

Seeing this, the Governor ordered the horsemen to dismount and attack them on foot. The purser dismounted with them, and so they attacked them, and again they entered a lagoon, and so we won the crossing from them. In that skirmish some of our people were wounded, since their good arms and armor did not help them; and there were men that day who swore they had seen two oak trees, each as thick as a man's lower leg, shot straight through by the Indians' arrows; and that is not something to marvel at, considering the force and skill with which they shoot, for I myself saw an arrow stuck in the base of a poplar that had penetrated it a full span.[1] All the Indians we saw, from La Florida to here, are archers, and since they are so large in body and go about naked, from a distance they look like giants. They are marvelously well-built people, very lean, and with great strength and agility. The bows they use are as thick as your arm, from eleven to twelve palms[2] long, and they shoot arrows at two hundred paces with such a steady hand that they never miss.

After we got through that crossing, one league farther on we reached another one of the same sort, except that it was so long— half a league from end to end—that it was much worse. We forded this one freely and without hindrance from the Indians, for they had used up all their store of arrows at the first crossing and had nothing to dare attack us with. The day after, while crossing a similar ford, I found tracks of people who were going ahead of us, and I warned the Governor, who was going in the rear. And so, although the Indians went after us, since we were on notice, they were not able to injure us. And when we emerged onto open ground, they still con-

1. *Jeme*; the distance from thumb tip to index finger tip, spread wide; about six inches. "Good arms and armor" (*buenas armas*): the Spanish term *arma* encompassed both offensive weapons and armor.
2. *Palmos*; one palm is the distance from thumb tip to the tip of the little-fingertip, spread wide (also called a span in English); by convention, a quarter of a *vara*, the Spanish yard, or about eight inches.

tinued to pursue us. We turned upon them twice, and we killed two Indians, and they wounded me and two or three other Christians. And because they took refuge from us in the woods, we could not hurt them or harm them.

In this way we marched for eight days. After that crossing that I have related, no more Indians went after us until one league farther on, which is the place where I said we were heading. There, as we continued along our path, Indians came out and, without being noticed, fell upon our rear. Hearing the shouts of a boy belonging to an hidalgo named Avellaneda, who was one of the men in the rear, Avellaneda turned back and went to their aid. And the Indians hit him with an arrow right at the edge of his breastplate armor, and the wound was such that the arrow pierced his neck nearly all the way through, and he died then and there, and we carried him to Aute. After nine days of marching, from Apalachen to there, we arrived.

And when we had arrived, we found all the people from there gone, and the houses burned, along with lots of maize and squash and beans, which had all been ready to begin to harvest.[3] We rested there for two days, and afterward the Governor begged me to go discover the sea, for the Indians said it was so near there; on that journey we had already discovered it from a great river that we had found along the way, which we had given the name of Rio de la Magdalena. Considering this, the next day I set out to discover the sea, accompanied by the commissary and Captain Castillo and Andrés Dorantes and seven horsemen and fifty foot. We marched until late in the afternoon, when we reached a cove or inlet of the sea where we found many oysters, at which the men rejoiced, and we gave many thanks to God for having brought us there.

The next morning I sent twenty men to reconnoiter the coast and see its disposition. They returned the next day at night, saying that those coves and bays were very large and went so far inland that they greatly hindered discovering what we wanted to find out, and that the coast was still at a great distance. Hearing this news, and considering how bad the position was there and how poorly equipped we were for discovering the coast, I returned to the Governor. And when we arrived, we found him sick, together with many others. The night before, Indians had fallen upon them and put them in great hardship because of the illness that had overcome them. They had also killed one of their horses. I informed the Governor about what I had done and about the bad disposition of the land. That day we stayed there.

---

3. The phrasing is ambivalent, but it seems that they found the fields burned as well.

Chapter 8. How We Left Aute

The following day we left Aute and walked all day long until we reached the place where I had been. It was an extremely difficult march, for neither did we have enough horses to carry the sick, nor did we know what relief[4] we could give them, for they labored under illness every day, so that it was a matter of great pity and anguish to see the difficulties and hardships into which we were plunged. Once we arrived there, we saw how little relief we had for going farther: for we did not know where to go, nor could our men have gone forward even if we did, because most of them were sick—so sick that few would have been of any use whatever. Here I leave off telling this story at greater length, because each person can imagine what might happen in a land so strange and so bad, and so utterly lacking in any means of relief, whether for staying or for getting away.

But as the surest relief is always God our Lord, and in Him we never lost faith, something occurred that made things more intolerable than all this, for among the horsemen the majority began leaving in secret, hoping to find relief by themselves while forsaking the Governor and the sick, who were helpless and disabled. But since there were many hidalgos and men of good lineage among them, they did not allow this to happen without alerting the Governor and Your Majesty's officials. And as we decried their intentions, and we put before them the time at which they were forsaking their captain and the sick and disabled, and above all separating themselves from Your Majesty's service, they agreed that they would stay, and that what happened to one would happen to all, and none would forsake another.

The Governor, having seen this, summoned everyone jointly and severally, asking their opinions about this dismal land, that we might get away and seek some relief, for there was no relief in that land, as a third of the men were gravely ill and getting worse by the hour, so that we all felt sure we would end up like them, with death as our only prospect, which in such a place seemed even more serious to us. After looking at these and many other impediments and attempting to find relief in many ways, we settled on one means that was very difficult to put into practice, which was to build ships on which we could leave.

It seemed impossible to everyone, because we did not know how to build them, nor were there any tools, or iron, or a forge, or oakum, or

---

4. In these pages, Cabeza de Vaca riffs on the word *remedio*, which has a range of meanings from "remedy, medicine," to "resources" to "aid" to a more general sense of "prospects" or "likelihood." Instead of translating each occurrence differently by context, this translation uses the word *relief* in an attempt to cover most of these meanings.

pitch, or cordage, or lastly, any one of the many things that were needed; nor anyone who knew anything about it, to put some expertise into the task; and above all, there was nothing to eat while they were being built or anyone who could work in the fashion that we have described. Considering all this, we agreed to think it over at greater length, and our talk ceased for that day, and everyone went off, commending the matter to God our Lord, that He might lead it on the path that would best serve Him.

The next day God willed it that one of the men began saying that he would make some wooden tubes, and some deerskins could be used to make bellows. And since we were at a point when anything with some superficial appearance of relief seemed good to us, we told him to get to work. And we agreed to take our stirrups and spurs and crossbows, and anything else we had of iron, and use them to make nails and saws and axes and other tools, so great was our need for them. And to relieve our need for some provisions during the time this work was being done, we settled on making four raids into Aute, with all the horses and men that could go, and on killing a horse every other day[5] and distributing it among those who were working on building the barks and those who were sick. The raids were carried out with such men and horses as were able, and from those raids they brought back as much as four hundred *hanegas*[6] of maize, though not without fights and skirmishes with the Indians. We had many palmettos gathered so that we could use their fiber and stems, twisting and preparing them to use in place of oakum for the barks[7] that they began to build, under the only carpenter we had in the company.

And we put so much diligence into it that, after beginning them on August 4, by September 20 there were five barks finished, each measuring twenty-two cubits,[8] caulked with palmetto oakum, and we tarred them with a sort of pitch that a Greek named Don Teodoro made from some pines. And using the same palmetto cloth, and the tails and manes of the horses, we made rope and cordage, and from our shirts we made sails. And from the junipers that grew there we

5. *Cada tercer día*, a Spanish idiom meaning every other day, not "every third day" as the phrase is commonly understood in modern English. Comparing the number of days that the group remained near Aute (forty-eight) with the number of horses they had to start with (thirty-six, by the translator's count), it seems that they must have killed a horse *at least* every other day, not every third day.

6. One *hanega* or *fanega*, the most common Spanish grain measure, was roughly one hundred pounds of grain; 1.6 bushels; or (originally) one sack, or one fourth of a *carga* (load), the amount of grain a mule could carry.

7. *Barcas*; small, flat-bottomed boats.

8. *Codos*; one cubit is the length from the elbow to the tip of the outstretched hand; sometimes standardized as twenty-four *dedos* (sixteen or seventeen English inches), but Spain also had a "royal cubit" of twenty-seven *dedos* (eighteen or nineteen inches) and a nautical cubit of thirty-three *dedos* (a little under two feet). Depending on the *codo* used, the barks were thirty to forty-two feet long.

made the oars that we thought necessary. And such was the land to which our sins had brought us that it was only with very great trouble that we could find stones to use for ballast and anchors in the barks; we had not seen any there at all. We also flayed the horses' legs whole and tanned the skin to make bags for carrying water.

During this time some were going around gathering shellfish in the nooks and inlets of the sea, at which the Indians fell upon them twice, killing ten of our men in plain view of the camp, without our being able to come to their aid; we found them shot through and through with arrows, for although several had good arms and armor, it was not enough to keep that from happening, since the Indians shot their arrows with all the skill and force that I mentioned above. And our pilots declared on oath that, from the bay we had named Bay of the Cross to this place, we had traveled two hundred and eighty leagues, more or less.[9] In all this land we saw no mountains nor heard news of any at all. And before we embarked, not counting our men that the Indians killed, more than forty men died from illness and hunger. By September 22, we had eaten up all the horses, and only one remained. And on that day we embarked in the following order: in the Governor's bark there went forty-nine men; in another one that he gave to the purser and the commissary went as many more; he gave the third one to Captain Alonso del Castillo and Andrés Dorantes, with forty-eight men; he gave another to two captains named Téllez and Peñalosa, with forty-seven men; he gave the other one to the inspector and to me, with forty-nine men. And after the supplies and clothing were put on board, the barks rose no more than one span above the waterline. Besides that, we were so crowded that we could not turn around. And the power of necessity is so great that it made us risk traveling like this and venturing out into such a troublesome sea, and without anyone among us having any knowledge of the art of seafaring.

Chapter 9. How We Set out from the Bay of Horses

That bay, the one from which we set out, is named the Bay of Horses. We sailed seven days among those coves in waist-deep water without seeing a sign of anything like the coast, until at the end we reached an island near the land. My bark went in the lead, and we saw, heading from the island, five canoes of Indians; they abandoned the canoes and left them in our hands when they saw that we were going after them. The other barks went on and came upon some houses

9. If true, this would have put them relatively near their ultimate goal, Puerto de las Palmas. In fact, it is no more than fifty or sixty leagues in a straight line from Tampa Bay (Bay of the Cross, *Bahía de la Cruz*) to Apalachee Bay, where they were now; but their wandering route must have greatly increased the distance they had walked.

on the same island, where we found many fish—dried mullets and their roe—which were a very great relief for the need we were suffering. After taking the canoes we went ahead, and two leagues beyond we passed through a strait between the island and the land, which we christened the Strait of San Miguel, because we passed through it on his day.[1] Issuing from it we reached the coast, where we used the five canoes I had taken from the Indians to mend the barks somewhat, making the canoes into washboards[2] and attaching them to the barks so that their sides rose two palms above the water line.

Then we went back to sailing all along the coast in the direction of the Río de las Palmas, our thirst and hunger growing every day, because our supplies were few and were getting very near the bottom; and we ran out of water, for the leather bags we made from the legs of our horses soon rotted and became useless. Sometimes, too, we would enter coves or bays that stretched very far inland; we found all of them shallow and dangerous. And so we sailed through them for thirty days, sometimes meeting Indian fishermen in them, poor and wretched people.

At the end of those thirty days, when we were in extreme need of water, sailing close to the coast one night we heard a canoe approaching. Once we saw it, we waited for it to arrive. And it would not come and face us. And although we called out, it would not turn back nor wait for us. And because it was night, we did not follow the canoe, and we went along our way.

At dawn we saw a small island. We sailed to it to see if we could find water, but our labor was in vain, for there was none. While we were at anchor there, a great storm overtook us, so that we stayed there for six days not daring to set sail. And since it had been five days since we had drunk anything, our thirst was so great that we were compelled to drink salt water. And some drank so heedlessly that all of a sudden five men had died on us. I tell this story so briefly because I do not think there is any need to relate in great detail all the wretchedness and hardships we found ourselves in; for by considering where it was that we were and the slim hope of relief we had, each one may imagine much of what we went through. And as we saw that our thirst was growing and the water was killing us, though the storm had not ceased we agreed to commend ourselves to God our Lord and risk the danger of the sea rather than await the certainty of death that thirst offered us.

1. I.e., Michaelmas, the feast day of Saint Michael the Archangel (San Miguel), which is September 29.
2. *Falcas*; boards attached around the rims of the boats to raise their sides and prevent water from washing over.

So we set out in the direction we had seen the canoe going on the night we had come through there. And on that day we often found ourselves foundering and so close to perishing that there was not one who did not think death was certain. It pleased Our Lord, Who at the hour of greatest need tends to show His favor, that at sunset we turned around a point of land and found great calm and shelter there. Many canoes came out to us and the Indians in them spoke to us and, not wishing to wait for us, turned back. They were large and well-built people, and they carried no bows or arrows. We followed them to their houses, which were close by, at the edge of the water, and we disembarked. And in front of the houses we saw many jars with water, and great quantities of cooked fish. And the lord of those lands offered all that to the Governor and, taking him with him, led him to his house. Their houses were made of woven mats, and seemed to be permanent. And after we entered the cacique's house, he gave us a lot of fish. And we gave him some of the maize we had brought, and they ate it in our presence, and they asked for more, and we gave it to them. And the Governor gave him many trade goods, and while he was with the cacique in his house, in the middle of the night, suddenly the Indians fell upon us and upon those who lay very sick on the beach. And they also attacked the house of the cacique, where the Governor was, and they wounded him in the face with a stone. Those who were in the house seized the cacique, but as his men were so near, he escaped them and left them holding a robe of sable pelts, which are the finest pelts that I think can be found in the world. And their smell can only be described as that of ambergris and musk, and it spreads so far that it can easily be sensed at a distance. We saw other pelts, but none to compare to these.

Those of us who were in the house, seeing that the Governor had been wounded, placed him aboard the bark, and we made sure that as many men as possible joined him on their barks. And some fifty of us remained on land to face the Indians, who attacked three times that night, so ardently that each time they made us retreat more than a stone's throw. Not one of us escaped without a wound; I was wounded in the face; and if instead of the few arrows that they had with them, they had been better provisioned with them, there is no doubt that they would have done us great harm. The final time they attacked, Captains Dorantes, Peñalosa and Téllez placed themselves in ambush with fifteen men and fell on them from the rear, causing them to flee; and so they left us.

The next morning I broke up more than thirty of their canoes, which we put to use to protect ourselves against a north wind that was blowing, for all that day we had to stay there in the great cold, not daring to set to sea because of how it was storming out there.

After this had passed, we embarked once more and sailed for three days. And since we had taken little water with us, and we likewise had few vessels for carrying it, we fell once more into our basic necessity. And as we continued along our way, we entered an estuary, and while we were there we saw a canoe with Indians approaching. As we hailed them, they came toward us. And the Governor, whose bark they had reached, asked them for water, and they offered some, provided we gave them something in which to carry it. And a Christian Greek, named Doroteo Teodoro (who has already been mentioned) said he would go with them. The Governor and others endeavored greatly to dissuade him, and they never could, but he insisted upon going with them no matter the case. So he went, and he took a black man with him. And the Indians left two of their company as hostages. At night the Indians returned and brought us many vessels, without any water, and they did not bring the Christians they had taken. And the ones they had left as hostages, when the others spoke to them, tried to jump into the water. But our men in the bark held them, and so the Indians in canoe fled. And they left us feeling very uneasy and sad for the loss of those two Christians.

Chapter 10. On the Skirmish the Indians Gave Us

When morning came, many canoes of Indians approached us, asking for the two companions who had remained in the bark as hostages. The Governor answered that he would give them to them as soon as they brought the two Christians whom they had taken. With those people came five or six lords, and they seemed to us the best-built people and the ones with the greatest authority and composure we had seen up to then, though not as large as the others of whom we have spoken. They wore the hair loose and very long, and were clothed in marten-skin robes of the sort we had taken earlier, and some of the robes were made in a very strange fashion, for they were trimmed with braided knots of lion-hued leather, which made them look very fine. They begged us to go with them, saying they would give us the Christians and water and many other things. And continually more canoes pressed toward us, endeavoring to block the mouth of that cove. And so for that reason, since the land was very dangerous to remain in, we set out to sea, where we remained with them till noon.

And since they would not give us the Christians, and for the same reason we would not give them the Indians, they began to hurl stones at us with slings, and sticks, and made signs of shooting arrows, though we only saw three or four bows among them all. While engaged in this fight, the wind picked up and they turned about and left us. And so we sailed that day until late afternoon, when my bark, which went ahead of the others, discovered a point of land projecting into the water, and on the other side a very large river[3] could be seen. And at a small island that the point made I had them drop anchor to wait for the other barks. The Governor refused to approach; instead, he entered a very nearby bay where there were many small islands. And there we gathered together and drew fresh water from the sea, because the river emptied into it like a torrent. And in order to toast some of the maize we had brought—because we had been eating it raw for the past two days—we went ashore on that island; but since we found no firewood, we all decided to go to the river beyond the point, one league from there. And as we went, the current was so strong that it absolutely would not let us approach, but rather it carried us away from the land.

And as we struggled obstinately to make the shore, the north wind blowing from the land began to grow so strong that it drove us out to the high sea, and there was nothing we could do about it. And half a league out, where we had been driven, we sounded, and found that with thirty fathoms[4] of rope we could not touch bottom, and we could not tell whether the current was the reason why we could not touch it. And so we sailed for two more days, struggling to make land, and at the end of that time, a little before sunrise, we saw many columns of smoke rising along the coast. Struggling to reach them, we found ourselves in three fathoms of water. And because it was night, we did not dare to make landfall, for we had seen so many columns of smoke that we believed some danger might again befall us there, and due to the deep darkness we would not be able to see what we should do. For that reason we decided to wait until morning, and when dawn broke, each bark was on its own, lost from the others.

I found myself in thirty fathoms, and continuing my journey late in the afternoon I saw two barks, and as I drew near them I saw that the first one I reached was the Governor's, who asked me what I thought we should do.

I told him that we ought to rejoin the other bark, which was ahead of us, and in no manner forsake her, and the three barks together should continue our journey, wherever God might take us.

He replied that that was impossible, because the bark was sailing too far out at sea, and he wanted to make landfall, and that if I

3. Apparently the mouth of the Mississippi.
4. *Brazas*; a fathom is the distance from fingertip to fingertip, with the arms spread wide; conventionally equal to six feet, though when measures were standardized in later centuries, the Spanish foot was slightly smaller than the British foot. The depth of the seafloor so near the mainland here is another indication that they are at the mouth of the Mississippi River.

wished to follow I should have the people of my bark take the oars and pull hard, for only by might of arms would land be reached. This was the counsel he had been given by a captain he had brought with him whose name was Pantoja, telling him that if he did not land that day he would not land for another six, and during that time we would necessarily die of hunger.

Seeing his determination, I took up my oar, and all the others in my bark who were able did the same, and we rowed until nearly sunset. But as the Governor had our healthiest and most robust men with him, there was no way we could follow or keep up with his bark. When I saw this, I asked him to throw me a rope from his bark to be able to follow, and he replied that it would be no small feat if they could reach land on their own that night. I told him that since I could see it was barely possible for us to follow and do what he had ordered, he should tell me what it was that he was ordering me to do.

He replied to me that this was no time for anyone to give orders to anyone else; that each one should do what best seemed to him the way to save his life; that this was he intended to do it. And having said this, he sailed on away from us with his bark.

As I could not follow him, I bore down upon the other bark that was out at sea, which waited for me. On reaching it, I found it was the one that Captains Peñalosa and Téllez led. And so we sailed together for four days, eating half a handful of raw maize each day as our ration. At the end of those four days a storm overtook us, which made the other bark perish, and by the great mercy that God showed us we did not sink utterly, for all the weather.

With it being winter, and the cold very great, and so many days that we had been suffering from hunger, and from the blows we had received from the waves, the next day the men began to lose their spirits entirely, so that when the sun set all those aboard my bark had collapsed on one another in a heap, so near dying that few remained conscious. Among them all, at that time there were not five men still standing. And when night fell, only the ship's master[5] and I were still able to sail the bark. And two hours after nightfall the master told me that I should take charge of it, because he was in such a state that he believed he would die that very night. So I took the helm, and after midnight I went to see if the master was dead. And he told me that, on the contrary, he was better, and that he would steer until daybreak. At that moment, truly, I would much more willingly have accepted death than see so many people before me in such a state. After the master took charge of the bark I rested

5. *Maestre*; the second in command on a vessel. Here, Cabeza de Vaca and the inspector, Solís, share joint command as captains of the small bark; the master is directly under them.

a little, very restlessly, nor was there anything further from my mind then than sleep.

Near the break of dawn it seemed to me I heard the crash of the sea swell, for as the coast was shallow, the noise was loud. Surprised at it, I called the master, who told me he thought we were near land. And we tested it and found we were in seven fathoms. And it seemed to him that we should keep at sea until dawn had broken. So I took up an oar and rowed along the strip of land, for we were one league offshore; and then we turned the stern to seaward. And close to land a wave took us and hurled the bark a horseshoe toss out of the water, and at the great jolt it made nearly all the people who were lying in the boat as if they were dead came to. And when they saw we were close to land, they began to clamber off the bark, crawling on hands and feet. And when they came onto land near some deep gullies, we built a fire and toasted some of the maize we had brought. And we found water from when it had rained, and with the warmth of the fire the men revived and began to take heart. The day we arrived here was November 6.

Chapter 11. On What Befell Lope de Oviedo among Some Indians

After the men had eaten, I sent Lope de Oviedo, who had more strength and was more robust than anyone else, to go over to some trees nearby there, climb one of them, and discover the land we were in and endeavor to bring back some news about it. He did so and found out we were on an island.[6] And he saw that the land looked like it had been pawed, the way land looks where there are cattle grazing, and from that it seemed to him that it must be a land of Christians, and so he told us.

I sent him back to look again much more closely, and see if there were any worn trails, and not to go too far because of the danger there might be. He went and, finding a footpath, followed it about half a league, and he found a few Indian huts, which were empty because the Indians were out in the fields. He took one of their pots, a small dog, and a few dried fish, and then turned back toward us.

And since it seemed to us that he was taking a long time, I sent two other Christians to look for him and see what had happened. They met him nearby and saw that three Indians, with bows and arrows, were following after him, calling him, and he likewise was calling them by signs. And so he came to where we were, and the Indians stayed a bit back, sitting on the beach itself. And half an

---

6. The consensus is that this is one of the barrier islands off of Galveston Bay, either Galveston Island itself or a smaller sandbar island (which may have shifted position since 1528) just south of it, near the outlet of Oyster Creek.

hour later, a hundred other Indian archers joined them, and now, whether they were big or small, our fear made them look like giants. And they stood near us, where the first three were.

It was pointless to suppose that there might be anyone among us who could defend himself, for there were hardly three of us to be found who could stand upright. The inspector and I stepped forward and called the Indians over, and they came to where we were, and we endeavored as best we could to reassure them and reassure ourselves. And we gave them beads and bells, and each of them gave me an arrow, which is a sign of friendship. And by signs they told us that the next morning they would come back and would bring us food, for at the moment they had none.

Chapter 12. How the Indians Brought Us Food

The next day, as the sun was rising, which was the hour the Indians had told us, they came to where we were as they had promised and brought us a lot of fish and some roots that they eat, and they are like nuts, some bigger, some smaller, most of which are gathered from the water with great difficulty. In the afternoon they returned and brought us more fish and some of the same roots, and they had their women and children come so they could see us, and so they became rich with the bells and beads that we gave them. And the following days they returned to visit with the same things as before. As we saw that we had been supplied with fish and roots and water and the other things we asked for, we all decided to embark once more and continue our voyage. And we dug the bark out of the sand into which it had sunk. And we were all forced to strip and undergo great hardships to set it in the water, for we were in such a condition that other, much lighter things would have been enough to give us trouble.

So, after we embarked, when we were two crossbow shots from shore we were hit by such a wave that we all were soaked, and as we were naked and it was very cold, we dropped our oars. And at the next wave that the sea hit us with, it overturned the bark. The inspector and two others clung to it to escape drowning, but quite the contrary happened, for the bark took them under and they drowned. Since the coast is very wild, a single sea swell pitched the others, enveloped in waves and half-drowned, onto the beach of the same island, and only the three whom the bark had taken under were missing. The rest of us who escaped—as naked as we were born; everything we had brought—lost. And though it all had little value, at that moment its value was great. And as it was already November then, and the cold was great, and we were in such a state that one could easily have counted all our bones, we looked like the figure of death itself.

Of myself I can say that since the month of May I had not tasted anything but toasted maize, and sometimes I had even been forced to eat it raw, for although the horses were killed while the barks were being built, I never could eat them, and not even ten times did I eat fish. I say this to explain myself, so that anyone might see what a state we were in. And on top of all that I have said, a north wind had arisen, so that we were closer to death than to life. It pleased Our Lord that, while searching for unburned wood from the fire we had made there before, we found burning embers, which we used to light great fires. And so we asked Our Lord for mercy and forgiveness of our sins, spilling many tears, each of us feeling pity not only for himself but for all the others that he saw in the same state.

And at sunset the Indians, thinking we had not left, sought us out again and brought us food. But when they saw us like that, dressed so differently than at first and looking so strange, they were so frightened that they turned back. I went after them and called them, and they returned, very frightened. I made them understand by signs that we had lost a bark and three of our men had drowned. And there before them they themselves saw two dead men, and the rest of us were on the same path. The Indians, on seeing the disaster that had overcome us and the disaster that still surrounded us with so much misfortune and wretchedness, sat down among us. And from the tremendous grief and pity they felt on seeing us in such a chance, they began to weep so loudly and so sincerely that it could be heard far away. And they went on like this for more than half an hour; and truly, when we saw that these men, so devoid of reason and so rude, like brutes, grieved so deeply for us, it made me and the others in my company feel even more emotion and regard for our own calamity.

When the lament had calmed down, I asked the Christians, and said that if it seemed well to them, I would beg those Indians to take us to their houses. And some of them who had lived in New Spain replied that we should not even mention it, for if they took us to their houses, they would sacrifice us to their idols. But seeing that there was no other relief to be had, and that by any other route death was surer and nearer, I disregarded what they said, and instead begged the Indians to take us to their houses. And they showed that this gave them great pleasure, and told us to wait a bit, for they would do what we wished. Soon thirty of them loaded themselves with firewood and went to their houses, which were far away. And we stayed with the others until nearly nighttime, when they took us and, carrying us along tightly gripped and in great haste, we went to their houses. And because it was so very cold, and they feared that on the way someone might die or faint, they made sure there would be four or five big fires at intervals, and at each one they warmed us, and once they saw that we had regained a little warmth and strength, they would take us to the next fire with such haste that our feet barely touched the ground. And in this way we got to their houses, where we saw they had built a house for us, and many fires in it. And about an hour after we arrived, they began to dance and to make a great celebration, which lasted all night long, though for us there was no pleasure, celebration, or sleep as we awaited the moment when they would sacrifice us. And in the morning they once more gave us fish and roots and treated us so well that we became reassured, and we lost some of our fear of sacrifice.

Chapter 13. How We Learned about Other Christians

That same day I saw one of the Indians with a trade good, and I recognized that it was not one of the ones we had given them. Asking where they had gotten it, they replied by signs that it had been given to them other men like us, who were over behind us. Seeing this, I sent two Christians with two Indians who would show them those people, and very nearby they ran into them, for they had also come to seek us, because the Indians who stayed there had told them about us; and these were Captains Andrés Dorantes and Alonso del Castillo, with all the men from their bark. And when they reached us, they were very frightened to see us the way we looked. And they felt great grief that they had nothing to give us, for they had no clothes but what they were wearing. And they stayed there with us, and they told us how, on the fifth of that same month, their bark had beached a league and a half from there, and they had escaped without losing anything. And we all decided together that we would repair their bark, and that all of us who had the strength and the inclination would leave in it; the others would remain there until they had convalesced, and then go as best they could along the coast, and they would wait[7] there until God led them with us to a land of Christians.

And as we planned, so we set to work. And before we could launch the bark, Tavera, a gentleman in our company, died. And the bark that we were planning to sail met its end, and could not stay afloat, and soon sank. And as we were left in the fashion I have mentioned, most of us naked, and the weather so rough for walking and for swimming across rivers and coves, nor did we have any provisions nor any way to carry it, we decided to do what necessity demanded, which was to winter there. And we also agreed that the four men who were the most robust would go to Pánuco, believing that we

---

7. *Esperar*; an ambiguous verb, meaning both "to wait" and "to hope, have faith." Another valid translation would be "and have faith there."

were near there, and that if God our Lord should be pleased to lead them there, they would give notice of how we were staying on that island, and of our need and hardships. These four were great swimmers. One was named Álvaro Fernández, Portuguese, a carpenter and sailor; the second was named Méndez, and the third Figueroa, who was born in Toledo; the fourth, Estudillo, born in Zafra. They took with them an Indian who was from the island.[8]

Chapter 14. How the Four Christians Left

These four Christians left, and a few days later the weather grew so cold and stormy that the Indians could not pull up the roots. And the narrow sluices[9] in which they used to fish no longer yielded anything. And as the houses were so open to the weather, people began to die. And five Christians who were encamped[1] on the coast got to the point that they ate each other up, until only one of them remained—who, being alone, had no one to eat him. Their names are these: Sierra, Diego López, Corral, Palacios, Gonzalo Ruiz. The Indians were so shaken by this case, and it caused such astonishment among them, that if they had seen it at the beginning they undoubtedly would have killed them, and we all would have been in great hardship.

In the end, after a very short time, out of eighty men who had come there in our two parties, only fifteen remained alive. And after all these had died, the local Indians got a stomach illness from which half of their people also died. And they believed that we were the ones who were killing them. And as they were so certain of this, they planned among themselves to kill those of us who had remained. Right when they were coming to carry this out, an Indian who was keeping me told them not to believe we were the ones killing them, for if we had such a power we would have avoided letting so many of our own people die, unable to relieve them; also, only a very few of us remained, and none did any harm or injury, so the best was to let us

---

8. This phrase as it appeared in V. The 1542 Zamora edition (hereafter Z) has "from the island of Avia." The island, whether or not we attach the dubious name "Avia" to it, remains unidentified.
9. *Canales* (Z); Small channels dug from a river or body of water to trap fish. Or in another sense of *cañales* (V), they may have been weirs or enclosures made of reeds, used to narrow a river for the same purpose. Or then again, if the *cañales* (V) reading is correct, they may not have been sluices at all but wetlands where *cañas* (water reeds or canes) grew, attracting fish.
1. *En rancho*; in the early sixteenth century primarily a military term that had not yet developed the set of meanings peculiar to Mexican Spanish, "rural community" and "large agricultural estate." Z changes the unfamiliar military term to "en Xamho," which is probably a printer's error: in sixteenth-century handwriting, *r* can easily be mistaken for *x*, and *nc* for *m*, leading the printer to misinterpret *rancho* as a place name, the unlikely "Xamho."

alone. And Our Lord so willed it that the other followed this advice and counsel and so their plan was stopped.

We gave this island the name *Isla del Mal Hado*, the Island of Ill Fate. The people on it are tall and well built. They have no weapons other than bows and arrows, at which they are extremely skilled. The men pierce one of their nipples from side to side, and some of them have both pierced. And they wear a cane in the hole they make, as much as two and a half palms long and as thick as two fingers.[2] They also have their lower lips pierced and place a thin piece of cane in it, about half a finger. The women work very hard. The settlement they make on this island lasts from October until late February. Their food supply is the roots I have mentioned, which they gather from underwater around November and December. They use sluices, and they only have fish during this season;[3] afterward, they eat the roots. At the end of February they leave for other parts in search of food, because the roots begin to sprout then and are not any good.

Of all the people in the world, they are the ones who love their children most and treat them best. And when it happens that the child of one of them dies, the parents and relatives mourn it, and so does the whole pueblo. And the wailing lasts a full year, for each day before the sun rises, first the parents begin to mourn, and after them the whole pueblo. And they do the same at noon and at nightfall. And at the end of the year of mourning, they do the child the honor of the dead, and they wash themselves and clean off all the soot they have been wearing. They mourn all their dead in this manner, except for the old, to whom they pay no attention, for they say that they have already passed their time and are no longer of any use; rather, they take up space and rob the children of their food.

Their custom is to bury the dead, excepting those among them who are physicians,[4] for these they burn, and while the fire is ablaze, everyone dances and makes a big celebration, and they grind the bones to powder. At the end of the year, when they do them their last honors, they all scarify their flesh at the ceremony, and give the relatives those powdered bones to drink in water.

Each man has one recognized wife. The physicians are the freest men; they can have two or three, and between these wives there is great friendship and harmony. When someone marries off his daughter, everything that the one who takes her as his wife kills by hunting or fishing, from the day he marries her onward, is all brought by his

---

2. *Dedos*; a traditional measurement equal to about one and a half inches.
3. *De para este tiempo*; Spanish uses the same word (*tiempo*) for the senses that English distinguishes as "time," "weather," and "season," depending on context.
4. *Físicos*; the word used here and again in the next chapter is a direct cognate of the common English term, but in Spanish it was considered obsolete by the 1700s and in that sense could be more precisely translated by the obsolete English term *leeches*.

woman to her father's house; he would not dare try it or eat any of it. And they bring him food to eat from his father-in-law's house. And all that time, neither the father-in-law nor the mother-in-law enter his house, and he may not enter his parents-in-law's or of his brothers-in-law's house. And if they happen to run into each other somewhere, they turn out of each other's way, the distance of a crossbow's shot, and while they are walking away from one another like this they lower their heads and keep their eyes on the ground, for they hold it to be an evil thing to see or speak with each other. The women have the freedom to communicate and converse with their parents-in-law and relatives. And this custom prevails everywhere from the island up to more than fifty leagues inland.

There is another custom, which is that when a son or a brother dies,[5] the people in the house where he died do not gather food for three months; instead, they let themselves starve. And their relatives and neighbors provide them with what they need to eat. And since so many of their people died during the time we were there, there was great starvation in most of the houses, because they were also keeping their customs and ceremonies. And those who did gather food could bring in only very little no matter how hard they labored because the weather was so rough. Therefore the Indians who were keeping me left the island and went over to the mainland in some canoes, to some bays where there were many oysters. And for three months of the year they eat nothing else, and they drink very bad water. They have far too little firewood and far too many mosquitoes. Their houses are built from woven reed mats, on piles of oyster shells; and they sleep on them naked; and they do not even have the oysters, except by chance.[6]

5. *Hijo o hermano*; may be taken to encompass both sexes, so the phrase could also be translated as "child or sibling." On the other hand, the reader will note that Cabeza de Vaca describes all these customs from a presumptively male point of view.
6. This sentence, and particularly its last two phrases (*y sobre ellos duermen en cueros; y no los tienen si no es acaso*), has posed difficulties for every translator who has tried to tackle it. One problem is the last bit, *si no es acaso* (except if it is perhaps), an unusual turn of phrase but not insoluble. More puzzling is the pronoun *los* in *y no los tienen* (and they do not have them), which has no clear antecedent. What is it that they do not have? The last noun mentioned is *cueros*, which normally means "hides" or "pelts," leading some translators to follow the lead of Smith: "The houses are of mats, set up on masses of oyster shells, which they sleep upon, and in skins, should they accidentally possess them." The problem is that the phrase *dormir en cueros* (literally, "to sleep in skins") always means "to sleep naked"; a search of text databases did not turn up any context in which it means "to sleep on hides." Eliminating *cueros* as the antecedent of "them" leaves only *ostiones*, "oysters," as a possibility; and so Pupo-Walker goes with: "Their houses are built of oyster shells, and they sleep naked on top of these shells if they happen to have any." Favata and Fernández try, rather unconvincingly, to have it both ways: "Their houses are made of mats and built on oyster shells, on which they sleep naked, putting animal hides on them if they happen to have any." In the end, this translation follows Pupo-Walker's interpretation, but the translator's guess is that a few words were inadvertently dropped in the transition from manuscript to printer text, and what we struggle to understand here is, in fact, accidental nonsense.

And so we lived until the end of April, when we went to the sea-shore, where we ate blackberries the whole month long, during which season they never ceased holding their *areítos*[7] and celebrations.

Chapter 15. *On What Befell Us on the Island of Ill Fate*[8]

On the island I have described they wanted to turn us into physicians without giving us any examinations or asking us for any diplomas, because they heal diseases by blowing on the patient, and with that puff of breath and their hands they drive the illness out of him. And they ordered us to do the same so that we would at least be of some use to them. We laughed at this, saying it was ridiculous and that we did not know how to heal, so they took away our food until we did what they told us to. And seeing our obstinate refusal, an Indian told me that I did not know what I was saying when I said that what he knew was useless, because the stones and other things that grow in the countryside have virtue;[9] and he said that by using a heated stone and drawing it across the stomach he could cure and take away pain, and that we who were men surely had greater virtue and power. In the end, we found ourselves in such dire necessity that we had to do it, without fear that anyone would exact punishment from us for it.

The way they have of healing themselves is this: when they see that they are sick they call a physician, and after they are well, they not only give him everything they own, they even look for things from their relatives to give him. What the physician does is make a few cuts on them where the pain is located and then suck around the cuts. They do cauterizations with fire, which is something they all take to be very efficacious, and I have experienced it, and it turned out well for me. After this, they blow on the spot where they have the ache, and with that they believe that they have taken out the illness. The way we treated the sick was by making the sign of the cross over them, and breathing on them, and reciting a Pater Noster and an Ave Maria, and praying as hard as we could to God our Lord that He might give them good health and inspire them to treat us somewhat well. It was by the will of God and His mercy that all those for whom we prayed told the others that they were well and healthy as soon as we made the sign of the cross over them, and that was why they treated us well, and would go without food in order to feed us, and

7. *Areítos*; ritual singing and dance; this is another exotic Taino word, adopted in the colonial Spanish of the Caribbean and Mexico to refer to indigenous religious festivals in general.
8. *Villa de Malhado*; per V, but Adorno and Pautz note this is clearly a typesetter's error. In the Gothic typeface used, *ysla* (with a long s, *yſla*) looks like *villa*.
9. *Virtud*; in the older, physical (not moral) sense, in both Spanish and English, a special power or efficacy, especially for healing.

gave us hides and other little things. So extreme was our hunger there that I often went three days without eating anything at all, and so did they, and to me it seemed impossible that life could go on, though afterward I met with other, greater famines and necessities, as I will relate later on.

The Indians who kept Alonso del Castillo and Andrés Dorantes and the others who were still alive belonged to a different language and a different kindred, so they had gone to a different part of the mainland to eat oysters; they remained there until April 1, and then they returned to the island, which was perhaps two leagues off shore at the broadest part of the channel, and the island is half a league wide by five long. All the people in this land go about naked. Only the women keep part of their bodies covered with a wool that grows on the trees. Adolescent girls cover themselves with deer skins. They are very freely giving of what they have with each other. There is no lord among them. All who are of the same lineage go about together. Two sorts of languages live among them: one group is named Capoques, the others are Han. They have the custom that, when they know each other and meet from time to time, before they speak, they stand weeping for half an hour, and afterward, the one who is being visited rises first and gives to the other everything he owns, and the other receives it. And then in a little while he goes away with it all, and sometimes, after receiving it, he even leaves without either having spoken a word. They have other strange customs, but I have told the main and most striking ones, so I will proceed to relate what else happened to us.

Chapter 16. How the Christians Left the Island of Ill Fate

After Dorantes and Castillo returned to the island, they gathered together all the Christians, who were somewhat scattered, and they found there were fourteen all told. I was across the way, as I have said, on the mainland, where my Indians had taken me and where I had caught such a severe illness that, even if anything else gave me some hope for life, that illness was enough to take it away from me altogether. When the Christians learned of this, they gave an Indian the sable robe that we had taken from the cacique, as we stated above, so that he should guide them to where I was, to see me. And so twelve of them came, because two had become so frail that they did not dare to take them along. The names of those who came are: Alonso del Castillo, Andrés Dorantes and Diego Dorantes, Valdivieso, Estrada, Tostado, Chaves, Gutiérrez, the Asturian cleric,[1] Diego de

---

1. *Esturiano clerigo*; Asturias is a province on the north coast of Spain. Esturiano is also a (rather rare) surname, so the phrase could alternatively be interpreted as "Esturiano the cleric."

Huelva, Estevanico the black man, Benitez. And when they reached
the mainland they found another who was of ours, named Francisco
de León, and the thirteen of them went along the coast. And after
they had gone by, the Indians with whom I was told me of it, and how
Jerónimo de Alaniz and Lope de Oviedo were still on the island. My
illness prevented me from following them, nor did I see them.

I had to remain with those same Indians from the island for more
than a year, and because they gave me so much work and treated me
so badly, I resolved to flee them and go to those who live in the woods
and the mainland, who are called the ones from Charruco, because I
could not stand the life I had with these others; because, among
many other hardships, I had to gather the roots for food from under
the water and from among the canes where they were buried in the
ground. And from doing this my fingers had become so worn out that
the touch of a straw was enough to make them bleed, and the reeds
cut me all over, because many were broken and I had to go in among
them with only what clothing I have said I was wearing.

That is why I set to work to go join the other Indians, and with
them things turned out a little better for me. And because I became
a trader, I endeavored to practice the trade as best I knew how. And
for that reason they fed me and treated me well and begged me to
go about from one part to another for things they needed, since
there is little movement or trade in the land on account of the wars
they constantly waged.

So with my trades and wares I would go as far inland as I wished,
and I would travel along the coast forty or fifty leagues away. The
main items of my trade were pieces of seashells, and hearts of seashells, and oyster shells that they use to cut a bean-like fruit that
they use for healing and in their dances and feasts, and that is
thing of greatest value among them, and sea beads and other things.
So that was what I carried inland. And in exchange and barter for
it, I brought back hides, and red ochre, which they use to daub and
dye their faces and hair, flint for arrowheads, paste and hard canes
for making arrows, and some tassels that are made from the hair of
deer, which they dye and turn red. And this trade suited me well,
because while practicing it I had the freedom to go wherever I
wished, and there was nothing I was obliged to do, and I was not a
slave, and wherever I went they treated me well and fed me for the
sake of my wares, and especially because while practicing it I was
trying to find out which way I should go to move forward. And I was
well known among them; they rejoiced greatly when they saw me and
I brought them the things they needed. And those who did not know
me endeavored and desired to see me because of my fame.

The hardships I suffered in this would take long to tell, from
danger and hunger to storms and frost, for they often overtook me

in the open field and alone, where through the great mercy of God our Lord I escaped. And for this reason I did not practice this trade in winter, for that was the season when they themselves, shut up in their huts and encampments, could not get by or take care of themselves. Almost six years I spent in that land, alone among them and naked as they all went. The reason I lingered so long was to take with me a Christian who was still on the island, named Lope de Oviedo. His other companion, de Alaniz, who had stayed with him after Alonso del Castillo and Andrés Dorantes had gone with all the others, died soon afterward. And to get him out of there, I went over to the island every year and begged him that we should go in the best way we could devise in search of Christians. And each year he stopped me, saying we would go next year.

In the end, I finally got him out. And I got him over the cove and four rivers that are there along the coast, because he could not swim, and so we went ahead with some Indians until we came to a cove that is one league across and very deep everywhere; and from the way it looked to us and what we saw, it is the one they call Espíritu Santo.[2] And on the other shore we saw some Indians who had come to meet ours, and they told us that farther on there were three men like us, and they told us their names. And when we asked them about all the others, they told us that they had all died of cold and hunger, and that the Indians farther on had themselves killed Diego Dorantes, Valdivieso, and Diego de Huelva for their own amusement, because they had moved from one house to another; and that other Indians, their neighbors with whom Captain Dorantes was now staying, had killed Esquivel and Méndez because of a dream they had dreamed.

We asked them how those who were alive were doing. They told us they were very ill-treated, for the boys and other Indians, who are very lazy and cruel among them, often kicked, slapped, and beat them, and such was the life they had with them.

We wished to find out about the country farther on and the supplies of food that might be found in it. They replied that it was very thinly settled, and that there was nothing to eat there, and that people died of cold because they had no hides and nothing with which to cover themselves. They also told us that, if we wished to see those three Christians, the Indians who held them would be coming in about two days to eat nuts one league from there, on the bank of the river.

2. Cabeza de Vaca was quite mistaken in this identification. Here he was most likely at Matagorda Bay. Bahía de Espíritu Santo (Bay of the Holy Spirit) was a name that other early Spanish explorers gave to the Mississippi River Delta.

And so that we might see that what they had said about the ill-treatment of the others was true, they slapped and beat my companion while we were with them, and I was not deprived of my share; and they hit us with many balls of mud that they threw at us, and every day they held arrows to our chests, saying they wished they could kill us like they had our companions. And fearing this, Lope de Oviedo, my companion, said he wanted to go back with some of those Indians' women, with whom we had forded the cove, who had remained a bit farther back. I strongly insisted he should not go, and did all I could, and I could not stop him by any means. And so he went back, and I remained alone with these Indians, who were named Quevenes, and those with whom he went away were called Deaguanes.

Chapter 17. How the Indians Came and Brought Andrés Dorantes and Castillo and Estevanico

Two days after Lope de Oviedo left, the Indians who held Alonso del Castillo and Andrés Dorantes came to the very spot they had told us about to eat those nuts[3] on which they subsist, grinding some grains with them, during two months of the year when they do not eat anything else. And they do not even have that each year, for the nuts come in only every other year; they are the size of the nuts from Galicia,[4] and the trees are very large, and there is a great number of them.

An Indian let me know that the Christians had arrived and that if I wished to see them I should steal away and flee to the other side of a wood that he pointed out to me, because he and other relatives of his were to visit those Indians, and they would take me with them to where the Christians were. I trusted them and resolved to do it, because they spoke a different language from that of my Indians. And putting the plan in action, the next day they went and found me in the place he had pointed out, and so they took me with them. When I got near to where they had their shelter, Andrés Dorantes came out to look who it was, because the Indians had also told him that a Christian was coming. And when he saw me he was very shocked, because for many days they had given me up for dead, and that is what the Indians had told them.

We gave many thanks to God for meeting each other again, and that day was one of the days of greatest pleasure we had in all our days. And when I got to where Castillo was, they asked me where I was going. I told him my goal was to go to a land of Christians, and

3. *Nueces*; in Spanish, *nuez* means both "walnut" specifically and "nut" in general. In Texas Spanish today, *nuez* usually means "pecan." The nuts here are wild pecans.
4. Walnuts.

that was the trail and the quest I was on. Andrés Dorantes replied that he had been begging Castillo and Estevanico for many days to go farther on, and that they did not dare do it because they did not know how to swim and they were afraid of the rivers and coves that they would have to cross, for there are so many in that land. And since God our Lord had been pleased to spare me through all my hardships and illnesses and lead me at last to their company, they resolved to flee, as I would take them across the rivers and coves we might run into. And they warned that I should not by any means give the Indians to understand or let them learn from me that I wanted to go on, because they would kill me right away, and for this purpose I would have to stay with them for six months, when it would be the season when those Indians went to another land to eat *tunas*.[5] These are fruits the size of eggs, and they are vermilion and black and taste very good. They eat them three months of the year, during which they eat nothing else at all. Because, during the season when they would gather this fruit, other Indians from farther on would come to them, and they would bring bows for trade and exchange; and when they returned, we could flee from our Indians and go back with the others.

Having come to this understanding, I stayed there, and they gave me as a slave to an Indian with whom Dorantes stayed, <who was cross-eyed, and his wife and their son and another Indian who was with them were all cross-eyed>.[6] These are called Mariames, and Castillo was with other neighbors of theirs called Iguaces.[7]

And while we were here, they told me about how, after leaving the Island of Ill Fate, they found the bark that the purser and the monks had sailed in, beached on the seacoast; and when they were crossing the rivers—there are four large rivers, with very strong currents—the barks in which they were crossing were swept out to sea, where four of them drowned; and they had gone on like that until they crossed the cove, which they crossed with great difficulty. And fifteen leagues farther on, they found another cove, and when they reached it two of their companions had already died over the sixty leagues they had walked, and everyone who remained was about to do the same, and on the whole journey they had eaten nothing but crawfish and rock grass.[8] And when they reached this last cove, they said, they found Indians in it eating blackberries; and

---

5. Another exotic Taino word adopted by Spanish (and also by English, in which it has been used since 1555). These are the fruits of the nopal cactus (*Opuntia*), also known in English as prickly pears or Indian figs; the same word can also refer to the cactus itself.
6. Throughout, lines enclosed in angle brackets appear only in V.
7. Also spelled Iguases, Yeguaces, and Yaguaces at various points in the two early editions.
8. *Yerba pedrera*; many wild plants in Spain share this common name; the most likely candidate in this context seems to be kelp or seaweed.

upon seeing the Christians, the Indians went from there to another promontory. And while they were endeavoring and searching for a way to cross the cove, an Indian and a Christian crossed over to them, and when he arrived they recognized him as Figueroa, one of the four men we had sent on ahead from the Island of Ill Fate.

And there Figueroa told them about how he and his companions had reached that place, where two of them and one Indian had died, all three from cold and hunger, because they had come and stayed there in the roughest weather in the world; and he said that the Indians had captured him and Méndez, and while he stayed with them Méndez had fled, heading in the direction of Pánuco as best he could, and the Indians had gone after him and killed him. And [Figueroa said], while he was with these same Indians he found out that among the Mariames there was a Christian who had come over from the other side, and he had been found with the ones called Quevenes, and this Christian was Hernando de Esquivel, born in Badajoz, who had been in the commissary's company. And he had found out from Esquivel how the Governor, the purser, and the others had met their end.[9]

Esquivel told him that the purser and the friars had beached their bark among the rivers, and, while they marched down along the coast, the bark of the Governor and his men had made land, and he [the Governor] went on with his bark until they reached that big cove, and there he went back to pick up his men and he crossed them over to the other side, and then came back for the purser, the monks, and all the rest. And he told him how, after they had disembarked, the Governor had revoked the authority he had granted to the purser as his lieutenant, and had given that office to a captain he had with him called Pantoja. And the Governor had stayed on his bark and had not wanted to get out on land that night. And a ship's master and a page who was sick had stayed with him, and aboard the bark they had no water and nothing to eat; and at midnight the north wind blew so hard that it carried the bark out to sea, without anybody seeing it, because they had nothing but one stone for an anchor; and they never heard from him again. And, seeing this, the people who had stayed on land went on along the coast, and since they found so much water blocking their way, they built rafts with great difficulty, on which they crossed to the other side. And as they went on ahead, they reached a wooded point at the water's edge, and they found Indians who, on seeing them approach, packed their houses into their canoes and crossed over from the other side of the coast. And the Christians, in view of the season—for it was in the

9. We are three layers deep in hearsay at this point: Cabeza de Vaca is telling the story that Dorantes told him about what Figueroa told Dorantes that Esquivel had told Figueroa.

month of November—remained in those woods, because they found water and firewood and some crawfish and seafood, where they slowly began to die from cold and hunger. On top of that, Pantoja, who had remained as lieutenant, ill-treated them.

Unable to stand this, Sotomayor, a brother of Vasco Porcallo (the one from the island of Cuba), who had come over in the fleet as camp master,[1] confronted Pantoja and struck him a blow with a stick from which he died, and so they went on perishing. And as they died, the others made them into strips of dried meat. And the last one to die was Sotomayor, and Esquivel made him into dried meat, and by eating him he stayed alive until March 1, when one of the Indians who had fled from there came to see if they were dead, and took Esquivel back with him. And while Esquivel was in the power of this Indian, Figueroa spoke to him, and he learned from him everything we have related here. And [Figueroa] begged him to come with him, so they could both head toward Pánuco; but Esquivel refused to do this, saying he had learned from the monks that Pánuco was behind them; and so he remained there, and Figueroa went back to the coast where he used to stay.

Chapter 18. On the Report He Gave from Esquivel

Figueroa gave this whole story as the report he had learned from Esquivel; and so, from person to person, it came to me, and through it the fate of the whole fleet can be seen and known, and the particular cases that occurred to each of the others. He also said that if the Christians wandered about there for a while they might see Esquivel, for he knew that Esquivel had fled the Indian with whom he had stayed and gone to others called Mariames who lived near there.

And, as I have just said, Figueroa and the Asturian had wished to go to other Indians who lived farther on. But since the Indians who held him sensed this, they went after them and beat them severely, and they stripped the Asturian naked and pierced one of his arms through with an arrow. And at last, they escaped by running away. The Christians stayed with those other Indians and arranged with them to be taken in as slaves, even though while they served them they were more ill-treated than any slaves or men of any sort ever were. For, not content with slapping and beating them and pulling out their beards for their own amusement, they killed the other three out of the six of them, merely because they moved from one house to another; these were the ones I mentioned above: Diego Dorantes,

---

1. *Maestre de campo*; this became a military rank, equivalent to colonel, in the Spanish army in 1534. It is unclear whether Cabeza de Vaca had the military rank in mind.

Valdivieso, and Diego de Huelva. And the other three who remained
expected to meet the same fate in the end.

As he could not bear that life, Andrés Dorantes fled and went over
to the Mariames, who were the ones with whom Esquivel had stayed,
and they told him about how they had held Esquivel there, and how
when he was there he had tried to flee, because a woman had
dreamed he would kill her son, and the Indians went after him and
killed him. And they showed Andrés Dorantes his sword and his
rosary beads and book, and other things of his.

These people do this because of a custom of theirs, which is that
they even kill their own children because of dreams, and they leave
their girls at birth to be eaten by dogs, and throw them away. The
reason why they do this is, according to them, that everybody who
lives in that land are their enemies and they are always at war with
them, and if they should marry off their daughters, their enemies
might multiply so much that they would overcome them and take
them as slaves; and for that reason they preferred to kill the girls
rather than let them give birth to children who would be their enemies. We asked them why they did not marry the girls off to themselves. They said that among them it was also an ugly thing to marry
girls off to their own relatives, and that it was much better to kill
them than to give them to their relatives or to their enemies. This
custom is practiced only by them and their neighbors called the
Iguaces; no other tribe in that land follows it. And when they must
get married, they buy their women from their enemies, and the price
each man gives for his woman is a bow, the best bow he might have,
and two arrows; and if he happens not to have a bow, he gives a net
measuring up to one fathom wide and one long. <They kill their
own children, and purchase those of strangers; their marriages last
only as long as they are content, and they undo a marriage for a
trifle.>

Dorantes stayed with these people; then a few days later he fled.
Castillo and Estevanico came over to the Iguaces on the mainland.
All these people are archers and well built, although not as large as
those we left behind us, and they have the nipple and lip pierced.
Their main source of food are two or three kinds of roots, which they
search for all over the land; these roots are very unhealthy and make
the men who eat them swell up. They take two days to roast, and
many of them are very bitter, and on top of all that they are gathered
with great difficulty. There is so much hunger among those people
they could not get by without these roots, and they walk two and
three leagues in search of them. Sometimes they kill a few deer, and
at times they catch a few fish; but that is so little, and their hunger
so great, that they eat spiders and ant eggs, and worms and lizards
and salamanders and snakes and vipers that kill any man they bite;

and they eat dirt and wood and everything they can get—deer dung and other things I will not mention; and I certainly believe that if there were any stones in that land, they would eat them. They preserve the bones of the fish they eat, and the bones of snakes and other things, to pulverize them all later and eat the powder.

Among them, the men do not bear burdens or carry anything of any weight; the women and old men carry it instead, being the people they hold in the smallest esteem. They do not love their children as much as the ones we spoke of above. There are some among them who practice the sin against nature.[2] The women are worked very long and hard, for out of the twenty-four hours in one day and night they get no more than six hours of rest, and they spend the better part of the night tending their ovens to dry the roots they eat. And from the break of day they begin to dig and to carry firewood and water to their houses and to sort out other things that they have need of.

Most of these people are great thieves, for although they are very freely giving among themselves, as soon as one turns his head his own son or the father will take anything he can get from him. They are great liars. And they are great drunkards, and for that they drink a certain thing.[3] They are so used to running that, without resting or getting tired, they will run from morning till night in pursuit of a deer. And in this way they kill many of them, because they follow them until they wear them out, and sometimes they take them alive.

Their houses are made of woven mats placed over four arches. They carry them on their backs, and they move every two or three days to search for food. They do not plant anything of any use. They are a very merry people: no matter how hungry they are, they do not cease on that account to dance or to celebrate their feasts and *areítos*. For them, the best times they have are when they eat tunas, for then they are not hungry, and they spend all their time dancing, and they eat them night and day. As long as the tunas last, they squeeze them and open them and spread them out to dry. And when they are dried, they put them in baskets, like figs, and they keep them to eat along the way when they go back, and they grind the peels and turn them into powder.

Many times when we were among them we went three or four days without eating, because there was no food. To cheer us up, they would tell us not to be so sad, for there would soon be tunas, and then we would eat many of them and drink their juice, and we would have full stomachs and be contented and merry and not at all hun-

---

2. The colonial-era Spanish term (both legal and cultural) for sexual relations between men.

3. *Una cierta cosa*; there is no indication of what this might be.

gry. And from the time they started telling us this until there were tunas to eat, it must have been five or six months. And in the end, we had to wait out those six months, and when it was time, we went to eat tunas.

We found a great quantity of mosquitoes around that land, of three kinds, all very bad and irksome, and for most of the summer they tormented us. And to protect ourselves from them, we would build many fires around the people, using damp and rotten wood so that the fires would not burn up and would give off smoke. And this protection gave us a further hardship, for all night long we did nothing but weep from the smoke that got in our eyes, and on top of this was the great heat all the fires caused us, so we would head to the shore to sleep. And whenever we managed to fall asleep, they would rouse us with blows so that we would get back to lighting the fires.

Those from farther inland have another remedy, just as intolerable and even worse than the one I have described, which is to go about holding firebrands, setting fire to all the fields and woods they come across, so that the mosquitoes will flee, and also so that lizards and other such things will emerge from underground so they can eat them. And they also usually kill deer by encircling them with many fires. And they also practice this to deprive the animals of pasture, so that need will force them to go in the direction they want them to go in search of it, for they never make a settlement with their houses except in places where there is water and firewood, and sometimes they all haul these necessities, and they go to find the deer, which most ordinarily roam where there is no water or firewood. And the day they arrive, they kill deer and whatever other things they can, and they use up all the water and wood in cooking their food and in the fires they make to protect themselves from the mosquitoes. And they wait until the next day to get something to take along on the road. And when they leave, the mosquitoes are so bad that they look like they have Saint Lazarus' disease (leprosy). And in this manner they satisfy their hunger two or three times a year, at the great cost that I have described. And since I have been through it, I can affirm that no hardship suffered in this world is its equal.

Across this land there are many deer and other birds and animals of the kinds I have described before. Cows reach this far, and I have seen them two or three times and have eaten their meat. And it seems to me that they are about the size of those in Spain. They have small horns, like Moorish cows, and their hair is very long, <like merino wool, or a *bernia*[4]>. Some are brownish and others

4. A woolen cloak that was coarsely woven to leave matted tufts of wool on its front. This account of cows is the first European description of the buffalo (American bison).

black, and in my opinion they have better and thicker meat than the cows from here. The Indians use the ones that are not full grown to make robes for covering themselves with, and they make shoes and shields from the older ones. These cows come from the north across the countryside as far as the coast of La Florida, and they spread all over the land for over four hundred leagues. And all along the way, through the valleys through which they come, the people who live there go down and live off of them, and they introduce great quantities of hides into the land.

Chapter 19. How the Indians Separated Us

When the six months that I was staying with the Christians while waiting to carry out our plans were up, the Indians went for tunas; our distance to where the tunas would be gathered was a good thirty leagues. And just when we were ready to run away, the Indians we were with began fighting with each other over a woman, and they punched and cudgeled and trounced one another. And they felt such great rage that each took up his house and went his separate way, so all of us Christians who were there had to separate, too, and we had no way to get together again until the next year. And during that time I fared very badly, both from great hunger and from the ill-treatment I received from the Indians, which was so bad that I had to flee three times from the masters I had, and they each went looking for me, endeavoring to kill me. And God our Lord, with His mercy, wished to protect me and save me from them. And when the season for tunas came again, we got together again on the same spot.

Just when we finished our plan to escape and picked the day, that same day the Indians separated us, and we each went our separate way; I told the other companions that I would wait for them in the tunas until moon was full. And that day was the first of September and the first day of the new moon.[5] And I warned them that if they did not come to the agreed spot at the set time, I would go on alone and would leave them. And so we separated and each went off with his Indians. I remained with mine until the thirteenth of the moon, and I was determined to flee to other Indians as soon as the moon was full. And on the thirteenth of the month, Andrés Dorantes and Estevanico came to where I was, and they told me how they had left Castillo with other Indians called Anagados, and that they were near there, and that they had gone through many hardships, and

5. After six years stranded on the coast, Cabeza de Vaca is keeping time by the moon and the changing seasons; he identifies the new moon closest to the end of summer as September 1. The actual date was September 8, 1534, according to the Julian calendar (September 18 according to the Gregorian calendar that we now follow).

that they had wandered around lost. And then the next day our Indians moved toward where Castillo was, and they were going to join together with those who held him, and to make friends with each other, for up until then they had been at war, and in this way we got Castillo back, too.

We were thirsty the whole time we were eating tunas; to relieve our thirst, we would drink the juice of the tunas, which we would squeeze into a pit that we had made in the earth, and once it was full we would drink from it until we were satiated. It is sweet and the color of *arrope*.[6] They do this for lack of other vessels. There are many types of tunas, and some of them are very good, although they all tasted good to me, and my hunger never left me enough time to choose among them or stop to consider which ones were the best. Almost all of these peoples drink rainwater that collects in certain spots, for although there are rivers, since they never settle down, they never have known or established water sources. Across the whole land there are large and handsome meadows, with good pasture for cattle, and it seems to me that this would be a very fertile land if it were tilled and inhabited by people of reason.[7] We saw no mountains in this land all the time we were there.

Those Indians told us that there were others farther on called Camoncs, who live toward the coast, and they had killed all the men who came in the bark of Peñalosa and Téllez, who had arrived so thin and feeble that even though they were being killed they offered no resistance, and so they finished them all off. And they showed us some of their clothes and armor, and they said the bark was beached there. This is the missing fifth bark, for we already said how the Governor's bark had been swept out to sea, and the bark of the purser and the monks had been seen beached on the shore, and Esquivel related the end they came to. As for the two barks in which Castillo and I and Dorantes had sailed, we have already told how they sank by the Isle of Ill Fate.

Chapter 20. On How We Fled

After we moved, two days later we commended ourselves to God our Lord and fled, trusting that, although it was late and the tunas were giving out, the fruits that remained in the countryside should be enough for us to cover a good portion of the land. While going on our way that day, in great fear that the Indians would follow us,

---

6. Grape juice or new wine boiled down to a syrup; if made from red wine, this would be a dark, slightly brownish red color.
7. *Gente de razón*; a key colonial category used to distinguish Europeans (considered "people of reason") from indigenous people (treated as legal minors, as if they were permanent children) and enslaved Africans (discriminated against in even more drastic ways).

we saw some columns of smoke. And going toward them, just after sunset we reached a place where we saw an Indian who fled as he saw us approaching him, refusing to wait for us. We sent the black man after him, and when he saw that he was coming by himself, he waited.

The black man told him we were going to look for the people making those columns of smoke. He replied that the houses were nearby, and that he would guide us there. So we followed after him, and he ran ahead to let them know we were coming. And at sunset we saw the houses. At a distance of two crossbow shots before we reached them we found four Indians waiting for us, and they received us well. We told them in the language of the Mariames that we had gone looking for them, and they showed that they rejoiced to have our company, and so they took us to their houses. And they lodged Dorantes and the black man in the house of a physician, and me and Castillo in the house of another.

These have another language and call themselves Avavares; they are the ones who used to bring bows to ours and trade with them. And though they are of a different nation and language, they understand the language of the ones we were with before. And they had arrived there on that very day with their houses. The pueblo offered us a lot of tunas right away, because they had already heard news of us and of how we healed and of the wonders that Our Lord worked through us. For even if there had been no other wonders, it was wonder enough to create paths for us through such an unpopulated land, and to give us people in places where so often there were none, and to free us from so many dangers, and not to allow us to be killed, and to sustain us when there was so much hunger, and to inspire those people to treat us well, as we will tell further on.

Chapter 21. On How We Healed Some Sick People

On the very same night we arrived, some Indians came to Castillo and told him that their heads ached badly, begging him to heal them. And after he made the sign of the cross over them and commended them to God, at that moment the Indians said that all their pain was gone. They went to their houses and brought us many tunas and a piece of venison, though we had no idea what it was. And as the news spread among them, many other patients came that night for him to cure, and each brought a piece of venison. And there were so many that we did not know where to store the meat. We gave many thanks to God, for His mercy and favors were increasing daily. And after the healings were done, they began to dance and perform their *areítos* and celebrations, until the next day when the sun rose. And the celebrations lasted three days, for our coming. And at the end of them, we asked them about the land farther on, and what people we might find there, and what food supplies there might be.

They replied that all through that land there were plenty of tunas, but they were already over, and no people would be there, because they had all gone to their houses after gathering the tunas; and that the land was very cold and there were very few hides in it. When we saw this, since winter and cold weather were already setting in, we agreed to spend it with these people.

Five days after we had arrived, they left to find more tunas in a place where there were people of different nations and languages. And when we had marched five days while suffering great hunger, because there were no tunas or any other kind of fruit on the way, we reached a river where we set up our houses. After we were settled, we went out searching for the fruits of some trees that are like vetches.[8] And since there are no paths anywhere throughout this land, I spent too much time searching for them; the people returned, and I remained alone, and when I went looking for them that night I got lost. And it pleased God that I found a burning tree, and I got through the cold that night by its fire, and in the morning I loaded myself up with firewood, took two firebrands, and went back to looking for the people. And I spent five days in this way, always with my fire and my load of wood, so that if the flames went out someplace where there was no firewood—which was the case in many parts—I would have what I needed to make new firebrands and would not be left without fire, for I had no other relief against the cold, since I went as naked as the day I was born.

And to get through the nights I had this relief: I would go to the copses in the woods by the rivers, and I would settle in them before the sun set. And I would dig a pit in the earth {with the butt of a log}[9] and fill it with a lot of dry wood, which is produced on many trees, of which there are a large number around there. And I would gather a lot of firewood from what had fallen from the trees and dried out, and around that pit I would make four fires, in a cross. And I was very careful to rebuild the fires now and then. And I would make bundles of the long straw that grows around there, and cover myself with them in that pit. And in this way I protected myself from the night cold. And one night, fire fell on the straw I was using to cover myself, and while I was asleep in the pit it began to burn very fiercely, and as quickly as I rushed to get out I still ended up with traces in my hair of the danger I had been in. During

8. Yeros or yervos; specifically the bitter vetch (*Vicia ervilia*), or in extended use any leguminous tree. There are several small, pod-bearing trees in south Texas that look similar the bitter vetch of Europe, including Texas ebony and various species of mesquite. The bean-like seeds of all these plants grow in long pods and can be processed into edible flour.
9. Throughout, lines in braces are found only in Z.

all that time I did not eat a bite, nor did I find anything that I could eat; and since I was barefoot, my feet bled a great deal. And God had mercy upon me, for in all that time the north wind did not blow, because otherwise I would have had no chance of surviving.

And at the end of five days I reached the bank of a river where I found my Indians; they and the Christians had already counted me dead, and they thought the whole time that some viper had bitten me. They all were greatly pleased to see me, especially the Christians, and they told me that so far they had marched with great hunger, and that was the reason they had not looked for me, and that night they gave me some of the tunas they had. And the next day we left there, and we went where we found many tunas, with which everyone satisfied their great hunger, and we gave many thanks to Our Lord, for relief never failed us.

Chapter 22. How They Brought Us More Patients the Next Day

Next morning many Indians came, and they brought five patients who were crippled and very ill, and they were coming to look for Castillo so that he would cure them. And every one of the patients offered his bow and arrows. And he accepted them and at sunset he made the sign of the cross over them and commended them to God our Lord. And we all prayed to Him as best we could to send them health, for He saw there was no other way of having those people help us so that we might get out of our miserable existence. And He carried it out with such mercy that, when morning came, they all woke up as good and healthy, and they left there in as good health, as if they had never had any ailment at all. This caused great wonder among them, and it moved us to give many thanks to Our Lord, and to recognize His goodness more fully, and to have firm faith that He would free us and guide us to a place where we might serve Him. And for my own part I may say that I always had entire hope for His mercy and that He would liberate me from captivity, and so I always said to my companions.

When the Indians had gone, taking away their healed Indians, we removed to where others were eating tunas. And these are called Cultalchuches and Malicones, which are different languages. And together with them were others called Coayos and Susolas, and from another part were others called Atayos who were at war with the Susolas, with whom they exchanged arrow shots every day.

And since throughout the land nothing else was talked about but the mysteries that God our Lord was working through us, they came from many parts for us to heal them. And two days after they had arrived there, some Indians of the Susolas came to us and begged

Castillo to go heal a wounded man and other patients, and they said that there was one among them who was quickly approaching the end. Castillo was a very fearful physician, especially when the cures were very fearful and dangerous, and he believed that his sins would prevent the cures from always turning out well. The Indians told me I should go heal them, because they thought well of me and they remembered that I had healed them during the nut harvest, and for that they had given us nuts and hides; and this had happened when I was coming to join the Christians. So I had to go with them, and Dorantes and Estevanico went with me. And when I drew close to the encampments that they had, I saw that the patient we were coming to cure was dead, for there were many people around him weeping and his house was torn down, which is a sign that the owner has died. So when I arrived I found the Indian with his eyes rolled back and without any pulse, and with all the signs of being dead, from what it seemed to me, and Dorantes said the same. I removed a woven reed mat that had been covering him, and as best I could I implored Our Lord to please give health to him and to all the others who had need of it. And after I had made the sign of the cross and blown on him many times, they brought his bow and gave it to me, and a basket of ground tunas. And they took me to heal many others who were ill with lethargy, and they gave me two more baskets of tunas, which I gave to our Indians, who had come with us. And having done this, we returned to our shelters. And our Indians, to whom I had given the tunas, remained there, and at night they returned to their houses and they said that the man who had been dead, whom I healed in their presence, had gotten up feeling well and had walked about, and eaten, and spoken with them, and that everyone I had healed was healthy and without fever and very cheerful.

This caused great wonder and shock, and in all the land nothing else was spoken of. All who heard the fame of it sought us out so that we would heal them and make the sign of the cross over their children. And when the Indians who were accompanying ours, the Cultalchuches, had to return to their land, before parting they offered us all the tunas they had for their journey, not keeping a single one. And they gave us flints as much as one and a half palms long, which they use for cutting, and among them these are things of great value. They begged us to remember them and to beg God to keep them always healthy, and we promised to do it, and with that they left, the happiest people in the world, having given us all the best they had.

We remained with those Avavares Indians for eight months, which we reckoned by the moons. During all that time they came from many parts to seek us, and they said that we were truly children of the Sun. Up until then Dorantes and the black man had not done

healings, but because we were so insistently begged by people coming from many parts to seek us, we all became physicians, though in
audacity and daring to undertake any cure, I stood out among them.
And we never treated anyone who did not say afterward that he had
gotten well. And they were so confident that they would get well if
we healed them that they believed that so long as we were there,
none of them would die.

These Indians and the ones we left behind told us a very strange
tale, and from the account that they sketched out for us it seemed it
had happened fifteen or sixteen years earlier. They said a man had
gone about through that land whom they call Mala Cosa,[1] who was
small in stature, and who had a beard, though they never could see
his face clearly; and whenever he came to a house, the hair of the
people in it would stand on end and they would tremble, and then a
burning firebrand would appear at the door of the house. And then
that man would enter and take anyone he wished, and would make
three great gashes in their sides with a very sharp flint knife, as
broad as a hand and two palms long. And he would stick his hand
through those gashes and pull out their entrails; and he would cut
off a piece of their entrails about one palm long, and he would throw
the piece he cut off into the burning embers. And then he would
make three gashes on one arm, the second one on the inner elbow,[2]
and would dislocate it. And soon afterward he would reset it, and
would place his hands on the wounds, and they told us that they
healed up at once. And [they said] that many times when they were
dancing, he would appear among them, sometimes dressed as a
woman, and other times as a man; and whenever he wished, he
would take the *bohío* or house and raise it up into the air, and soon
afterward he would fall down with it and make a great crash. They
also told us that many times they tried to feed him, but he never ate
the food at all; and they would ask him where he came from and
where he had his house, and he would show them a fissure in the
earth, and he said his house was down there.

We laughed very much at these things they used to tell us, making fun of them. And when they saw that we did not believe it, they

1. The story of Mala Cosa as described by Cabeza de Vaca seems to be a mélange of North
American trickster stories and Spanish folk beliefs about the devil. It may be significant
that in rural Mexico *cosa mala* (evil thing) is a euphemism for the devil, used in spoken
language because mentioning the devil's real name aloud might lead the Evil One to
appear in person. Such folk beliefs were discouraged by the official church and rarely
appeared in print before the twentieth century, but there is at least one occurrence of
the euphemism in a line of spoken dialogue in Vicente Espinel's picaresque novel *Vida
del escudero Marcos de Obregón* (1618), Relación primera, descanso V.
2. *Sangradura*; described by the DRAE (1739) as "the inner part of the arm, where it
bends, and where it is bled." The cubital vein at the inner elbow is still the preferred spot
for collecting blood donations.

brought many of those that they said he had taken, and we saw the traces of the gashes he had made, in the places and in the manner they recounted. We told them that he was an evil being, and we explained as well as we knew how that, if they would believe in God our Lord and be Christians like us, they would not have any fear of him, nor would he dare come and do those things to them, and they might be sure that as long as we were in the land he would not dare to appear there. They rejoiced greatly at this and lost much of the terror they had felt.

These Indians told us they had seen the Asturian and Figueroa with other Indians who lived farther along on the coast, whom we called "the people of the figs."[3]

None of these people recognized the seasons by the sun or the moon, nor do they keep a count of the months and years, but they understand and distinguish between the seasons when fruits begin to ripen, and the season when fish die, and when stars appear, in all of which they are very skilled and practiced.

Among these people we were always well treated, though we had to eat what we dug out of the ground, and we carried our loads of water and firewood. Their houses and their food supplies are like those of the previous ones, though they are much hungrier, for they get no maize or acorns or nuts. We always went about naked like them, and at night we covered ourselves with deer skins.

For six of the eight months we were with them, we suffered from great hunger, for they do not get fish either. And at the end of that time the tunas were beginning to ripen, and without letting them notice it we went on to others who lived farther ahead, named Maliacones. These people lived one day's travel away, which was where I and the negro went. Three days later, I sent him back to get Castillo and Dorantes. Once they came, we all departed together with the Indians, who were going to eat the tiny fruit of some trees on which they subsist for ten or twelve days while the tunas are coming in. And there they joined up with these other Indians called Arbadaos, whom we found to be very sick and feeble and swollen, so much so that we were greatly amazed. The Indians with whom we had come went back the same way, and we told them that we wished to remain with the others, at which they showed grief; and so we remained in the countryside with the others, near their houses. And when they saw us, they gathered together after having talked among themselves, and each one of them took his own by the hand and led us to their houses. We suffered more from hunger with these than with the others, for all day long we did not eat more than two fistfuls of

---

3. *Higos*; another Spanish term for tunas or prickly pears.

that fruit,[4] which was green; it contained so much milky sap that it burned our mouths, and as water was very scarce, it made anyone who ate them very thirsty. And since the hunger was so great, we bought two dogs from them and in exchange for them we gave them some nets and other things, and a hide I used to cover myself.

I have already said that through all this land we went about naked, and since we were not accustomed to it we shed our skin twice a year, like snakes. And the sun and the wind gave us great dry scabs on our chests and backs, which greatly tormented us because of the great loads we had to carry, which made the ropes cut into our arms. The land is so rough and so overgrown that often when we made firewood in the woods, after we finished hauling it out we would be bleeding all over from the thorns and shrubs we would run into, which would cut us wherever they touched. Sometimes it happened that I had made firewood in a place where, after it had cost me a lot of blood, I could not haul it out either on my back or by dragging it. When I found myself in these hardships, I had no other relief or consolation but to think on the passion of our redeemer Jesus Christ and on the blood he shed for me, and to ponder how much greater his sufferings must have been from the thorns than those I was enduring.

I traded with these Indians by making them combs, and with bows and with arrows and with nets. We would make woven reed mats, which are the things they have great need of. And though they know how to make them, they do not busy themselves at all, because in the meantime they have to be searching for food. And when they are engaged in weaving mats, they suffer greatly from hunger. At other times they would order me to scrape skins and tan them. And the greatest prosperity I found myself in there was the day they gave me some skin to scrape, because I would scrape it hard and eat the scrapings, and that was enough to keep me for two or three days. It also happened to us among these Indians, and among the ones we had left behind, that we would be given a piece of meat and we would eat it raw. Because if we started to roast it, the first Indian who came along would take it and eat it. It did not seem good to us to risk it like that; also, we were not in such a state that we were worried about eating it broiled and could not get it down just as well raw.[5] Such was the life we led there; and the bit of sustenance that

4. The tree and its "tiny fruit" (*frutilla*) are unidentified, though several candidates have been proposed, including the Texas persimmon (*Diospyros texana*) and the agarita (*Berberis trifoliatla*), both of which are shrub trees that produce edible berrylike fruit that can be astringent if eaten green. Other suggested fruits are the bean-like seeds of the mesquite or the Texas ebony; these seem less likely, given the more accurate descriptions of both foods elsewhere in the narrative.
5. This is another difficult sentence to interpret; in the original: "*y también no estábamos tales que nos dábamos pena comerlo asado, y no lo podíamos tan bien [también] pasar*

we got, we had to earn with the trade goods we made with our own hands.

Chapter 23. How We Left after Eating the Dogs

After we ate the dogs, since we felt we had enough strength to go on, we commended ourselves to God our Lord that He might guide us and took our leave of those Indians. And they set us on the path toward others of their language who were nearby. And while we were walking on our path it rained, and all that day long we walked in the rain. And beyond that, we lost the trail and ended up in a great woods. And we gathered many tuna leaves,[6] which we roasted that very night in an oven that we made, and we put so much fire under them that in the morning they were ready to be eaten. After we had eaten them, we commended ourselves to God and left, and we found the trail we had lost.

Once past the woods, we found other Indian houses. When we reached them, we saw two women and adolescent boys, who were frightened that people were walking through the woods, and on seeing us they fled from us and went to call the Indians who were walking through the woods. When they came, they stopped to peer at us from behind some trees, and we called them, and they approached in great fear. After we had spoken to them, they told us they were very hungry and that nearby there were many houses belonging to them; and they said that they would take us to them.

And that night we reached a site where there were fifty houses, and the people were frightened at seeing us and showed a great deal of fear. After they had been somewhat set at ease about us, they approached us with their hands to our faces and bodies, and then they passed their hands over their own hands and bodies. And so we stayed there that night, and when morning came they brought the sick people they had, begging us to do the sign of the cross on them, and they gave us of what they had to eat, which were roasted tuna leaves and roasted green tunas. And because of how well they treated us, and because they gladly and willingly gave us everything they

---

como crudo." I have taken it as corroborating the general sense of the passage, which is that they gave up on the idea doing things differently from the people they were with, so that they did not try to insist on cooking meat before eating it. Adorno and Pautz interpret it in the opposite sense: "and besides, we were not such that it troubled us to eat it roasted, but neither were we able to swallow it raw," implying that they didn't eat the meat at all, either broiled or raw; this strikes me as a plausible translation but an unlikely situation, given their constant state of hunger and their willingness to discard other Spanish conventions for the sake of survival.

6   The large, fleshy pads of the nopal or tuna cactus are often eaten when tender, when they are known as nopalitos; but older pads can also be roasted and eaten in a case of need. Though Cabeza de Vaca does not mention it, they must have learned this roasting technique from one of the indigenous groups they had stayed with over the previous seven years.

had, and rejoiced to be left without food for having given it to us, we stayed with them for a few days.

And while we were there, others came from farther on. When they were ready to leave, we told the first ones that we wanted to go with these others. This made them very sad, and they fervently begged us not to go. In the end, we took our leave of them, and we left them weeping at our departure, because it made them tremendously sad.

Chapter 24. On the Customs of the Indians of That Land

From the Island of Ill Fate up to this land, all the Indians we saw have the custom that, from the day their wives feel pregnant, they do not sleep together until they have raised their children for two years; and they suckle their children to the age of twelve years, for by then they are old enough that they know how to gather their own food. We asked them why they raised them like that, and they said it was because of the great hunger that existed in that land; for it often happened, as we ourselves had seen, that they would go two or three days without eating, and sometimes four, and that was the reason why they let them suckle, so that they would not die in times of famine, and even if some might avoid death, they would turn out very delicate and feeble. And if some of them should happen to fall ill, they let them die in the countryside, unless it is a son; and as for all the others, if they cannot keep up with them, they are left behind; but to bring a son or brother[7] they carry him and bear him on their backs.

All these [Indian men] have the custom of leaving their wives when there is disagreement between them, and they remarry with whomever they wish; this is true among the young men, but those who have children remain with their wives and do not leave them. And in some pueblos, when they quarrel and bicker with one another, they punch and cudgel each other until they are very tired, and then they separate and make peace. Sometimes women separate them, stepping in between them, for men never step in to separate them; and no matter how great their passion, they never introduce bows or arrows into it. And after they have punched each other and the bickering is over, they take their houses and women and go out to live in the countryside and apart from the others until their anger has passed. And when they are over their anger and free from wrath, they return to the pueblo, and from then on they are as close

7. *Hijo, hermano*; the Spanish words are masculine, but are also (in generic contexts) assumed to include both genders, making the sentence somewhat ambiguous; these words could perhaps be translated with the gender-neutral terms *child* and *sibling*. Cabeza de Vaca's default point of view is male, however, so the use of gender-neutral terms would seem to introduce an aspect not justified by the original text.

friends as if nothing had happened between them, nor is there any
need for someone to build their friendship, because that is how they
do it. And if the men who are quarreling are not married, they go stay
with other neighbors of theirs [that is, with neighboring groups]; and
even if they are their enemies, they receive them well and rejoice
with them and give them gifts of what they have, so that, when their
anger has passed, they return to their pueblo, and they return rich.

They are all people of war, and as cunning at guarding themselves from their enemies as if they had been raised in Italy and in
continuous war.[8] When they are in parts where their enemies can
attack them, they set up their houses on the edge of the roughest
and densest woods they can find around there, and next to the
woods they dig a trench, and they sleep in it. All their men at arms
are hidden by brushwood, and they make holes in it for shooting
arrows, and they are so well covered and concealed that even when
[their enemies] are almost on top of them they cannot be seen. And
they make a very narrow trail and go into the center of the woods,
and there they make a place for their women and children to sleep.
And when night falls, they light fires in their houses, so that if there
happen to be spies, they will think that that is where they are. And
before sunrise they light the same fires again, and if their enemies
chance to fall upon those same houses, those who are waiting in
the trench leave it and do them great harm from the entrench-
ments, yet those outside the trenches cannot see them or find
them. And when there are no woods where they can hide like this
and prepare their ambushes, they settle on flat ground, in the part
that seems best to them, and surround themselves with entrench-
ments covered with brushwood. And they open holes through
which they can shoot arrows at the Indians, and they put up these
defenses for nighttime.

When I was with the Deaguanes[9] and they were not on their
guard, their enemies came at midnight and fell upon them, killing
three and wounding many others, so that they fled from their houses
into the woods. And as soon as they sensed that the others had gone,
they went back to their houses and gathered all the arrows that the
others had shot at them, and they followed them as stealthily as they
could, and that night they came upon their houses unnoticed. And
when the early morning hour came, they attacked, and they killed
five of them, not counting many others who were wounded, and they
made them flee and leave their houses and bows behind, and everything else they owned. And a short time later, the women of the

8. Spain was involved in an almost continuous series of wars on the Italian peninsula
from 1494 to 1559. Cabeza de Vaca himself fought in the Italian Wars in 1510–11.
9. So the name was spelled earlier; here both Z and V have *los de Aguenes*. There is no
way to determine which variant (if either) is closer to the group's actual name.

ones called Quevenes came back and reasoned between them and made them friends, though sometimes women are the cause of war. All these people, when they have personal enmities, when they do not belong to a single family, kill each other at nighttime by trickery, and they perform great cruelties with one another.

Chapter 25. How the Indians Are Ready at Arms

These are the readiest people for arms of all the ones I have seen in the world, for if they suspect something from their enemies, they lie awake all night with their bows right next to them and a dozen arrows; anyone who sleeps will try his bow, and if he finds it unstrung he will tighten the string as much as necessary. They often go out of their houses crouching low to the ground in such a fashion that they cannot be seen, and they look and spy in every direction to see what is there. And if they sense anything, in a moment are they all out in the field with their bows and arrows, and so they stay until it is day, running back and forth, wherever they see it is necessary or think their enemies might be. When day comes, they unstring their bows once more until they go out hunting. The strings of their bows are made of deer sinews.

Their way of fighting is crouched low to the ground, and while they are shooting at each other they go about constantly talking and leaping from one end to the other, dodging the enemy's arrows, so well that in such places they receive little harm from crossbows and arquebuses. Rather, the Indians laugh at those weapons, because they are no use against them on flat fields where they roam freely. They are good in narrow passes and places with water; everywhere else, horses are what will subdue them, and what the Indians universally fear. Anyone who has to fight against them must be very cautious that they not sense any weakness in him or greed for what they own; and so long as the war lasts, he must treat them very harshly, for if they sense fear or any greed, these are the people who know how to recognize the times for revenge, and they take strength from their foes' fear.

When they have shot their bows in a war and used up all their arrows, they all go home, each their own way, without one side pursuing the other, even though one side might have many men and the other few; that is their custom. Often they are shot all the way through with arrows and they do not die from their wounds, so long as they are not hit in the bowels or heart; rather, they readily recover. They see and hear more, and have sharper senses, than any other men I believe exist in the world. They have great endurance for hunger and thirst and cold, being more accustomed and used to it than others.

I wished to report this here because, apart from the fact that all men desire to know the customs and practices of others, those who some day may come to face them should be informed of their customs and stratagems, information that is usually rather advantageous to have in such cases.

Chapter 26. Of Their Nations and Languages

I also want to enumerate their nations and languages that exist from the Island of Ill Fate to the last ones, {the Cuchendados}.[1] On the Island of Ill Fate there are two languages: one group is called Capoques, the other is called Han. On the mainland, facing the island, there are others called Charruco, and they take their name from the woods where they live. Farther on, along the seacoast, are others called Deaguanes, and in front of them others named the people of Mendica. Farther on, on the coast, are the Quevenes, and in front of them, within the mainland, the Mariames. And following along the coast, there are others called Guaycones, and in front of them, within the mainland, the Iguaces. After these are others called Atayos, and behind them are others, Acubadaos, and there many of these farther on in this direction. On the coast live others called Quitoles, and in front of them, within the mainland, the Chavavares. These are joined by the Maliacones, and others, Cultalchuches, and others called Susola and others who are called Comos. And farther along the coast are the Camolas; and on the same coast, farther along, are others whom we call the people of the figs.

All those peoples have dwellings and pueblos and diverse languages. Among these, there is a language in which, when they call men, for "look here" they say *arre acá*, and they call dogs by saying *shoh*.[2]

All over the land they get drunk on a certain smoke, and they will give everything they have for it. They also drink another thing that they extract from the leaves of trees like live oaks, which they toast in jars over the fire; after they have toasted them, they fill the jar with water and then keep it on the fire, and when it has boiled twice they pour it into a vessel, and they work to cool it down, using a gourd cut in half. And when it is full of foam, they drink it as hot as they can stand it. And from the time they pour it out of the jar until they drink it, they keep shouting out, "Who wants to drink?" And when the women hear these shouts, they immediately stand still, not daring to

1. Many of the group names in this paragraph have variations between the two editions, and even within the same one; here I generally use the forms from Z.
2. One suspects that, of all the vocabulary Cabeza de Vaca must have learned, he includes only these two words for the sake of comic relief: in Spanish, these were the calls used to get horses or cattle to move and stop, the equivalent of *Giddyap!* and *Whoa!* (*Shoh* is spelled *xo* in old Spanish; I have represented it phonetically for English speakers.)

move; even if they are carrying a very heavy load they do not dare to do anything else. If one of the women should happen to move, they dishonor her and thrash her, and in a great rage they spill the water that they were about to drink, and they spit up what they have already drunk, which they do very easily and without any embarrassment. The reason they give for this custom is that, when they want to drink that water, if the women move from the spot where they first hear the shouts, then an evil thing gets into their bodies from that water, and not long afterward it causes them to die. And the whole time the water is boiling, the jar has be covered. If it happens to be uncovered and some woman passes by, they pour it out and do not drink that water. It is yellow, and they drink it for three days without eating. And each day, each person drinks an arroba[3] and a half of it.

And when women have their periods, they only gather food for themselves, because no other person else will eat any of what they bring.

During the time I was thus among them, I saw one devilry,[4] which is that I saw one man married to another man, and these are womanish, impotent men. They go about covered up like women, and they do the duty of women, and they {do not} use the bow[5] and they carry great loads. Among these people we saw many such men—womanish, as I have said; and they are stouter than other men, and taller; they can bear up under very heavy loads.

Chapter 27. On How We Moved and Were Well Received

After we parted from those whom we had left weeping, we went with the others to their houses. And we were well received by the people in the houses there, and they brought their children so that we would touch them with our hands, and they gave us a lot of mesquite[6] meal. This mesquite is a fruit that is very bitter while on the tree, and looks like a carob pod; it is eaten with earth, and with that it becomes sweet and good to eat. The way they make it is this: they

3. A liquid measurement that varied according to province and the liquid being measured from two and a half to four gallons; also, a weight equivalent to twenty-five pounds.
4. *Diablura*; the Spanish and English words are not only close cognates but underwent a similar "devaluation" in meaning, from "the work of the devil" (meant quite literally in the Middle Ages) to "kids' mischief" in the eighteenth and nineteenth centuries, before more or less falling out of use in the twentieth century. Cabeza de Vaca's usage is somewhere along this continuum.
5. There is a key (and unresolvable) difference here between the two early editions: Z says they "do not use the bow," V says they "use the bow."
6. A tree that the Spanish came to know in Mexico, adopting its Náhuatl (Aztec) name *mizquitl* into Spanish as *mezquite*, from which it was adopted into English. The word was new to Cabeza de Vaca, who spelled it *mezquiquez*. The five closely related species of mesquite (genus *Prosopis*) are hardy leguminous trees, native to Mexico and the U. S. Southwest and well adapted to arid climates. As Cabeza de Vaca notes, they bear long seed pods that look very similar to those of the more distantly related Mediterranean leguminous tree the *algarroba* or carob (*Ceratonia siliqua*).

dig a pit in the ground, as deep as each person wishes. After the fruit has been put in this pit, they use a log as thick as a person's leg and one and a half fathoms long to pound it until it is well ground; and besides the earth that sticks to it in the pit, they bring more fistfuls and throw them into the pit, and they pound it again for a while, and then they empty it into a vessel that looks like an *espuerta* [a large two-handled carrying basket]. And they pour in enough water to cover it, so that there is water on top. And the one who pounded it tastes it, and if it does not seem sweet to him he asks for earth and stirs it in. And he does this until he finds it sweet. And they all sit down around it, and each person sticks in his hand and takes out as much as he can, and they throw the seeds back onto some hides, and the husks. And the one who pounded it gathers them and throws them back into that *espuerta*, and he pours in water like he did before, and again they squeeze out all the juice and water that they can get out of it, and they toss the seeds and husks back on the hides. And in this way they do each pounding three or four times. And those who take part in this banquet, which for them is very great, end up with huge bellies from all the earth and water they have swallowed. And the Indians turned this into a great celebration for us, and among them there were great dances and *areítos* for as long as we stayed there.

And at night when we slept by the gate to the encampment where we were staying, each one of us was guarded by six men with great care, so that no one dared come in to see us until the sun had risen. When we were ready to leave them, some women arrived there from another group who lived farther on. After we were informed by them where their houses were, we left there, though they begged us very much to stay there the rest of that day, because the houses we were going to were far away, and there was no path to them; and those women had arrived exhausted, and by resting they would go with us the next day and guide us; and so we took our leave. And a bit later these women, who had come with other women from the same pueblo, came after us. But since there were no roads across the land, we got lost right away, and so we wandered four leagues. And at the end of four leagues, we approached a watering hole to drink, and there we found the women who had followed us, and they told us about everything they had gone through to catch up with us. We set out from there, taking the women along as guides, and when it was already afternoon we crossed a river that reached up to our chests; it must be about as wide as the river of Seville,[7] and it had a strong

---

7. I.e., the Guadalquivir, the only navigable river in Spain, more than five hundred feet wide in the center of the city. The only river in south Texas or northern Mexico large enough to fit this description is the Rio Grande. Krieger (2002: 56) uses archaeological evidence to suggest a crossing point at the modern Falcon Reservoir, about halfway

current. And at sunset we arrived at one hundred Indian houses, and before we could reach them all the people came out of them to receive us with so much shouting it was frightening, and making loud slaps against their thighs. They carried pierced gourds filled with pebbles, which is the thing for their great celebrations, and they only bring them out to dance or to heal, nor does anyone dare hold them but themselves. And they say that those gourds have healing virtues and that they come from the sky, because they do not grow around that land, nor do they know where they grow, except that the rivers bring them when they rise and overflow.

They were so afraid and frenzied that, to get to touch us before others could, they pressed and squeezed us so much that they came close to killing us. And, without letting our feet touch the ground, they carried us to their houses. And they crowded us so much and pressed us in such a way that we shut ourselves up in the houses they had prepared for us, and we would not by any means allow them to make more celebrations with us that night. Among themselves, they spent that whole night in *areítos* and dances. And the next morning they brought us all the people of that pueblo so that we would touch them and make the sign of the cross over them, as we had done to the other with whom we had stayed. And after that was done, they gave many arrows to the women from the other pueblo who had come with their women.

The next day we left there, and all the people of the pueblo went with us, and when we came to other Indians we were well received, as we had been by the earlier ones. And so they gave us of what they had and the deer they had killed that day.

And among these we saw a new custom, which is that when people came to be healed, the ones who were with us would take their bows and arrows from them, as well as their shoes and beads, if they had any. After taking them, they would bring those things before us so that we would heal those people. And when they were healed, they would go away very contented, saying that they were well.

So we left those people and went to others, by whom we were very well received, and they brought us their sick, who on having the sign of the cross made over them said they were healed. Anyone who was not healing believed that we could heal him. And at what the others whom we had healed told them, they put on so many festivals and dances that they did not let us sleep.

---

between Laredo and Matamoros; in this area the Rio Grande widens to about four hundred feet and becomes shallow enough to be waded across in some seasons.

Chapter 28. On Another New Custom

Having left these people, we went to many other houses, and from this point there began another new custom, which was that, while people received us very well, those who went along with us began to do them great harm, for they would take away their belongings and plunder their houses, leaving them with nothing. We felt very sorry at this, to see the ill-treatment afforded those who had received us so well, and also because we feared that this would be or would cause some disturbance or commotion between them. But since we had no standing to fix this, nor to dare punish those who did it, for the time being we had to bear with it until we might have more authority among them. Then, too, the Indians themselves who lost their belongings, recognizing our sadness, consoled us, saying that this should not give us grief; that they were so happy to have seen us that they considered their belongings well spent, and that going forward they would be paid by others who were very rich.

On this whole journey we were given great trouble by the number of people following us. And we could not escape them, though we endeavored to do so, because the crush of people[8] to get to touch us was so great, and they were so insistent on doing it, that for more than three hours we could not finish with them so they would leave us alone.

The next day they brought all the people from the pueblo to us. The greater part of them are blind in one eye from clouding, and others are totally blind from the same, which shocked us. They are very well built and with very good features, whiter than any others of all those we had seen until then.

Here we began to see mountains,[9] and it seemed as if they swept down in a chain from the direction of the North Sea. And so, from the report that the Indians gave us about this, we believe they are fifteen leagues from the sea.

From there, we departed with these Indians toward the mountains just mentioned. And they led us through where some of their relatives were, and they wanted to lead us only through places where their relatives lived and did not want their enemies to attain the

---

8. *Priessa*; following the third definition in DRAE (1737), "this is also the name for the crowd that runs after something being distributed; for example, it is said: There was a great *priessa* for bread." The word is cognate with the English *press*, which had a similar meaning at the time. In more recent usage, *prisa* means "hurry, haste, rush."

9. The first mountains they were likely to see are the small chains just north of modern Monterrey; several peaks in these chains are over thirteen hundred meters (4,250 feet) and visible on the horizon from the Falcon Reservoir area, where they seem to be running from north to south; i.e., parallel at that point to the Rio Grande, which Cabeza de Vaca knew to be heading toward the "North Sea." They lie more than 130 miles from the Gulf, however, which is a good deal more than fifteen leagues by any calculation.

great benefit that they thought it was to see us. And as soon as we arrived, those that were going with us would plunder the others. And since they knew the custom, before we could arrive they hid a few things. And after they had received us with a lot of celebration and rejoicing, they took out what they had hidden and came to present it to us. And these were beads and ochre and a few little bags of silver.[1] We, according to the custom, gave it immediately to the Indians who had come with us, and after they gave it to us their dances and celebrations began, and they sent for others from another nearby pueblo to come see us; and in the afternoon everyone came, and they brought us beads and bows and other little things, which we also distributed.

And the next day, as we were trying to leave, all the people wanted to take us to other friends of theirs who lived at the edge of the mountains, and they said that there were many houses and people there, and that they would give us many things. But since it was out of our way, we did not want to go see them, and we took the way along the plains near the mountains, which we believed were not far from the coast.

All the people of the coast are very bad, and we felt it better to traverse the land, because the people who live farther inland have better dispositions and treated us better, and we felt certain that we would find the land more thickly settled and with better food resources. Finally, we did this because by traversing the land we would see many of its particular circumstances; because, if God our Lord were pleased to spare one of us and lead him to a land of Christians, he would be able give news and a report of it.

And when the Indians saw that we were determined not to go where they were leading us, they told us that in the direction we wanted to go there were no people, nor tunas or anything else to eat. And they begged us to stay there that day, and so we did. Right away they sent two Indians to search for people along that way that we wished to go. And the next day we departed, taking many of them along with us. And the women went carrying loads of water, and our authority among them was so great that none dared to drink without our permission. Two leagues from there we ran into the Indians who had gone to search for people, and they said that they had not found any, at which the Indians showed sorrow and once more begged us to

1. Adorno and Pautz show that this was most likely marcasite (in the next chapter, V corrects *plata*, "silver," to *margaxita*, "marcasite"). Until the mid-nineteenth century the various iron sulfides then known as marcasites were thought to be formed from the "vapors" of various metals, including lead, silver, and gold; a discovery of "silver marcasite" would thus have been taken as de facto proof of the existence of silver. There was, in fact, some silver in these mountains, as well as lead and zinc; San Gregorio de Cerralvo (1577) was the first mine founded in Nuevo Leon.

go through the mountains. We would not do it, and seeing our resolution they took leave of us, though with great sadness, and returned
downstream to their houses. And we marched upstream. And a little
bit from there we ran into two women carrying loads, who stopped as
soon as they saw us and put down their loads, and brought us some
of what they were carrying, which was cornmeal, and told us that
farther along that river we would find houses and many tunas and
more of that cornmeal. And so we took our leave of them, for they
were going to the others, where we had just left. And we walked until
sunset. And we reached a pueblo of perhaps twenty houses, where
they received us with weeping and great sadness, for they already
knew that wherever we arrived, the people were all plundered and
robbed by those who accompanied us. And since they saw us alone
they lost their fear, and they gave us tunas and nothing else.

We stayed there that night, and at dawn the Indians who had left
us the day before fell upon their houses. And since they caught them
unawares and feeling secure, they stripped them of everything they
had, for they had nowhere to hide anything, at which they wept bitterly. And to console them, the robbers told them that we were children of the Sun, and that we had the power to heal the sick and to
kill them, and other lies even bigger than these, as they know how to
come up with so well when they feel it suits them. And they told
them they should treat us with great reverence, and should take care
not to anger us about anything, and that they should give us everything they had, and should endeavor to lead us somewhere where
there were a lot of people, and that wherever we went to, they should
steal and plunder what the others had, for that was the custom.

Chapter 29. On How They Stole from One Another

After they had informed and taught them well what they were to do,
they returned and left us with the new ones, who, bearing in mind
what the others had told them, began to treat us with the same fear
and reverence as the others. And we traveled with them for three
days, and they took us to where there were many people. And before
we could reach them, they sent word that we were coming, and they
said everything about us that the others had taught them, and added
many other things besides; for all these Indian people are very fond
of fictional tales and great liars, particularly when they think it will
be to their benefit. And we drew near their houses, all the people
came out to receive us with great cheer and celebration, and among
other things two of their physicians gave us two gourds. And after
that we began to carry gourds with us, and we added this ceremony
to our authority, which is a great thing among them. Those who had
accompanied us plundered the houses, but as the houses were many

and they were few, they could not carry off everything they took, and they left more than half to waste.

From here, we went inland along the foot of the mountains for more than fifty leagues, at the end of which we found forty houses. And among other things they gave us, Andrés Dorantes got a large, wide copper bell[2] with a face depicted on it, and they displayed this, for they thought highly of it. And they said they had gotten it from some of their neighbors. Asked where they had gotten it, they said that they had brought it from up north, and that there were many of them there, and that it was held in great esteem. And we understood that wherever it had come from there was metalworking and casting in molds.

And with that, we left the next day and crossed a mountain range seven leagues wide, the stones of which were iron slags.[3] And that night we came to many houses built on the banks of a very beautiful river.[4] And the owners of these houses came to receive us halfway, with their children on their backs. They gave us many little bags of <silver> and powdered kohl,[5] which they use to paint their faces. And they gave many beads and many cowhide[6] robes, and they loaded all those who came with us with everything they had. They ate tunas and pine nuts; across that land there are short pine trees whose cones are like small eggs, but the pine nuts are better than those of Castile because they have very thin shells. When the nuts are green, they grind them and make balls, and so they eat them; and if they are dry, they grind them in the shell and eat them pulverized. And those who received us there, as soon as they had touched us, ran back to their houses; then they circled around us, and never stopped running, back and forth. In this way they brought us many things for our journey.

Here they brought to me a man and told me that a long time before he had been wounded by an arrow through his right shoulder blade,[7] and the arrowhead was stuck above his heart. He said that it

2. *Cascabel* rather than a *campana*; i.e., a spherical bell with a rock or other object inside to make it ring, like a jingle bell or sleigh bell, as opposed to an open bell with a clapper.
3. Krieger (2002: 69) points out that the Sierra de la Gloria, just south of Monclova, Coahuila, fits this description exactly, though it is about twenty miles ("seven leagues") *long* rather than *wide*. It was the original source of the iron ore used in the Monclova steel industry, and the papershell piñon trees mentioned a few lines later grow on its sides.
4. The tributary of the Nadadores River that flows through the center of Monclova.
5. *Alcohol*; which at the time referred (in both Spanish and English) to the powdered antimony or galena that is still used in the Middle East as a cosmetic. The existence of kohl was taken as another indication that silver might also be present. "Silver": V has "marcasite."
6. I.e., buffalo hide. Buffalo may have lived in this part of Coahuila in small numbers, or the people may have obtained the hides by trade.
7. The text says *Espalda derecha* (right shoulder blade), but for the arrow to be "above" (*sobre*) the heart, one might think it was the left shoulder. Perhaps it was not quite so near the heart or perhaps Cabeza de Vaca described right and left from the observer's point of view.

tormented him, and on account of it he was always sick. I touched him, and I felt the arrowhead, and saw he had it stuck through the cartilage, and using a knife I had, I opened his chest up to that place. And I saw that he had the arrowhead in sideways, and it was very difficult to remove. Again I cut deeper, and inserting the point of the knife, with great difficulty I removed it. It was very long. With a deer bone, practicing my medical trade I gave him two stitches <and having done that, he began bleeding out on me, and with the scrapings from a hide I stanched the blood>. And when I had removed the arrowhead they asked me for it, and I gave it to them. And the whole pueblo came to see it, and they sent it along inland so that the people who lived there might see it. And because of this they put on many dances and celebrations, as they usually do. And two days later I removed the Indian's two stitches, and he was healed, <and his wound seemed like nothing more than one of the lines in the palm of the hand>. And he said that he felt no pain or aching at all. And this healing gave us such a reputation throughout that land that they revered and extolled us for all they were worth.

We showed them the rattle we had gotten, and they told us that many metal plates like it lay buried in the place where it was from; and that it was a thing that they valued highly [there]; and there were permanent houses in that place. And that place, we believe, is on the South Sea, for we have always heard that that sea is richer than the North Sea.

We left these people and traveled among so many sorts of people, with such diverse languages, that memory does not serve to describe them all. And always one group plundered the next, and so both those who lost and those who gained were very content. There were so many in our company that we could not control them at all.[8] In the valleys through which we were going, each of them carried a club some three palms long, and they all fanned out as a flank. And whenever some hare jumped out—for there are quite a lot around there—they quickly closed in upon it, and so many blows fell on it that it was a wonder. In this way they made the hare jump from one to the other, which in my view was the loveliest hunt one could imagine, for many times the hares would come right to one's hands. And when we stopped at night, they had given us so many hares that each of us had eight or ten loads of them. Those who carried bows did not appear before us; rather, they took off for the mountains to hunt deer. And at night when they came back, they would bring each of us five or six deer and many birds and quail and other game.

8. *En ninguna manera podíamos valernos con ellos*; following the definition of *No poderse valer con alguno* in the DRAE (1739), "Phrase that means not being able to subjugate someone to one's intentions."

In short, everything those people hunted and killed, they set before us, without daring to take anything themselves, even if they were dying of hunger—for that was their custom ever since they began to walk with us—unless we made the sign of the cross over it first.

And the women brought many woven mats, with which they built houses for us, his own for each of us, together with all the people attached to him. And when that was done, we would order them to roast those deer and hares and everything else they had taken. And this, too, they did very quickly in some ovens that they built for the purpose. And we would taste a bit of everything, and give the rest to the highest-ranking man[9] among the people who came with us, ordering him to distribute it among them all. Each one would come to us with the share he had received so that we would blow on it and make the sign of the cross over it, for otherwise they would not dare eat any of it. And we often had three or four thousand persons with us. And our hardships were great, for we would have to blow on and make the sign of the cross over everything that each of them would eat or drink, and they would come to ask our permission for many other things that they wanted to do, so it is easy to see how beleaguered we were. The women brought us tunas and spiders and worms and whatever could be found, for even if they were dying of hunger, they would not eat a single thing unless we had given it to them.

While traveling with these people, we crossed a big river that came from the north. And after we had crossed some thirty leagues of plains, we found many people who were coming from far away to receive us. And they came out onto the trail along which we had to walk, and they received us in the same way as the earlier ones.

Chapter 30. On How the Custom of Receiving Us Changed

From here on there was a new way of receiving us, with regard to the plundering, for those who came out along the trails to bring us something for those who were coming with us were no longer robbed; but after entering their homes, they themselves offered us everything they had, and the houses along with it. We gave it all to the high ranking men, for them to distribute it among them. And always those who had been plundered would follow us, so that the number of people out to make up for their losses grew. And they would tell people to watch out and not hide anything they owned, because they could not do it without our knowledge, and we would straight away make them all die, <because the sun told us to>. So greatly did they terrify them that for the first few days they were

---

9. *El principal*; another synonym for *señor* and *cacique*, though it was used more flexibly and, in established Indian pueblos under colonial rule, could refer to members of the indigenous government regardless of cacique status.

with us they would do nothing but tremble and would not dare speak or lift their eyes up to the sky.

These people guided us through more than fifty leagues of unpopulated land with very rugged mountains—they were so dry that there was no game in them, so that we suffered great hunger— and at the mountains' end, a very large river, whose water reached up to our chests. And from here on, we began to have many of the people coming along with us suffering from the terrible hunger and hardship they went through in those mountains, which were arduous and wearisome in the extreme.

These same people led us to some plains at the end of the mountain chain, where people came to meet us from a long distance. And they received us like those who had come before, and they gave so many of their belongings to those who came with us that, unable to carry it all, they left half of it. And we told the Indians who had given it to take it back and carry it away so that it would not stay there, wasted. And they replied that by no means would they do so, for it was not their custom once they had offered something to take it back. And so, giving it no value, they left it all to waste.

We told these people that we wanted to go toward sunset, and they replied that in that direction the people were very far away. And we ordered them to send and let them know that we were going there, and they tried their best to refuse, because the others were their enemies, and they did not want us to go to them; but they did not dare do otherwise. And so they sent two women, one of their own and one whom they had captured from those others. And they sent these women because women can trade even when there is war.

And we followed the women, and we stopped at a place where it had been agreed we should wait for them, but after five days they had not returned. And the Indians said that they must not have found anybody. We told them to take us north. They replied in the same way, saying that there were no people there except very far away, and that there was nothing to eat and no water to be found. And for all that, we insisted, saying we wanted to go there. They still tried their best to refuse, so we grew angry. And I went off one night to sleep in the countryside, apart from them; but right away they came to where I was. And all night long they stayed up, not sleeping, full of fear and talking to me and telling me how frightened they were, begging us not to be angry any more, saying that even if they knew they would die along the way they would take us anywhere we wanted to go. And since we still pretended to be angry, and because their fear would not lift, a strange thing occurred, which was that on this same day many of them fell ill. And the next day, eight men died. Throughout the land where this became known, they were so afraid of us that when they saw us it seemed they would die of terror. They begged us not to be angry and not to wish for more of them to die. And they were quite convinced that we were killing them merely by wishing it. And the truth was that we felt as sorry as we possibly could about this; because, beyond seeing the ones who were dying, we were afraid that they all might die, or leave us there alone, out of fear, and that all the other groups of people farther on would do the same when they saw what had happened to these. We begged God our Lord to remedy this. And so all those who had fallen sick began to get well.

And we saw something that was very astonishing: that the parents, brothers, and wives of the dying felt deep sorrow at seeing them in that state; and after they had died, they showed no emotion whatsoever, nor did we see them weep or talk with one another or make any other demonstration of feeling, nor did they dare approach the dead until we ordered them to be taken for burial. And in more than fifteen days that we stayed with them, we never saw any of them talk with one another, nor did we see any child laugh or cry; rather, because one child cried, they carried it far away from there, and they used some sharp mice teeth[1] to scarify it from its shoulders almost all the way down its legs. When I saw this cruelty I was angered by it and asked them why they did it. And they replied to me that it was to punish the child for having cried in front of me. They would instill all these fears they had into all the others who newly arrived to meet us, so that they would give us everything they had, because they knew that we did not take anything and would give it all to them. These were the most obedient people we met throughout that land, and in the best condition. And in general they are very graceful.

The sick had convalesced and we had already been there three days when the women we had sent out returned, saying that they had found very few people, and that everyone had gone after the cows, as it was the season for them. And we ordered those who had been sick to remain, and those who were well to go with us, and that two days' travel from there, those same women would go with two of us and get people and bring them to the trail so that they could receive us.

And with that, the next morning all the most robust were leaving with us. And after three days' journey we halted. And the next day Alonso del Castillo left with Estevanico, the black man, taking the two women as guides. And the one who was a captive led them to a

1. Thomas Hester notes that "a number of rodent (rabbit) mandibles" were found by archaeologists in the area, where they formed part of a bundle that "is sometimes called a 'shaman's kit' or a 'medicine kit'" Hester, "Artifacts, Archaeology, and Cabeza De Vaca in Southern Texas and Northeastern Mexico" available at www.swrhc.txstate .edu/cssw/resources/cdvresources. "It": the Spanish word used here for the child, *criatura*, is grammatically feminine, so the feminine pronoun (*ella*, "she") is used, but the child's actual sex is never specified.

river that flowed through some mountain chains where there was a pueblo[2] in which her father lived. And these were the first houses we saw that had the likeness and manner of being houses. Here Castillo and Estevanico arrived and, after having spoken with the Indians, at the end of three days Castillo returned to where he had left us, and he brought along five or six of those Indians. And he said that he had found inhabited houses, permanent houses, and that those people ate beans and squashes, and that he had seen maize. This was the thing that most cheered us in the world, and we gave endless thanks to Our Lord for it. And he said that the black man was coming with all the people of the houses to wait by the trail, near there.

For that reason we set off, and after walking a league and a half we ran into the black man and the people who were coming to receive us, and they gave us beans and many squashes to eat and gourds to carry water in, and cowhide robes and other things. And as these people and the people who were coming with us were enemies and did not get along each other, we took leave of the latter, giving them everything that had been given to us, and we went on with the former. And six leagues from there, when night was already coming on, we reached their houses, where they made many ceremonies with us. Here we stayed one day, and the next day we left, and we took them with us to other permanent houses, where the people at the same foods as these.

And from there on we found another new usage: that the people who knew of our approach did not come out to receive us on the trails, as the others had done; rather, we would find them in their homes, and they would have other houses ready for us. They would all be seated, and all would have their faces turned to the wall and their heads bowed and the hair pulled over their eyes, and their belongings gathered in a heap in the middle of the house. And from here on they began to give us many robes of hides, and they had nothing that they would not give us. These are the people with the finest bodies we saw, the liveliest and most skillful, and the ones who best understood us and answered what we asked them. We called them the Cow people, because most of the cows die near there, and because for more than fifty leagues upstream along that river the people go killing many cows. These people go completely naked, like the first ones we met. The women go covered with some deer skins, as do a few men, especially the ones who are old, who are of no use in war.

2. This town is generally thought to be the indigenous settlement at Junta de los Ríos (modern Presidio, Texas, and Ojinaga, Chihuahua), where the Rio Conchos meets the Rio Grande.

It is a well settled land. We asked them how it was that they did not grow maize. They replied that they did not do it so as not to lose what they sowed, because for two years in a row it had not rained, and the weather had been so dry that everyone had lost their crops, and that they did not dare sow any more until it had rained very hard first. And they begged us to tell the sky to rain, and to beg it, and we promised that we would do so. We also wanted to know where they had brought that maize from. They told us it was from where the sun sets, and it was found all over that land, but the closest place was in that direction.

We asked them the best way for us to go, and to tell us all about the road, because they did not want to go there. They told us that the road was upstream along that river northward, and that in seventeen days of travel we would not find anything else to eat but a fruit {that grows on some trees and}[3] that they grind between stones. And even after this action has been performed, the meal cannot be eaten, it is so harsh and dry. And that was true, for they showed it to us there and we could not eat it. And they also told us that while we were going upstream, we would always be traveling among people who were their enemies and who spoke the same language that they did, and that they would have no food to give us, but that they would receive us very willingly and give us many cotton blankets, hides, and other things that they had; but that it still seemed to them that we should not take that road.

In doubt as to what we should do and which road we might take that would be most appropriate and advantageous for us, we stayed with them for two days. They fed us beans and squash. Their way of cooking them is so new that, as such, I wished to set it down here, that it might be seen and known how diverse and strange are the devices and artifices of human men. They do not possess pottery, and in order to cook what they want to eat they fill a large half gourd with water. And they put many stones of the sort that heat up most easily into the fire, and the stones absorb the fire.[4] And when they see that the stones are burning hot, they take them out with wooden tongs and put them into the water that is in the gourd, until they make it boil from the fire that the stones carry. And when they see that the water is boiling, they put into it whatever they are going to cook. And all this time they do nothing but take out some

---

3. In Z this phrase continues: "and that they call *chacan*." The text in V reads "a fruit that they call *chacan* and that they grind between stones." Adorno and Pautz argue convincingly that the phrase "that they call *chacan*" (*que llaman chacan*) is a misprint for "that they grind" (*que la machacan*), which V then reduplicated.

4. Fire was one of the four basic elements, according to the European physics of the time; when a stone became red hot it was thought to have absorbed the fire from the burning wood.

stones and put in other, burning hot ones, so that the water will boil and cook what they want<, and that is how they cook it>.

Chapter 31. On How We Followed the Maize Road

After we had been there for two days, we decided to go search for the maize. We did not want to follow the road of the cows because it runs north, and for us that would mean taking a very long way around, because we always felt certain that by heading toward sunset we would have to find what we desired.

So we followed our route and traversed the whole land until we came out on the South Sea. And the fear of the great hunger we would have to suffer (and we truly did suffer it) during the full seventeen days of marching that they had told us about was not enough to keep us from going this way. On each of those days going upstream we were given many cowhide robes. And we did not eat any of that fruit; instead, what sustained us was about a handful of deer fat per day, which we always endeavored to save for such cases of need.

And so we got through all seventeen days of marching, at the end of which we crossed the river and marched seventeen days more toward sunset, through some plains and between some very tall mountain chains that rise there. There we met some people who eat nothing but a kind of powdered straw for a third of the year. And as it was that season when we marched through there, we also had to eat it, until, when those days of marching were over, we found some permanent houses[5] where there was plenty of maize gathered, and they gave us great quantities of this maize and of ground maize, and of squashes and beans and cotton blankets. And we loaded those who had led us there with all this, so they went home the most contented in the world. We gave many thanks to God our Lord for having led us there, where had found such a large supply of food.

Among these houses there were some that were made of earth, and all the others were of woven cane mats. And from here we traveled more than a hundred leagues overland, and we always found permanent houses and a great supply of maize and beans. And they gave us many deer and many cotton blankets, better than those of New Spain. They also gave us many beads made out of a coral found in the South Sea; many turquoise stones, very good, which they get from up north; and in short, they gave us all they had, and [to Dorantes, / they gave me five] emeralds[6] shaped into arrowheads, and they

5. Perhaps near Casas Grandes, Chihuahua.
6. In both Spanish and English, *esmeraldas* (emeralds) referred at the time to any precious or semi-precious green stone, including malachite and jade. These green stones were highly prized in Mesoamerican cultures, where they were known in Náhuatl as *chalchihuitl* (adopted in Mexican Spanish as *chalchihuites*). Z has "to Dorantes, emeralds"; V has "they gave me five emeralds." "Turquoise": the ancient civilizations of

use these arrows in their *areítos* and dances. As they seemed very good to me, I asked where they had gotten them from. And they said that they brought them from some very high mountains up north, and they bought them in exchange for feathered headdresses and parrot feathers. And they said that up there, there were pueblos with many people and very large houses.

Among these people we found the women more decently arrayed than in any other part of the Indies we had seen. They wear cotton chemises that reach down to the knee, and over them half-sleeved garments with skirts of scraped deerskin that touch the ground. And they launder them with certain roots that are good at cleaning, and so they care for them very well; they are open in front and closed up with laces. They wear shoes.

All these people came to us that we might touch and make the sign of the cross over them. And they were so insistent about this that we endured it with great difficulty, because all of them, sick and healthy, wanted to have the sign of the cross made on them. Many times it happened that some of the women who came to us would give birth, and as soon as the child was born they would bring it to us so that we would make the sign of the cross over it and touch it. They would always accompany us until they had left us in the care of others. And among all these people it was held to be very certain that we came from the sky,[7] {because everything they do not understand and about which they have no information as to where it comes from, they say comes from the sky}.

While we were traveling with these people, we would walk all day long without eating until nighttime. And we would eat so little that they were shocked to see it. They never sensed tiredness in us, and the truth is, we were so inured to hardship that we never sensed it either. We had great authority and gravity among them. And to maintain this, we rarely spoke to them. The black man spoke to them always; he inquired about the roads we should follow, what pueblos there were, and all the things we wanted to know.[8] We crossed through a great number and diversity of languages. With all of them God our Lord favored us, because they always understood us and we understood them. And so we would ask and they would answer by

---

Mesoamerica obtained turquoise by trade with the Puebloan peoples of New Mexico. In this stage of the journey, Cabeza de Vaca and his comrades have moved into the sierras of northern Chihuahua and Sonora, an area of settled agricultural villages that communicated with the cultures of Mesoamerica to the south (and are sometimes included in the definition of Mesoamerica) and the Puebloan cultures to the north.

7. *Cielo*; could also be translated as "heaven"; Spanish uses the word for both concepts, in physical and religious contexts alike.

8. This detail provides more evidence that Estevanico belonged to the Spaniards but was by no means considered one of the Spaniards; with his ambivalent social position and human status, they were happy to use him as their go-between.

signs, as if they spoke our language and we theirs; for, although we knew six languages, we could not use them everywhere, because we found more than a thousand differences.

Throughout these lands, those who were at war with others would quickly make peace in order to come receive us and bring us everything they had. And we left the whole country like that, <at peace,> and we told them, using signs that they understood, that in Heaven[9] there was a man we called God, who had created Heaven and earth, and that we worshiped Him and considered Him our Lord, and that we did all He ordered us to do, and that all good things came from His hand, and that if they would do the same, things would go very well for them. And we found them so well disposed that if there had been a language in which we could have made ourselves perfectly understood, we would have left them all Christians. We gave them to understand this as best we could. And from there on, when the sun rose, with great shouting they would lift their clasped hands to Heaven and then pass them all over their body, and they would do the same at sunset. They are good-tempered people and industrious at following anything when well prepared.[1]

Chapter 32. On How They Gave Us Deer Hearts

In the pueblo where they gave us the emeralds, they gave Dorantes over six hundred open deer hearts, which they always keep an abundance of for their sustenance. And for this reason we gave their pueblo the name of Corazones and it is the entryway to many provinces that lie toward the South Sea.[2] If any people went looking for the sea around here and did not enter the pueblo, they would perish. For on the coast they have no maize, and they eat ground pigweed,[3] straw, and fish that they catch on the sea in rafts, for they do not possess canoes. The women cover their shameful parts with grass and straw. They are a very abject and sad people.[4]

We believe that near the coast, along the route of those pueblos that we traveled through,[5] there are more than a thousand leagues

9. Also "the sky."
1. (Bien aparejada); ambiguous: the phrase might apply to "anything" (cualquier cosa), meaning that the people are good at doing anything that has been carefully explained to them, or to "these people" (gente), meaning that they are ready to do anything asked of them.
2. Many sites have been suggested for this settlement, mainly among Pima Bajo peoples in the western foothills of the Sierra Madre, southern Sonora, in the vicinity of the Río Yaqui. Krieger proposed Suaqui; Adorno and Pautz suggest an area about twenty miles east, around Onavas. "Corazones": hearts.
3. Bledos; refers to various weeds with edible leaves used for animal fodder or as food in times of hunger, including Chenopodium album (lamb's quarters, white goosefoot) in Europe and several species of amaranth in the Americas.
4. Almost certainly the Seri of coastal Sonora. Their language is unrelated to any other known language families.
5. Reading traximos as trajinamos.

of inhabited land. And they have a large food supply, because they plant beans and maize three times a year. There are three kinds of deer; those of one kind are as large as the yearling bulls of Castile. The permanent houses of all the people here are *bohíos*. And they have poison that they get from certain trees the size of apple trees, and they need only pick the fruit and rub it over an arrow; and if there is no fruit, they break a branch and do the same with its milky sap. There are many of these poisonous trees, which, if they crush their leaves and wash them in some stagnant water, the deer and any other animals that drink the water will burst right away.

We stayed three days in this pueblo, and one day's journey from it there was another one where we were surprised by so much rain that we could not cross a river because of how high it rose, and we remained there two weeks. During this time Castillo saw on an Indian's neck a small buckle from a swordbelt, and a horseshoe nail sewed onto it. He took it from him and we asked him what it was; they said it had come from the sky. We then asked who had brought it from there. And they answered that some men who had beards like ours had come from the sky and reached that river, and that they had horses and lances and swords and had speared two of them. And, as nonchalantly as we could manage, we asked them what had become of those men. And they told us that they had gone to sea, and that they plunged their lances underwater, and that they too plunged themselves under, and that afterward they saw them going on top toward the sunset.[6]

We gave many thanks to God our Lord for what we had heard, for we had few hopes of ever getting any news of Christians. On the other hand, we found ourselves greatly perplexed and saddened to think that those people might only be some who had come by sea to discover. But in the end, since we had such certain news of them, we hastened our march, and we kept finding more news of Christians. And we told them that we were going in search of those people in order to tell them not to kill or enslave them or take them out of their country or do them any other harm, and they were very glad of this.

We walked a lot of land, and we found it all deserted, because its inhabitants were fleeing to the mountains, not daring to keep their houses or till their fields for fear of the Christians. This was something that filled us with great sorrow, seeing the land so fertile and so lovely and so full of waters and rivers, and to see the settlements

6. *Hacia puesta del sol*; if this reading (from V) is correct, they were seen heading west; Z has "until sunset" (*hasta puesta del sol*). "Going on top" (*ir por cima*): the context seems to imply that they are walking (or perhaps sailing) over the water, but Adorno and Pautz interpret this phrase as "go[ing] overland." This report and the general fear of Spaniards in the area recall the slave raids that were carried out as far as the Yaqui River in 1533 under Diego de Guzmán, a brother and underling of the notoriously brutal conqueror of western Mexico, Nuño de Guzmán. Such memories become more present as the four survivors head south into regions still occupied and subject to constant slave raids.

abandoned and burned, and the people so emaciated and sick, all fleeing and in hiding. And since they were not planting, given so much hunger they sustained themselves on tree bark and roots. Part of this hunger affected us all along this journey, because they could hardly supply us with food, being so dispossessed[7] that it seemed they wanted to die. They brought us beads and blankets from what they had hidden from the Christians and gave them to us. And they even told us how on other occasions the Christians had invaded the land and had destroyed and burned the pueblos and taken away half the men and all the women and children; and that those who could escape by flight had run fleeing away. As we had seen them, so terrorized that they did not dare stop anywhere and they neither would nor could plant or till the land, it seemed that they were resolved instead to let themselves die, and that they held this preferable to waiting and being treated with as much cruelty as they had been up until then. And they showed the greatest pleasure with us, though we feared that when we reached those who were at the frontier with the Christians and at war with them, they would ill-treat us and make us pay for what the Christians were doing against them. But since God our Lord was pleased to lead us to them, they began to fear and respect us as the earlier ones had, and even a bit more, which astonished us more than a little; from which it can clearly be seen that, in order to entice all these people into being Christians and into obedience to His Imperial Majesty, they must be attracted with good treatment, and that this way is surest, and the other is not.

They took us to a pueblo on the crest of a mountain range that can only be reached after a very rugged climb. And there we found many people gathered together, taking shelter out of fear of the Christians. They received us very well and gave us as much as they had, and they gave us more than two thousand loads of maize, which we gave to those wretched and hungry people who had led us up to that point. And the next day we dispatched four messengers across the land, as we were accustomed to doing, so that they would call and summon as many people as they could to a pueblo at three days' march from there. This done, the next day we set off with all the people who were at that place. And we always found traces and signs of where the Christians had slept.

At midday we ran into our messengers, who told us that they had not found any people; that all the people were off in the woods, hidden and in flight, so that the Christians might not kill them and enslave them; and that the night before they had seen the Christians,

---

7. Z has *desnaturado*, an archaic legal term that meant "deprived of the rights and privileges of a native and citizen of some City or Kingdom" (DRAE 1732). V changed this word to *desventurado*, "wretched, miserable, unfortunate."

watching them from behind some trees to see what they were doing, and they saw how the Christians were carrying off many Indians in chains. At this, those who had come with us were perturbed, and some of them turned back to sound the alarm through the land that Christians were coming, and many more would have done so if we not had told them to stop and have no fear, at which they felt reassured and were very glad. At the time there were Indians with us from a hundred leagues away, and we could not get them to go back to their houses. And to reassure them we slept there that night. And the next day we marched and slept on the road. And the following day, the ones we had sent as messengers guided us to where they had seen the Christians. Arriving late in the afternoon, we clearly saw they had told the truth. And we could tell that the men had come on horseback by the posts to which they had tied their horses.

From here, which is called the Río de Petután, to the river that Diego de Guzmán reached,[8] there may be, to there from where we learned of the Christians, eighty leagues. And from there to the pueblo where we were caught by the rain, twelve leagues; {and from there to the pueblo of Corazones there were five leagues;} and from there to the South Sea[9] there were twelve leagues. Throughout that land, wherever there are mountains we saw many signs of gold and kohl, iron, copper, and other metals. The area where the permanent houses are is hot country, so much so that even in January it is very hot. From there toward the south of the land, which is uninhabited as far as the North Sea,[1] is very unlucky and poor, where we suffered great and incredible hunger. And those who live and wander around that land are extremely cruel people, evil in disposition and customs. The Indians who have permanent houses, and those farther back, pay no attention to gold and silver, nor do they find that there is any possible use for them.

Chapter 33. How We Saw Traces of Christians

Once we saw clear traces of Christians and understood how near we were to them, we gave many thanks to God our Lord for wishing to redeem us from such sad and wretched captivity. The delight we felt at this can be guessed by anyone who considers the time we spent in that land, and the dangers and hardships we suffered. That night I begged one of my companions to go after the Christians, who were moving through the area where we had left the land reassured. And

8. The Yaqui. The Río de Petután, or more properly, Rio de Petatlán, is now called the Sinaloa River.
9. The Pacific (or here, the Gulf of California).
1. I.e., the entire route of the four men's journey, from the Gulf of Mexico (part of the "North Sea," or Atlantic system) to southern Sinaloa.

they were three days away. They thought it a bad idea, refusing because of exhaustion and hardship, although either of them could have done it better than I, being more robust and youthful. But seeing their will, the next morning I took the black man and eleven Indians with me,[2] and on the trail I found following the Christians I passed three places where they had slept. That day I walked ten leagues. And the next morning I came upon four Christians on horseback, who felt greatly startled to see me, so strangely dressed and in the company of Indians. They stood there looking at me for a long stretch of time, so astonished that they neither spoke to me nor found the words to ask me anything. I told them to lead me to where their captain was, and so we went on half a league from there to see Diego de Alcaraz, who was the captain.

And after I had spoke to him, he told me that he was quite lost there, because for many days he had not been able to capture Indians, and there was nowhere to go, because they were beginning to feel necessity and hunger.

I told him that Dorantes and Castillo had remained behind, that they were ten leagues from there, with many people who had led us. He dispatched three horsemen at once, with fifty Indians of the ones they had brought.[3] And the black man went back with them as their guide. And I remained there and asked them to give me a certified statement of the year, month and day that I had arrived there, and the manner in which I had come, and they did so.

From this river to the pueblo of the Christians named San Miguel, which is under the jurisdiction of the province called New Galicia, there are thirty leagues.[4]

Chapter 34. On How I Sent for the Christians

After five days, Andrés Dorantes and Alonso del Castillo arrived with those who had gone for them. And they brought with them more than six hundred people, who came from that pueblo that the Christians had caused to flee up into the woods and who were in hiding about the land. Those who had come with us up to that place had taken them out of the woods and turned them over to the

2. Here is another phrase underlining the fact that, after all the years they have spent together, Cabeza de Vaca does not consider Estevanico, "the black man," to be one of his "companions."
3. I.e., victims of earlier slave raids on indigenous villages.
4. The Spanish *villa* (town) of San Miguel Culiacán was for many years the main Spanish settlement on the Pacific coastal plain north of Acapulco. It was named after an important preconquest settlement that continued to exist as an Indian pueblo after the conquest and that still exists and is also confusingly named Culiacán (or Culiacancito). According to Peter Gerhard (*The Northern Frontier of New Spain*, 1982: 261), the Spanish town was originally founded about thirty miles southeast and moved only in the 1550s to its present site, nine miles east of the "original" Culiacán.

Christians, and they had sent away all the other people whom they had brought up to there.

When they arrived at where I was, Alcaraz begged us to send out and summon the people of the pueblos along the banks of the river, who were off in hiding throughout the woods of the land, and to order them to bring food—though that was unnecessary, because they always took care to bring us as much as they could. And we sent out our messengers at once to summon them, and six hundred persons came, and they brought all the maize they possessed. And they brought it in the clay-sealed pots in which they had buried and hidden it. And they brought absolutely everything they had; but we would only take the food from all of it, and we gave all the rest to the Christians to distribute it among themselves.

And after this, we had many bitter quarrels with the Christians, because they wanted to make slaves of the Indians we were bringing. In our anger at this, when we departed we left behind many Turkish bows that we were bringing, and many pouches and arrows, among them the five emeralds, for we forgot about them and so we lost them. We gave the Christians many cowhide robes and other things we were bringing, and we had a lot of trouble with the Indians, trying to get them to return to their houses and plant their maize. They wanted only to keep going with us until they had left us with other Indians, as their custom said; because if they returned without doing this, they feared they would die; for as long as they were going with us, they did not fear the Christians or their lances. This saddened the Christians, and they had their interpreter tell the Indians that we were some of their own, and that we had gotten lost a long time back, and that we were people with little luck or valor, and that they were the lords of that land, who had to be obeyed and served.

But the Indians gave little or no weight to what they were told. Instead, they talked among themselves, saying that the Christians were lying, for we had come from where the sun rises, and the others from where it sets; and that we cured the sick, and they killed those who were healthy; that we came naked and barefoot, and they came dressed and on horseback and with lances; and that we coveted nothing and instead quickly gave away everything we were given, and the others had no other aim but to steal everything they could, and they never gave anything to anyone.[5] And in this way they related all our deeds and held them up for praise, as the opposite of the others. Thus they replied to the Christians' interpreter, and they also made it

5. Sunrise and sunset are associated in many Native American cultures (and many other cultures around the world) with the world of the living and the world of the dead, respectively. The other contrasting attributes (giving life, health, and goods vs. taking them away) reinforce this association.

understood to the others through a *lengua*[6] they had among them whom we could understand. Those who use that language we call Primahaitu, <which is like saying Basques,>[7] which for more than four hundred of the leagues we traveled we found in use among them, and there was no other throughout those lands.

In the end, the Indians could never be convinced that we belonged to the other Christians, and only with great trouble and insistence could we make them return to their houses; and we ordered them that they should be reassured and should settle in their pueblos and should plant and till the land, which after being depopulated was already full of undergrowth—and it is without a doubt the best land to be found in these Indies and the most fertile and abundant in food supplies. And they plant three crops a year. They have many fruits and very lovely rivers, and many other excellent sources of water. There are signs and great indications of gold and silver mines. The people of this land have very good dispositions. The ones who are friendly serve the Christians very willingly. They are very graceful, much more so than those of Mexico. And in short, this is a land that lacks nothing to make it very good. When we took leave of the Indians, they told us they would do what we ordered and would settle in their pueblos, if the Christians let them. And I so say and affirm as certainly true that if they should not do it, it will be the fault of the Christians.

After we had sent off the Indians <in peace, and expressed our thanks to them for the hardships they had endured with us>, in a cunning trick[8] the Christians sent us off with an alcalde named Cebreros and three other Christians: which shows how much men can be deceived by their own thoughts, for we had gone to seek their freedom, and just when we thought we had achieved it for them, the opposite occurred. To separate us from conversation with the Indians, they led us through uninhabited woods so that we would not see <or understand> what they were doing {or how they would treat them}, because they had resolved together to fall upon the Indians, whom we had sent off reassured and in peace.[9]

---

6. Tongue, language, and interpreter. In this paragraph, the word shifts meaning from "interpreter" (the Christians' *lengua* is clearly their interpreter) to "language," or perhaps better, "lingua franca" in the next sentence. Here it is unclear: the Indians seem to be speaking "in a language" (*por una lengua*), but then Cabeza de Vaca says "*whom* we could understand," not "*which* we could understand" (*con quien nos entendíamos*) and *whom* is in the singular in Spanish, so it is one person, not all the Indians. Perhaps the Indians of Sinaloa had their own interpreter who spoke the lingua franca of Sonora and Chihuahua, which Cabeza de Vaca and his companions had learned.
7. Added in V. The Pima Baja (O'ob) and other languages spoken from northern Sinaloa through Sonora and Chihuahua are closely related and to some extent mutually intelligible.
8. *Debajo de cautela*, following the definition in the DRAE: "Guile, cunning, and artfulness at deception."
9. This paragraph was considerably reordered between Z and V; this translation follows the sentence structure of Z.

And as they planned, so they did. They led us through those woods for two days, with no water, lost, and with no trail. We all expected to die from thirst, and seven men suffocated from it on us, and many friends[1] brought along by the Christians could not reach the place where we found water that night until midday on the following day. And we marched with them twenty-five leagues, more or less, at the end of which we came to a pueblo of Indians at peace.[2] And the Alcalde who was leading us left us, and he went ahead another three leagues to a pueblo called Culiacán, where Melchior Díaz was Alcalde Mayor and captain of that province.

Chapter 35. On How the Alcalde Mayor Received Us Well the Night We Arrived

When the Alcalde Mayor learned of our departure and arrival, he set out right away that very night and came to where we were, and he wept with us, praising God our Lord for having shown such mercy toward us. And he spoke to us and treated us very well. And on behalf of Governor Nuño de Guzmán and himself he offered us everything he had and everything he could do. He expressed his deep condolences at the bad reception and ill-treatment we had met with from Alcaraz and the others. And we felt certain that if he had been there at the time, what was done to us and to the Indians would have been prevented.

With that night over, the next day we set off {for Ahuacán},[3] and the Alcalde Mayor entreated us to stay there, saying that by doing so we would be rendering a great service to God and Your Majesty, because the land was depopulated, untilled, and all quite destroyed, and the Indians were hiding and on the run in the woods, refusing to come back and settle down in their pueblos; and that we should have them sent for, and should order them in the name of God and Your Majesty to come back and settle on the plains and till the land.

To us, this seemed very difficult to put into effect, because we did not have any of our Indians with us, nor any of those who used to accompany us and take care of these things. In the end we hazarded two Indians for this from among the ones who were kept captive there; they were from the local people and had been with the Christians when we first reached them, and they had met the people who accompanied us and learned from them how much authority and dominion we had exercised through all those lands,

---

1. *Amigos*; the conquest-era term for indigenous allies of the Spanish.
2. *Indios de paz*; the conquest-era term for conquered indigenous communities, as opposed to those that were still waging active war against Spanish interests (*indios de guerra*).
3. According to Adorno and Pautz (p. 255), Ahuacán was an indigenous pueblo three leagues from the town of San Miguel Culiacán.

and the miracles we had worked, and the patients we had healed, and many other things. And we sent others from the pueblo with these Indians so that they would all go together to summon the Indians who were rebelling up in the mountains, and those from the Río de Petlatlán, where we had found the Christians, and would tell them to come to us, because we wished to talk to them. And so that they would go securely, and the others would return, we gave them one of the gourds we used to carry in our hands, which were our chief insignia and tokens of high rank. And with that, they went and roamed about there for seven days, at the end of which they came back, and they brought with them three lords of the rebels in the mountains, who were bringing fifteen men. And they brought us beads and turquoises and feathers. And the messengers told us that they had not summoned the natives from the river that we had started from, because the Christians had once more made them flee into the woodlands.

And Melchior Diaz told the interpreter to speak to the Indians in our name and to tell them that he came in the name of God, Who is in Heaven, and that we had wandered through the world for nine years, telling all the people we had met to believe in God and serve Him, for He was the Lord of everything that exists in the world; and that He gave rewards and recompense to the good, and eternal fiery punishment to the bad; and that when the good died, He took them up to Heaven, where no one ever died, or felt hunger, or cold, or thirst, or any other want, but only the greatest glory that could be imagined; and that those who refused to believe in Him or obey His commandments, He thrust them under the earth together with the demons, into a huge fire that would never go out, but would torment them forever; and that, beyond this, if they would become Christians and serve God our Lord in the way we ordered them to do, the Christians would accept them as brothers and would treat them very well, and we would order the Christians not to affront them or take them from their lands, but to be their great friends; but that if they refused to do this, the Christians would treat them very badly and would carry them away as slaves into other lands.

To this they replied to the interpreter that they would be very good Christians and would serve God.

Upon being asked whom they worshiped and to whom they sacrificed, and whom they asked for water for their maize fields and health for themselves, they replied, to a man who was in the sky.[4]

We asked them what his name was, and they said that it was Aguar, and that they believed he had created the world and everything in it.

4. See n. 7, p. 74.

Again, we asked how they knew this, and they replied that their fathers and grandfathers had told them, that they had known of it for a very long time, and they knew that water and all good things were sent by him.

We told them that we called the one of whom they spoke God, and that they should call Him that, and should serve and worship Him as we ordered, and they would do very well by it. They replied that they understood all this very well, and that they would do so.

And we ordered them to move down from the mountains, and come in security and at peace, and settle all the land, and build their houses; and among their houses they should build one for God, and should set at its entrance a cross like the one we had there, and when the Christians came there they should go out to receive them with crosses in their hands, without bows and without weapons, and should take them into their houses and feed them whatever they had to eat, and in this way they would do them no harm, but rather would be their friends. And they said that they would do as we ordered. And the captain gave them blankets and treated them very well; and so they returned, taking the two who were captives and had gone as messengers. This took place in presence of the notary they have there and many witnesses.[5]

Chapter 36. On How We Had Churches Built in That Land

After the Indians went back, when all the people of that province who were friends of the Christians learned we were there, they came to see us and brought us beads and feathers. We ordered them to build churches and set up crosses in them, because up until then they had not done so. And we made them bring the children of the high-ranking lords to be baptized. And right away the captain pledged an oath of fealty to God not to make or to allow anyone else to make any raids at all, nor to take any slaves throughout the land and the people we had secured, and that he would keep and fulfill this vow until His Majesty, and Governor Nuño de Guzmán or the Viceroy in his name, should decree what might better serve God our Lord and His Majesty. After the children were baptized, we set off for the pueblo of San Miguel, where, once we arrived, Indians came and told us how many people were coming down from the mountains and settling on the plains, and building churches and crosses and everything we had ordered them to do.

5. The settlement founded by these Pima Bajo people is Bamoa, Sinaloa, on the Petatlán or Sinaloa River about eighty-five miles northwest of Culiacán. See Cynthia Radding, *Wandering Peoples: Colonialism, Ethnic Spaces, and Ecological Frontiers in Northwestern Mexico, 1700–1850* (1997: 30), and Edward Spicer, *Cycles of Conquest: The Impact of Spain, Mexico, and the United States on the Indians of the Southwest, 1533–1960* (1962: 87–88).

And each day we got news of how that was being done and carried out more completely.

And after we had been there for two weeks, Alcaraz arrived with the Christians who had gone on that raid. And they told the captain how the Indians had come down from the mountains and settled on the plains; and they had found pueblos full of people that had formerly been depopulated and deserted, and the Indians had come out to receive them with crosses in their hands, and had taken them to their houses, and given them of what they had, and they had slept with them there that night. They were shocked by this new state of things and by the fact that the Indians would tell them they were already secure, and he ordered that no harm be done to them, and with this they departed.

May God our Lord in His infinite mercy grant that, in the days of Your Majesty and under your power and sway, these people may become, truly and of their full free will, subjects of the true Lord Who created and redeemed them. We hold it certain that so it shall be, and that Your Majesty shall be the one who shall bring it about—which will not be difficult to do; because in the two thousand leagues that we walked overland and crossed the sea in barks, and in the ten months more after our rescue from captivity that we walked without stop across the land, nowhere did we find sacrifices or idolatry.[6] During this time, we crossed from one sea to the other, and according to the information that we were able to deduce with great diligence, from one coast to the other, at the widest point, there may be two hundred leagues.[7] And we were able to deduce that on the South Sea coast there are pearls and great wealth, and all that is best and richest is near there.

We stayed in the town of San Miguel until May 15; the reason for our long stay there was because from there to the city of Compostela,[8] where Governor Nuño de Guzmán resided, there are one hundred leagues, all of it depopulated and filled with enemies. And we had to go with our men, so twenty horsemen went, accompanying us as many as forty leagues. And from there on six Christians came with us, who brought five hundred enslaved Indians. Having reached Compostela, the Governor received us very well,

6. Religious practices that formed a legal basis for wars of conquest, which in northwestern Mexico were largely pretexts for slaving raids.
7. This is a fairly accurate estimate—it is just over six hundred miles in a straight line from their original goal, Soto la Marina on the Gulf Coast, to Culiacán on the Pacific Coast—but given the state of their general knowledge, it is hard to imagine that this accuracy was more than a lucky coincidence.
8. Compostela: founded in 1531 as the first capital of Nueva Galicia, located at the site of modern-day Tepic, capital of the state of Nayarit. Indigenous rebellions in 1540, after Cabeza de Vaca's visit, forced the Spanish to move Compostela to its current location, a better-defended site about twenty-five miles south of Tepic.

giving us what clothes he had for us to dress in; but for many days I could not wear those clothes, nor could we sleep anywhere but on the floor. And after ten or twelve days we left for Mexico.[9] And all along the way we were well treated by the Christians. And many came out to see us along the roads, and they gave thanks to God our Lord for having freed us from so many dangers. We reached Mexico on Sunday, one day before the eve of Saint James, where we were very well treated and received with great pleasure by the Viceroy and the Marqués del Valle. And they gave us clothing and offered everything they had, and on Saint James's Day they held a celebration with *juego de cañas* and bulls.[1]

Chapter 37. On What Happened When I Tried to Return

After we had rested in Mexico for two months I tried to come over to these kingdoms, and as I was going to embark in October there came a storm that scuttled the ship, and it was lost. And seeing this, I decided to let the winter pass, because that is a very rough season for sailing in those parts. And after winter was past, around Lent, Andrés Dorantes and I set out from Mexico for Veracruz, where we would embark. And there we stayed, waiting for the weather, until Palm Sunday, when we embarked, and we stayed on board more than two weeks for lack of weather. And the ship we were on was taking on a lot of water. I left it and switched to one of the others that were set to come back, and Dorantes stayed on that one. And on April 10, three ships set sail from the port, and we sailed together for one hundred and fifty leagues. And on the way the other two ships took on a lot of water, and one night we were separated from their convoy, because their pilots and ship's masters—as we later learned—did not dare go any farther with their ships, and they returned once more to the port from which they had set out without our noticing it or learning what had happened to them. And we continued our voyage. And on May 4 we reached the port of Havana, where we stayed, waiting for the other two ships and thinking they would come, until June 2, when we left, in great fear of running into the French, who only a few days before had taken three of our ships.[2]

9. I.e., Mexico City, the capital of colonial New Spain.
1. As practiced at the time, this entertainment consisted mainly of the fun of crowds of people trying not to be trampled or gored by young bulls set loose in the plaza. The feast day of Saint James is July 25; they arrived in Mexico City on Sunday, July 23, 1536. "*Juego de cañas*" a stylized simulated battle between teams on horseback, using long canes in place of spears; usually held the city's main plaza, in front of the main church or cathedral.
2. This took place during the Italian War of 1536–38, which pitted France against Spain's Charles V in a contest for control of Turin and Milan.

And as we pulled near the island of Bermuda, we were hit by one
of the storms that tend to overtake all those who pass through there,
which is according to the people who travel by that island, and for
one whole night we considered ourselves lost. And it pleased God
that, when morning came, the storm ceased and we continued our
journey. Twenty-nine days after we set sail from Havana we had gone
the one thousand one hundred leagues that they say there are from
there to the pueblo of the Azores, and as we were passing the next
day by the island called Corvo, we met with a French ship.[3] At the
midday hour he began to pursue us with a caravel that he had taken
from the Portuguese. And they gave us chase. That evening we saw
nine more sails, and they were so far out that we could not tell
whether they were Portuguese or more of the same that pursued us.
And when night fell the French was a cannon shot from our ship,
and as soon as it was dark we changed our course to get away from
him. And as he was so close to us he saw us and took our course, and
we did this three or four times. And he could have taken us if he had
wished, but he left it for morning. It pleased God that when dawn
broke, we found the French and ourselves together, and surrounded
by the nine sails that I said we had seen the evening before, which we
recognized as belonging to the Portuguese navy. And I gave thanks
to Our Lord for having escaped the hardships of the land and the
dangers of the sea.

When the French recognized it as the Portuguese navy, he let go
of the caravel that he had taken, which was loaded with black men;
he had brought it along so that we would think they were Portuguese and wait for them. And when he let it go, he told its master
pilot that we were French and belonged to their convoy. And as he
said this, he set sixty oars to his ship; and so, by oar and by sail, he
pulled away, and he ran so fast it cannot be believed. And the caravel that he had let go went to the galleon[4] and told the captain that

---

3. Perhaps a privateer (i.e., a private ship commissioned by the French Crown to attack
the enemies of France, including private Spanish ships), but Cabeza de Vaca calls it a
cossario, "pirate," rather than a *corsario*, "privateer." The Azores are not a "pueblo" in
any ordinary usage of the word, except in the sense that this previously uninhabited
Atlantic island chain had been settled by the Portuguese beginning in the 1430s. The
westernmost islands in the chain are Flores and Corvo. They lie about 3,175 statute
miles from Havana, traveling in a straight line (which passes through Bermuda). Terceira (which appears a bit later in the story) is in the middle of the Azores.
4. The lead Portuguese ship. There are at least three types of ships involved in this story.
The French pirate ship and the lead Portuguese ship are both galleons, a large and
relatively fast ship, though neither as large nor as fast in the 1530s as later galleons
would be. The Portuguese are supported by several caravels, a much smaller, lighter,
faster, and more maneuverable ship whose invention in the 1400s made the Portuguese
voyages of exploration and trade possible; these fifteenth-century models would be
fighting caravels, designed as military escorts for trade with the Indies (East and West);
the one that the French pirate captured may be an old trading model, captured after a
slaving raid on the coast of Africa. The Portuguese fleet is escorting three vessels—
naos or "carracks," the largest cargo ships of the era, which were used to initiate the

our ship and the other one were French. And when our ship approached the galleon, and when the whole fleet saw that we were bearing down on them, thinking for certain that we were French, they armed themselves for war and bore down on us. And having pulled close, we saluted them. Recognizing that we were friends, they saw how that pirate had tricked them into letting him escape, by saying that we were French and part of his convoy; and so four caravels went after him.

After the galleon reached us and we greeted them, the captain, Diego de Silveira, asked us where we were coming from and what merchandise we were carrying. We replied that we were coming from New Spain, and that we were carrying silver and gold. And he asked us how much we had. The ship's master told him that we had about three hundred thousand castellanos.[5]

The captain replied: "*Boa fe*, that you come back very rich, but you bring very bad ship and very bad artillery, oh! son of a bitch! here a French renegade, and what a good morsel he lost, swear to God. Now you have escaped, then, follow me and do not part from me, for by help of God I will put you in Castile."[6]

And soon afterward the caravels that had gone in pursuit of the French returned, because it seemed to them that he was going full speed, and so as not to leave the fleet, which was escorting three vessels that had come loaded with spices. And so we reached the island of Terceira, where we stayed resting for two weeks, taking in supplies and waiting for another vessel that was coming loaded with cargo from India, which made up the convoy of three vessels that the fleet was escorting. After the two weeks were over, we sailed from there with the fleet, and we reached the port of Lisbon on August 9, the eve of Saint Lawrence's Day, in the year 1537.

And because what I have stated in the foregoing report is true, I have signed it with my name:

Cabeza de Vaca

(The report from which this was taken was signed with his name, and with his coat of arms.)

Portuguese trade with India through their entrepôt in Goa beginning in 1515. The Spanish ship is described only by the generic term *navío*.

5. Spanish gold coins of the era. This is quite a fortune: some forty-eight thousand troy ounces of gold, or its equivalent in silver at the official rate of one ounce of gold to eleven of silver.

6. Cabeza de Vaca reports the captain's speech in a sort of "Portuñol," a hybrid of Spanish and Portuguese that may indicate the captain's attempt to speak Spanish, Cabeza de Vaca's attempt to write in Portuguese, or some mixture of the two.

Chapter 38. On What Happened to the Others Who Went to the Indies

Since I have made my report about everything as stated above on the journey, entering and leaving the land, up to returning to these kingdoms, I likewise wish to give an account and report on what the other ships and the people who stayed on them did, which I have not recalled before because we never got news of them until after we had left, when we found many of those men in New Spain and others over here in Castile, and learned from them what had happened, the outcome, the way it took place.

After we left our three ships—for one ship had already been lost on the wild coast—they remained in great danger, and some one hundred persons remained on board with few supplies, among whom were ten married women. And one of those women had told the Governor many things that afterward happened to him on the journey, before they took place. She had told him, when he was about to march overland, that he should not go, because she believed that neither he nor any those who went with him would ever come out of it; and that if any of them did come out, then God would work great miracles through him; but she believed that few would escape, or none at all.

The Governor then replied to her that he and all who went inland with him were going to fight and conquer many and very strange peoples and countries, and that he felt quite sure that in conquering them many would have to die, but those who remained would have good fortune and become very rich, because of the information he had of the wealth that existed in that land. And he continued by begging her to tell him: those things past and present she had mentioned, who had told them to her?

She replied and said that in Castile, a Moorish woman from Hornachos had told it to her—which is something she had told us before we left Castile, and all along the voyage everything had happened just as she had told us.

After the Governor had left Carvallo, a native of Huete, in Cuenca, as his lieutenant and captain of all the ships and people he was leaving there, we set off from them, the Governor leaving orders that all the ships should withdraw as soon as at all possible and continue their voyage direct to Pánuco, always hugging the coast and searching for the port as well as they possibly could, in order to stop there when they found it and wait for us.

During the time that they were getting onto the ships, they say that all those who were there quite clearly saw and heard how that woman told the others that, since their husbands were heading inland and putting their lives in such great danger, they should not take them into account at all, and that they should soon see whom they would marry next, because that was what she planned to do. And so she did: she and the other women married or lived with those who had remained on the ships. And after we left there, the ships set sail and continued their voyage, and they did not find the port ahead and so they returned. And five leagues down from where we had disembarked they found the harbor that stretched seven or eight leagues inland; and it was the same one we had discovered, where we found the boxes from Castile, as told before, that contained the bodies of dead men, who were Christians. And in this harbor and along this coast cruised the three ships and the other that had come from Havana and the brigantine, searching for us for nearly a year. And since they did not find us, they went to New Spain.

That harbor is the best one in the world; it stretches inland for seven or eight leagues; and it has six fathoms at the mouth and it has five near land; and its bottom is silt; and there are no tides inside it or raging storms; just as there is room in it for many ships, it has a very large number of fish. It lies a hundred leagues from Havana, which is a Christian pueblo in Cuba, and it is directly north of that pueblo. And the breezes are constant here, and ships can go back and forth from one to the other in four days, because they can travel in both directions by flatting in the sails.[7]

And now that I have given an report of the ships, it will be good for me to say who the men are whom Our Lord was pleased to rescue from these hardships and where they are from. The first is Alonso del Castillo Maldonado, born in Salamanca, son of Doctor Castillo and of Doña Aldonza Maldonado. The second is Andrés Dorantes, son of Pablo Dorantes, born in Béjar and citizen of Gibraleón. The third is Álvar Núñez Cabeza de Vaca, son of Francisco de Vera and grandson of Pedro de Vera who conquered the Canary Islands, and his mother was named Doña Teresa Cabeza de Vaca, born in Jérez de la Frontera. The fourth is named Estevanico; he is an Arab black man, born in Azamor.[8]

---

7. A *quartel*; following the definition of DRAE (1726) for *aquartelar*. The *Oxford English Dictionary* (OED) cites this definition from *Practical Navigator* (1772): "To *flat in*, to draw in the aftermost lower corner or clue of a sail towards the middle of a ship, to give the sail a greater power to turn the vessel." Cabeza de Vaca's point is that by turning the sails it was easy to sail in both directions between Cuba and Florida, a feat that was difficult in many places due to prevailing winds.

8. The four survivors of the Narváez expedition are listed in an order that inadvertently mirrors the trajectory of Iberian expansion. Castillo's hometown is the site of Spain's oldest university, Salamanca, founded in 1134; his father's title, "doctor," indicated that he was a doctoral graduate of the university, almost certainly in a field that had nothing to do with medicine. Dorantes came from a small mountain town in the province of Salamanca, but he had established residence in the southern city of Gibraleón, only a few miles from the port that Columbus departed from in 1492 and in a region conquered by the Christian kingdom of Castile in the 1250s. Cabeza de Vaca's mother was from a southern Spanish city that was the staging ground for many expeditions to the Americas;

FIN

This book was printed in the magnificent, noble, and ancient city of Zamora by the honored gentlemen Augustín de Paz and Juan Picardo, book-printing partners, citizens of this city. Expenses paid by the virtuous gentleman Juan Pedro Musetti, book merchant, citizen of Medina del Campo. Completed on October 6 in the year of the birth of our Lord Jesus Christ 1542.[9]

his paternal grandfather, as he proudly notes, was one of the leaders of the conquest of the Canaries, the first major overseas expansion of the nascent Spanish empire, in 1481–83. (Note also taking his mother's last name, rather than his father's, was characteristic of the fluid approach to surnames in sixteenth-century Spain; many people adopted the most distinguished surname they could find in any branch of their family tree.) Estevanico, who as a slave was not given a surname at all (the narrative neglects to mention his enslavement, but other documents of the era state that he belonged to Dorantes, who sold him to another Spaniard in Nueva Galicia after the end of their ordeal), was sold into slavery by the Portuguese in the city of Azamor or Azemmour on the Atlantic coast of Morocco, which was under Portuguese control from 1486 to 1541.

9. This is the colophon from Z. The colophon from V reads simply: "Thanks be to God. Printed in Valladolid by Francisco Fernández de Córdoba. Year 1555."

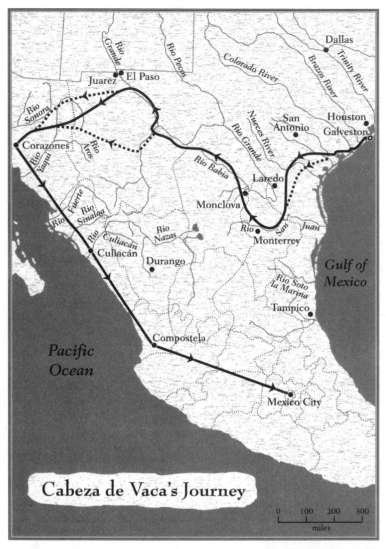

Overview of the castaways' trek across south-central North America from near the mouth of Guadalupe River in Texas, where they spent their final season in the fall of 1534 in the custody of Indian bands, to near the Gulf of California, where they eventually encountered members of the Spanish army who escorted them to Mexico City in late 1536. Adapted from Krieger (2002: Map 4).

CONTEXT

Alternative Narratives and Sequels

GONZALO FERNÁNDEZ DE OVIEDO Y VALDÉZ

From General and Natural History of the Indies (1535)[†]

Book 35

CHAPTER I · THE RELATION OF WHAT TOOK PLACE BETWEEN THOSE
WHO SURVIVED THE UNFORTUNATE EXPEDITION UNDER CAPTAIN
PÁMPHILO DE NARVÁEZ, AND OF WHAT HAPPENED ON THE COAST
AND LANDS TO THE NORTH.

Álvar Núñez Cabeza de Vaca, and Alonso del Castillo, and Andrés
Dorantes alone, and a black named Esteban, survived of the whole
fleet of the governor Pámphilo de Narváez. And this Cabeza de Vaca
was the treasurer and official of Your Majesty: he who says that from
Xagua, which is a port or *ancón* on the island of Cuba, on the fifteenth of February 1527 [1528], had written to your Majesty about
what had happened to them there, and about the loss of two ships
with sixty men and all there was in them. And those people and ships
being lost, and more than twenty horses that were with them, they
agreed to winter there at the port of Xagua, where Cabeza de Vaca
says they remained from the sixth of November of the said year, with
four ships and all of the people, until the twenty-second of the month
of February of the following year of 1528, when the governor [Narváez]
arrived there. Who [Narváez] embarked to continue his trip in four
ships and a brigantine, with four hundred men and eighty horses.

They continued by sea until the twelfth day of the month of
April, Tuesday of Holy Week, when they arrived at the Mainland,
and they followed the coast until Holy Thursday, and anchored on
the coast in a shallow bay and at the end of it they saw some huts.

[†] From *We Came Naked and Barefoot: The Journey of Cabeza de Vaca Across North
America*, trans. Alex D. Krieger, ed. Margery H. Krieger (Austin: University of Texas
Press, 2002), pp. 243–65. Reprinted by permission. All bracketed phrases by Alex D.
and Margery H. Krieger.

And the following day, Holy Friday [April 15], they landed with the most people they could bring out in the small boats and disembarked next to the huts, in which they found no people because they [the Indians] had abandoned them. One of the huts was so large that it could hold three hundred people, and the others were small. They found many fish nets and among them [the huts] was found a timbrel of gold.

The following day the governor set out flags for Your Majesty and took possession of the land and brought together Your Majesty's officers and friars, who were there and all the people who had landed, and he presented the royal credentials that he carried, and these were obeyed by all, and the said governor [was] accepted as governor and captain general. And the officers presented, their [credentials] and the same were accepted as officers of Your Majesty. And soon the order was given to disembark all the people and horses, which were extremely fatigued because it had been many days since they had embarked, and they had even lost nearly half of them at sea.

Next day, Sunday, Easter Day, the Indians of that town came and talked to the Christians without being understood; but it seemed that they menaced them and told them to leave that land and made angry gestures; and after doing this they left. The following day, in order to see the land and examine what it was like, the governor sent six horsemen and forty men on foot toward the northeast, until they arrived that day at a bay that enters the land,[1] and from there they turned back to the people [who had remained at the ships] and the governor with them, for he was one of the six horsemen.

The following day the governor sent [out] a brigantine that they had, to find the way along the coast of Florida and look for a port that the pilot Miruelo said he knew about, to where these people [could be] carried (in which he [the pilot] was wrong, and he did not know where it was). And he [Narváez] told him [the pilot] that while searching he would cross to the island of Cuba, and go to the town and port of Havana in search of another ship that they were waiting for from there, in which forty men and twelve horses were coming. And if they found it, both ships were to bring from Havana all the cargo they could, and carry it to where the Christians and governor were.

This task [giving the order] completed, the Christians left there and went to the bay which it was said they had discovered, and followed its coast. They traveled four leagues from where they started, and found some Indians, and took three of them and the Spaniards

1. This was undoubtedly one of the arms of Tampa Bay. Cabeza de Vaca is much clearer on this.

showed them a little maize, asking them where it came from. And those Indians guided them to a town at the end of that bay, and showed them a little maize they had planted there, which was the first they saw in that land. There they found some large boxes from Castile, and in each of them a dead man, and [the] corpses [were] covered with some painted hides; and it seemed to the commissary and friars that those [Indians] were idolatrous, and the governor had them [the corpses] burned. In addition, they found pieces of shoes and linen, and of cloth and some iron; and questioning those Indians, they said with signs that they found them in a ship that had been lost on that coast and bay.

He [Narváez] showed them a little gold, and they said there was none in that land, but far from there, in the province called Apalache, there was much gold in great quantity, according to what they gave [the Spaniards] to understand with their signs. And everything they showed these Indians, that to them [the Indians] it appeared that the Spaniards valued, they said that there was much of it in Apalache.

With this simple information, they left there, taking with them those Indians. Ten or twelve leagues from there they found up to twelve or fifteen houses where there was maize, and they stayed two days without seeing any Indian. And they agreed to turn back to where they had left the purser and other people with the ships. On arriving, they related what they had found by land, which was not more than what has been said.

Next day, the first of May, the governor brought together the King's officers and the commissary, and decreed, before a notary, that he had intentions of entering the country inland, and that the ships were to go along the coast, and asked them [the officers] what they thought of this. And the treasurer, Cabeza de Vaca, told him that he should not leave the ships without first leaving them at a [known] port and town, and that this being done, the governor and those he commanded could go inland. They would have a place, or a given part of the country, to return to, to look for the [remaining] people when it was convenient. And that for many reasons it seemed to him [Cabeza de Vaca] that he [Narváez] should not penetrate inland, because that country where they had gone inland following information from the Indians, from what the Christians had seen, was poor land and unpopulated; and also because they were waiting for the brigantine and the ships which it is said [above] were to come from Havana with supplies. And furthermore, because the pilots did not know or even understand in what place they were; and for other reasons that appeared reasonable to the treasurer, he said that what the governor [proposed] should not be done.

The commissary said that his opinion was that they should go inland, [but keep] close to the coast until arriving at the port that

the pilots said would be fifteen leagues from there, on the way to
Pánuco, and that they could not pass it [the port] without touching
it because it [the bay where the port was] entered the land twelve
leagues, and that there they would wait for the ships and for them
[the people on them?]. And that they [the whole expedition] should
not embark again because this would be to tempt God, since during
the trip at sea [from the beginning], they had suffered so many
misfortunes and hardships to arrive there.

The purser and overseer agreed with the commissary, and the governor decided to do it thus. But the treasurer, on seeing his determination, asked [Narváez] many times not to enter [the interior], for the
reasons he had given, and others which he emphasized in his request.
[He asked] him [Narváez] not to forsake the ships and the people
who were in them, without first leaving them at a known and populated port, and that after this he could do whatever he thought [best].
And thus he [Cabeza de Vaca] asked the notary who was present to
give testimony. But the governor answered that because there was
no port there, nor a suitable place to settle on account of the steril-
ity of the land, he was abandoning the town that he had founded,[2]
and was going in search of a port and land to settle, and said that
he would ask [the notary] to testify to this. And soon he ordered all
the people [except the ships' crews] to prepare to go with him, and
that the ships were to provide themselves with what was needed.

The next day they left there, taking forty horsemen and two hundred sixty men on foot. And with him went the said officers and the
commissary and other officers. They went inland and traveled fifteen
days with one pound of bread and half a pound of bacon as [daily]
ration, until they arrived at a river that they crossed by swimming.
And [while they were] crossing it, there came toward them two hundred Indians with whom they fought, and they captured five or six of
them; who took them to their homes that were nearby. [There] they
found much maize in the fields ready to eat. Next day the officers
and friars asked the governor to send [someone] to reconnoiter the
sea and [look for] the port, if there was one; and he sent the treasurer
and Alonso del Castillo to go with forty men. And thus they went
marching, because they could not take the horses, and traveled
through some low places [baxos] of the sea coast, through estuaries,
about two leagues, and arrived where the river passed, the [same]
river they had passed the day before inland. Because it was deep,
they could not cross it and returned to the camp [al real].

The next day the governor sent a captain with six horsemen and
forty men on foot to cross the river, through where they had come

2. Clearly this was not a town but the place where the flags had been planted and possession declared in the name of the king.

[the day before] and to explore that bay and [see] if there was a port, and he did thus. And he found that it was shallow and ships could not enter there. When the report was made, they departed from there to search for the province of Apalache, taking with them as guides the Indians they had made prisoners. And they traveled until another day after Saint John in June, when they arrived at Apalache which was the thing they most desired in the world, both because of the long trip and for the great need of supplies. And because though in some places they would find maize in the country, many times they traveled four or five days without finding any, besides because of the great amount of gold which it was said there was in that province.

When they arrived at the town, the Spaniards attacked with great audacity in order to enter it; but they did not find anyone to oppose them. And they took the women and boys, and there were no men because all of them were away. There were at that town forty houses, small and well sheltered because of the cold and the storms which occur in that country. They found many deer skins and some blankets of coarse thread; there was a great amount of maize in the fields and much dry maize in the town.

The land through which the Spaniards passed is flat and [has] firm sand lands, and many pine groves [pinares] though they are scattered and separated one from the others. There are many lakes and very many deer throughout the whole land, through the many groves and [also] fallen trees because of the great storms and hurricanes, which very often occur in that region. And thus they saw many trees split from top to bottom on account of the many thunderbolts striking there. And throughout the whole journey, after they passed the river mentioned, they did not find people who would dare to wait for them.

After two days that they had been in Apalache, the Indians came peacefully and their chief with them, and asked for their women and children, and all of them were given back. The governor kept the chief with him. But the next day they attacked and even set fire to the huts where the Christians were, and there might have been up to two hundred Indians. But as the Spaniards were awake they came out rapidly and boldly against them, and they [the Indians] took refuge in the thickets [monte] and to the mountains [?] and they could not take [capture] any of them; but they killed two or three of them. Then the next day came another two hundred Indians from another part and from other towns and people, and in the same [manner] the Christians went out against them, and in the same way they took refuge and fled, as the first ones.

The governor and the Spaniards stayed at this town twenty-six days, during which they made three explorations [entradas] inland.

And all of the land they saw was very poor and with few people, and had very bad passages [*passos*] and lakes, and very dense forests of tree. [They asked] the chief and other Indians whom they had with them from before about their lands and towns. They said that all [of that land] was of fewer people and food than that [the place] where they were, and that this [Apalache] was the main thing there is in that country, and that farther ahead there are many uninhabited lands and swamps and lakes, and very great forests. They asked them if there were towns and people toward the sea and they said that at eight days' travel from there there was a town which was called Aute, whose [people] were their friends, and who had much maize and beans, and was near the sea.

Because of what they [the Indians] told them and what they [the Spaniards] had seen in the explorations they made, that the country in which they were was not as they had been told, and that there was no hope of finding anything better farther ahead, and that where they were they [the Indians] had started to wound their people [the Spaniards] and make war on them, and that they [the Indians] had killed a chief whom the friars had brought from New Spain, and wounded others of their companions on their way to drink, and [because] they [the Indians] were hidden in the lakes and great density of the forest where they shot with arrows everyone who went there, the Spaniards agreed, at the end of the twenty-six days, to depart for Aute.

Does it seem to you, reader, that it was a good time these Christian sinners were having? I would like to be told what those friars and Pámphilo de Narváez preached to those Spaniards who went there so blindly, leaving their countries behind [to go] after false words (and though many of them died they never take warning). Who had certi-fied to having seen that gold they were seeking? What [kind of] pilots had they, such experts in navigation, that they did not even know the land, nor did they know how to identify the places they were? And what guides and interpreters did they take?

Oh, what rash madness! What greater crime can a leader commit than to conduct people to a land where neither he nor any other of his people had been? I well believe that Pámphilo must have remem-bered more than once that advice I gave him in Toledo. Truly I am [have] marveled many times and even been disgusted with those captains, seeing that on the one hand they are astute and clever and courageous men, and on the other hand, though they have seen many broken heads of other people, through which [experience] they should have learned, they do not fear or take warning of any danger. And may God will that those who suffer thus, would pay only with their lives, without their souls receiving detriment! But I doubt the salvation of most of them, because there have been quite a few days that I lived in these Indies and I have seen that they are based for the greatest part on that cursed greediness, laying aside the scruples that to their consciences would be profitable and worth accepting.

Since at the beginning I praised Pámphilo for being a good soldier and later captain, I am forced to give my own account of him in this case. I say that I have seen many courageous men with the lance or the sword in hand, but [when] removed from there have no control [of themselves], and I could point out some of them. Fighting is the least important, because honorable men who do not fight when it is convenient to their honor are very rare; and there are more captains who know how to fight and to command a few than [there are] to govern an army; and there are more captains who are fit to be commanded than who know how to command. Pámphilo, as long as Diego Velasques commanded him,[3] within the island of Cuba, knew how to serve and do what he was commanded. When he left there [Cuba] and went to New Spain, in book XXXIII [of Oviedo's *Historia*] can be seen the record given [about him][4] and in this [book] XXXV you will read how his government ended.

Let us proceed to the rest. This is a thing that though it has no remedy or correction contains something of a warning, or this narrative will create one for the future captains and governors and the governed, if they should not want to deceive themselves closing their eyes to understanding. Because in this treatise they will find what to fear or what those who will take charge of new tasks like this should distrust, since every day I see [how] they procure them and bring men like sheep without knowing where they take them, nor where they go, nor whom they follow.

CHAPTER 2 · IN WHICH ARE CONSIDERED THE MANY HARDSHIPS AND NEEDS THAT THE GOVERNOR, PÁMPHILO DE NARVÁEZ AND THESE PEOPLE SUFFERED; AND HOW THEY BUILT FIVE BARGES IN ORDER TO GO WHERE THEY COULD SETTLE; AND HOW THEY [THE INDIANS] WOUNDED THE GOVERNOR WITH A ROCK; AND HOW THERE WERE SEEN MARTEN OF VERY FINE SABLES; AND HOW THE GOVERNOR WITH HIS BARGE PARTED AND WENT A DIFFERENT WAY FROM THE REST OF THE COMPANY, AND TWO OF THEM [THE BARGES] WERE LOST AND THE OVERSEER AND OTHERS WERE DROWNED; AND OTHER VERY SORROWFUL THINGS ARE NARRATED.

Above, in the previous chapter, it has been told how these people were determined to depart for Aute, and thus they put it into practice. Whereby they left Apalache, and traveled eight or nine days

3. Diego Velasques was governor of Cuba at the time of Cortés' conquest of Mexico.
4. Narváez was a rival of Cortés. Narváez challenged him and was defeated and imprisoned by Cortés in New Spain.

until they arrived at Aute. And in the bad passes and lakes they found, the Indians attacked them and wounded five or six Spaniards and some horses, and killed one Spaniard. On arriving at Aute, they found all the houses burned. Where [from Aute] two days after, the governor sent the treasurer Cabeza de Vaca and Andrés Dorantes and Alonso del Castillo, with nine men on horseback and fifty on foot to go in search of the sea, and he [Narváez] remained with the other people there [at Aute], because a great number of Christians were ill, and each day they became sicker. And thus these noblemen parted with the company mentioned, and took the commissary with them.

It may well be believed that this reverend father [the commissary] would [now] be contented with the call he had left in Spain in order to come to seek [to earn] in these places those lap cloths or miters [bishop's honors] which caused them [the religious] to waste their time and the lives of some of them [in the Indies]. Even those who have served God forget [this], after they have accepted these dignities which the least among them attain. And may God will that souls would not be endangered, in spite of the fact that the ones who are not moved by these interests or ambition or desire for prelacies, but only to serve God better in the conversion of these Indians, have an honest and meritorious and holy desire, and these are the ones who obtain [spiritual] fruit; but may God help the rest of them.

The day they [Cabeza de Vaca and the other men] departed from there [Aute] they arrived at some low places [baxos] of the sea where they stayed that night. The next day in the morning they sent twenty men to explore the coast, and they said that they had not been able to see it, because it was very far away.

After this they returned to the camp [at Aute], where they found the governor, and the purser, and the overseer quite sick, and many others. And after they rested there one day, the next day they [the entire expedition] departed for the place where they [the party of Cabeza de Vaca] had discovered or found the sea, taking with them all the maize they could; and they arrived with great trouble, because the sick, who were many, were of no use. And here they stayed two days searching and thinking what way they had to save their lives and leave that land, since to think of building ships in which to travel seemed to them an impossible thing, because they did not have nails, oakum, tar, or any other things that were necessary for it. And as necessity had already led them to this extreme, they destroyed the stirrups of the horses and the bridles and spurs in order to make tools, and they made some pipes of wood, and with deer skins they made some bellows, and of the things mentioned they made tools. And because the people were weak and were not able to work, they killed a horse every third day which [only] those who worked and the sick divided and ate; and thus in order to eat of that meat, others [also] worked. And in four or five sallies [*entradas*] that the horsemen and the stronger ones made to Aute, they brought much maize which was enough for eating while they were there and even to take with them.

Thus they began to build barges [*barcas*] after four days of the month of August, and they caulked the barges with palmetto scutes, and of these they [also] made ropes and pitched them with tar which they made from pine trees, of which there are many. And of their shirts they made sails, and of the skin of the horses' legs they made bags to carry water. While the barges were being built, the Indians killed ten Christians who were fishing along those low places of the coast near the camp, without [their companions] being able to help them, shot through and through with arrows.

From the place where they left the ships to the place where they built the barges, and everywhere else that these Christians traveled, there would be about two hundred eighty leagues, a little more or less (in the opinion of those who traveled it) and throughout this whole country they did not see any mountains nor did they have any news about any. The people are very large, of good appearance and genteel disposition, and all of them are arrow shooters [bowmen] and great marksmen. Their bows are ten or twelve palms long, and almost as thick as the wrist of the arm (at the handles or near them), and are very strong and of beautiful wood; and it is something to terrify and an incredible thing, if not seen [with one's own eyes] what those arrows pierce through.

They finished five barges after twenty days of the month of September,[5] which were twenty cubits in length.[6] And there about forty men, a little more or less, died of illness. Of these barges the governor took one for himself and forty-eight men, and gave another one to the purser and the friars with forty-seven men, and gave another to the treasurer and the overseer with forty-eight men. And to Captain Tellez and to Peñalosa and Alonso del Castillo and Andrés Dorantes he gave the other two [barges], and in each of them there were forty-eight other men.[7] When the horses had been eaten, they embarked on the twenty-second of September. As the barges were

5. It took from about August 5 until September 20, or forty-seven days, to build the five barges.
6. *Codos*, or cubits, are a measure of length equal to the distance from the elbow to the end of the middle finger. If this measure was about eighteen inches, the barges were about thirty-three feet long. The Spanish *codo* may have been a little less than eighteen inches, as these people were generally of small stature.
7. Oviedo's list suggests that the numbers in each barge were as follows: 49 men in barge 1; 53 men in barge 2; and 50 men each in barges 3, 4, and 5. Thus he gives a total of 252 men.

small, they were extremely loaded with the supplies and clothing and weapons, and did not float more than one *xeme* above the water.

Thus they traveled through those low places [shallows] for seven days, until those unfortunate people arrived at a small island which is near the Mainland, and on it they found some dwellings and there they took five canoes. And that day they departed for the coast, which until then they had not seen; and there, they stopped the barges and with the canoes they made bulwarks [for the barges] and the barges grew and rose two palms more (above the water) and they continued their trip. This done, they entered many bays [*ancones*] they met at the coast, and in the low places they met, the land always appeared ahead [they could not see the water?], as they were sailing thus, without knowing where they were going.

One night a canoe came toward them and went following them a while and they [the Spaniards] turned to it and talked to [those in the canoe], but they [the Indians] did not want to wait. And as these [canoes] are very swift, those of the canoe went away, and the Christians followed their former course. Next day in the morning a storm struck them, and they came to an island, and did not find water on it, of which they had great need. There they stayed three days, and as there had been five [days] they had not drunk [water], some of them drank much salt water, and on account of this five or six men died suddenly. And seeing that the thirst was unbearable, and the storm had not ceased they agreed to go toward that place where they had seen the canoe go that has been mentioned.

They commended themselves to God and placed themselves in obvious danger of death; and they crossed. And at the time when the sun was setting, they arrived at a point where there was shelter and less sea, and some canoes came out to them and they talked to them [the people in the canoes]. They followed them for about a league to where they had their houses at the tongue or coast [?] of the water. And before them [the Indians] they had many pitchers [*cantaros*] and *ollas* filled with water, and much fish. And when the governor landed the chief came out to him and took him to his house and offered him of the fish and water he had there, as a reward for which the Spaniards gave them beads and hawk-bells [*cascabeles*] and of the maize they had in the barges.

That same night, the chief being with the governor, many Indians attacked the Christians, and killed three men who were lying sick at the coast, and wounded the governor in the head with a rock. And those who were there with him [the governor] seized the chief who tore himself free and left in their hands a robe [*manta*], which he had over him. [The robe was] of very good marten sables, which according to what Cabeza de Vaca the treasurer says were excellent, the best that he had seen, and even all the other Spaniards said the same. And they [the marten skins] smell like musk. And they took other robes of marten but they were not the same [kind].[8]

Because the governor was wounded and sick, they put him into the barges together with all the sick and weak there were. The Indians attacked them three times that night, and finally left the Christians alone. And there were many of the Indians wounded with knives, and many wounded Spaniards that night. And they were there until two days later, during which time they could not see any Indians.

From there they departed in their barges, and in three or four days they entered some lagoons [esteros] and met a canoe with some Indians, and asked them for water, and gave them a vessel in which to bring it. And with them [the Indians] went two Christians. The Indians who had stayed in the barges as ransom tried to throw themselves into the water [to escape] but they [the Spaniards] seized them. The next day in the morning other canoes began to come, and the Christians left the lagoons [to sail] toward the sea. In a little more than an hour there were twenty canoes and three or four principal Indian lords [señores] in them, and they wore over themselves some blankets of those very fine marten sables, and [wore] their hair long and loose. They asked for the Indians the Christians had, and the Christians asked them for the two Spaniards, and the Indians asked them to go with them to their houses, and they did not want to do it because the country was much covered with water and full of lagoons. As they [the Spaniards] did not want to give them the Indians, because these did not return the [two] Christians, the Indians began to shoot some rods [varas] and some arrows. And thus they had a battle with them until they [the Indians] left them.

Ours [the Christians' barges] went ahead and traveled another two days, at the end of which the barge in which the treasurer [traveled] arrived at a point made by the coast, and behind it there was a river which was flooded, very grown and large and a little island behind. The barge of the governor and the other [barges] anchored at some islands which were nearby; and the treasurer went to them and told them how he had discovered that river. Because they had not found firewood to roast maize there and for two days they had eaten it raw, they agreed to go and enter that river, from which at sea sweet [fresh] water was collected. And being near it, at the mouth, the great current pushed them more into the sea.

They navigated that night and the next day until night, when they found themselves at three fathoms deep. Having seen that afternoon

8. It may be doubted that the true marten lived on the Gulf coast in the sixteenth century. The furs may have been obtained by trade from far inland, or the animals referred to may have been beaver or otter, both of which are known in this area and have fine furs.

many smoke signals [*ahumadas*] on the coast, they did not dare to land at night. They anchored, and as the current was strong and they did not have [real] anchors except some weights [*betalas*] of rock, the currents took them out to sea that night, and when it began to be day, they did not see land, nor did any barge see another.

Thus the treasurer, Álvar Núñez Cabeza de Vaca, who is the one who narrates this, proceeded on his trip. At the hour of noon he saw two of the barges, and meeting the first one he recognized that it was that of the governor. They spoke, and the governor asked the treasurer his opinion about what should be done. [The treasurer] told him to get the other barge which appeared [nearby], and that all three of them together would go wherever he commanded, and he [Narváez] answered he wanted to land by force of oars, and for the treasurer to do thus with his barge [also]. And this way he followed him [Narváez] for about a league and a half, and as the people were weak and tired, and for three days they had eaten nothing but raw maize, and [only] a handful of it for ration, they could not keep up with it [the barge] of the governor, which was swifter and lighter, and was less loaded. The treasurer asked the governor to give a rope [to pull them] and he said he could not do it; for him to do what he could, that it was not the time to wait for anybody, but that each one should try to escape alive.

This was not the answer of the memorable count of Niebla, don Enrique de Guzman, who to rescue others, putting them into his barge, gathered so many of them in it, that they all drowned in Gibraltar. The treasurer and those who were with him did not ask Narváez to take them into his barge, but to give them the end of a rope so that his barge would help the other to move; and that once he would give it [the rope] to them, it would be at his will to let them loose when he wanted, if it was convenient to him.

Coming back to the narrative, hearing the unmerciful answer of the governor Pámphilo, the treasurer followed him a while until he lost sight of him. Then the treasurer went to the other barge which was further into the sea, which waited, and this was that of Peñalosa and Captain Tellez. Thus these two barges together navigated three hours until night. Because of the great hunger they had, and on account of becoming wet the night before with the waves of the sea, the people were fallen [on the floor of the barge] and there were not five useful men. Thus they passed that night, and at the quarter [of an hour before] dawn the mate of the barge of the treasurer threw the sound and found a depth of seven fathoms. Because the breaking of the waves was very great, they stayed at sea until dawn, and found themselves at a league from land. And they directed the prow toward it [land], and it willed God that they were saved.

Then the treasurer sent a man to some trees which appeared so that from above he would see the land, and he came back and said they were at an island. Then he went up again to see if he could find a trail or a sail, and came back in the afternoon and told what he had found and brought some fish, and behind him came three Indians, and after these another two hundred, all of them archers [*flecheros*]. They had their ears pierced and through them some pieces of cane.

The treasurer and the overseer went to them and called them and they came, and the Christians gave them of the things [*rescates*] they had, and each one of the Indians gave an arrow as a sign of friendship, and said with signs that next day when the sun rose, they would bring something to eat for the Christians. And they did thus: because then next day in the morning they came back and brought fish and some roots of those they ate, and the following day they did the same.

There they [the Christians] provided themselves with water and embarked to continue their trip. In order to put the barge into the sea they undressed themselves, and when doing this, putting it into the sea, the water struck them by the prow and wet one side [*banda*] where they were rowing, and with the water and cold they let the oars go, and the barge turned around. And soon a wave struck them another blow and turned it [over], and the overseer and two others clung to it and it took them under and drowned them. The rest escaped, naked, without salvaging anything they had.

They remained that day on the coast with very great cold until the afternoon, when the Indians came to see them. And finding them thus, they began crying with [for] the Christians, as if they were sorry for their trouble, and thus the treasurer asked them to take them to their dwellings (and they did it) where they stayed the night.

The next day in the morning the Indians told them that there were others like the Christians nearby, for which reason the treasurer sent two men to find out who they were, and they found that they were Alonso del Castillo and Andrés Dorantes and all the people who were in their barge, which in the same manner had wrecked at the same island on the fifth of November. And that [barge] of the treasurer had come out [landed] the next day on the [same] coast. These [other Christians] shared with the treasurer and his company of their clothes and food, which was indeed little.

CHAPTER 3 · IN WHICH ARE TREATED OTHER NEW HARDSHIPS OF
THESE PEOPLE, AND HOW THE CAPTAIN, PÁMPHILO DE NARVÁEZ,
WAS LOST, AND HOW THESE SPANIARD SINNERS CAME TO BE IN SUCH
A NEED OF FOOD THAT AMONG THEM SOME CAME TO BE THE FOOD
OF OTHERS. AND OTHER MISFORTUNES ARE NARRATED [SUCH AS]
NEVER [HAVE BEEN] HEARD OR SUFFERED, NOR AS LONG AND
CONTINUOUS AS THESE PEOPLE HAD, WITH WHICH MOST AND
ALMOST ALL OF THEM ENDED [DIED].

When the treasurer Cabeza de Vaca and those of his barge gathered
with those of the other [barge], which also was wrecked, as it was
mentioned in the preceding chapter, they agreed to fix up [adobar]
their barge [Dorantes' and Castillo's] and leave in it. And setting to
work, the best they could they fixed it up and placed it in the water;
but they could not float in it because of leakage [de broma] and other
faults. Thus they were wrecked [again] and agreed to winter on that
island because it was not possible to do anything else.

They sent a nobleman named Figueroa, and with him three other
Christians and an Indian, so that they would go to Pánuco (believing
that they were near Pánuco) to carry word as to where and how the
others remained. But after five or six days the people began to die,
and hunger was so great that five men ate one another. Also, an ailment of the stomach struck the natives of the land so that half of
them died, and seeing this the Indians had thought of killing those
few Christians who remained alive, and [the Indians] said that they
[the Christians] had brought that disease and plague to their land. It
willed God that one of their leaders said that it should not be done
thus, nor should they believe that those Christians had brought that
disease to them, since it was seen that they also had died and there
were very few of them left, and that if the Christians had brought
that disease to them, they [the Christians] would not have died. Thus
because of what that leader said they did not kill the Christians.

According to how they [the Spaniards] were, it was crueler to keep
the Spaniards alive and not to kill them, than to preserve them with
that mercy in such penance and hunger and torment, since they were
[had been] two or three days without eating a bite. And because all
were sick and died as the natives died, they agreed to cross to the
mainland to some overflowed places and ponds [paludes] to eat oysters, which the Indians eat for three or four months of the year,
without eating any other thing. They [the Indians] suffer great hunger and tremendous trouble in defending themselves day and night
from the mosquitoes, because there are so many that it is unbearable
to suffer them, and they have neither firewood nor water, except salt
water. Another four months of the year they eat herbs from the fields
and blackberries; and another two months they chew some roots.

And they eat some very large spiders and lizards and snakes and mice (sometimes they have deer), and for another two months they eat fish which they kill in canoes. They also eat some other roots which are like truffles [*turmas de tierra*], which they get from the water. Those people are very well disposed and the women work a great deal.

To eat of these oysters the Indians crossed Alonso del Castillo and Andrés Dorantes to the mainland, where they stayed until the end of the month of March, of the year 1529, when they returned to the same island. And they [Castillo and Dorantes] gathered the Christians they found alive, who were no more than fourteen, [and left two] of the Spaniards because they were extremely weak and without any strength. The treasurer Cabeza de Vaca was at the other part of the land, very ill and without hope of surviving. They crossed the bay [*ancón*] and came along the coast.

The treasurer stayed there where he was [for] five and a half years, digging from morning to night, getting out roots with a *coa* or stick which the Indians use for that [purpose], under the land and under the water, and carrying every day a load or two of firewood on his back over his flesh and skin without having any clothes, but [naked] as a slave or Indian. Thus he served the Indians in the work already mentioned, and in the other things they ordered him [to do], and in carrying their houses or apparels [*hatos*] on his back, because every three or four days they move, because this is their custom.

They do not have their own settled place because of the great hunger they have throughout that whole land, searching for roots. They do not eat maize at all, or have any, nor do they plant anything of this life.[9] The land is very healthy and temperate, except when the north [wind] blows in the winter, when even the fish freeze, inside the sea, from the cold.

Andrés Dorantes said that he saw snow and hail together in one day, and that the hunger suffered there is as great as it can be imagined, and that farther ahead they found it [the hunger] even greater. He says that these people suffer more with death than any other he had seen, and that thus they cried over the dead with great sorrow and attention.

Seeing that his work was so heavy and excessive, this gentleman [Cabeza de Vaca] began to barter among them, and to bring to them from other places what they did not have and needed. And [having an] understanding of this, he entered sometimes inland, and followed the coast forty leagues ahead. [The] three times he went [this way] he passed a bay [*ancón*] which he says he believes to be, because of the signs [*senas*] of it, the one called of the Espíritu Santo.

---

9. In *ni se siembra cosa alguna desta vida*, possibly Oviedo meant that they planted nothing whatever in their whole lives.

Two times he came back those forty leagues to [try to] bring [out] a Christian [Lope de Oviedo] who had survived. [He was] one of the two [who were] very weak that Castillo and Dorantes had left there when they departed from the island. The other one was already dead. And he [Lope de Oviedo] was brought out the last time and Cabeza de Vaca brought him from this to another part of the said bay of the Espíritu Santo ten leagues [ahead], to other Indians who were at war with those who had passed from the bay of Espíritu Santo.

[These Indians] told them [Cabeza de Vaca and Lope de Oviedo] their names [the names of Dorantes and the others] and that they had killed three or four other Christians, and that the rest had died nearby from hunger and cold, and that those who were alive were very mistreated. And they [the Indians] told these two Christians much bad news besides this (I mean to this Dorantes and compan-ion he had rescued),[1] and would aim with arrows at their hearts, and threatened them that they were to kill them. And fearful of this, the other Christian [Lope de Oviedo] went back [to Malhado] and left Dorantes, who could not stop him. And after he [Cabeza de Vaca] had remained there for two or three days, he departed from there secretly and met two Indians who took him where Dorantes and Alonso del Castillo were.

Andrés Dorantes,[2] then, arriving where these two Christians, and others who will be mentioned later, were, waited there for an Indian of his. And the first day of April the said Andrés Dorantes and Alonso del Castillo and Diego Dorantes and Pedro Valdivieso departed from there. And the Asturian priest and a black[3] were on an island behind where they had lost the barges, where they had gone on account of the great hunger they had there.

The Indians took them again [across] the bay in a canoe to [take them] where they had lost the barges, and [where] there were those few Christians who had escaped the hunger and the cold of winter; and there they took [met] another six Christians. Thus there were twelve in all. Two [others] remained on the island [since] on account of their weakness they could not take them along, plus Cabeza de Vaca and another Christian [who] were farther inland, whom they could not recover to bring [along either].

The Indians went [took them] across another *ancón* for certain things they [the Spaniards] gave them. And from there they walked two leagues to a large river, which was beginning to grow [rise]

1. Editor's note: Oviedo is apparently confusing Dorantes with Cabeza de Vaca in these two sentences.
2. Editor's note; Here Oviedo confounds us all by going back more than five years to the time when Dorantes, Castillo, and Estevan, with ten others, left Malhado and traveled along the coast toward Pánuco. The remainder of the chapter recounts their adventures.
3. Editor's note: Oviedo seems to refer here to Estevan.

because of the floods and rains, and there they built rafts, in which they crossed with great trouble because there were few swimmers among them.

From there they went three leagues to another river [the second] which flowed very powerfully and [was] flooded, and with such fury that the sweet [fresh] water came out for a very great distance into the sea. There [also] some rafts were built, and they crossed it on them. And the first one [raft] passed well, because they helped one another, and the second one took them out to sea, because since they were weak and tired on account of the hard winter and the traveling. They did not eat anything but an herb which they called *pedrera* (of which there are plenty along the coast) from which they make glass in Spain[?], and some crayfish which breed [*que crían*] in caves at the coast, and which are almost nothing but shell.

Those who were on that raft had no strength to come out safe. There two men were drowned, and another two came out [saved themselves by] swimming. And the raft went out to sea more than a league with the current, with a man clinging to it. When he [this man] saw himself out of the current he placed himself on top of it [the raft] and made a sail of his own person, and the wind blew from the sea, and turned him back to land, and he escaped.

There were now left but ten of the twelve that had departed [from Malhado]. There [after crossing the second river] they found another Christian who also went with them. After they had walked three or four leagues, they met another river [the third] and there they found another barge of their five, which they recognized as the one in which the purser Alonso Enriquez and the commissary [sailed], but they did not learn what had happened to the people in it. And they walked another five or six leagues to another [the fourth] large river, where there were two settlements [*ranchcos*] of Indians who fled.

From the other side of the river Indians came to the Christians and recognized them, because through there they [the Indians] had already seen those of the barge of the governor and that of Alonso Enriquez. And assuring themselves they took them [the Christians] across the river in a canoe. They took them to their dwellings, where they had not a thing to eat, but gave them a little bit of fish with which they spent [survived] that night.

Next day they departed from there, and the fourth day they arrived at an *ancón*, and during this walk two men died from hunger and fatigue. In this way they were left but nine people.[4] This bay was

4. Editor's note: After crossing the second river, they had found and added to their party another man, making a total of thirteen. Thus Oviedo's math is right though he continues to speak of the original twelve.

wide, and was almost a league in width, and makes a point toward the part [in the direction of] Pánuco, which comes out to the sea almost a fourth of a league, with some cliffs [mogotes] of white sand. [These are] large, which reasonably ought to appear from afar in the sea, and for this [reason] they suspected that this was the river of Espíritu Santo. There they saw [found] themselves very tired because they could not find a way to pass. But finally they found a broken canoe, and fixing it up the best they could, in two days they stayed there they crossed the bay, and proceeded on their way very fatigued with hunger. Most of them were swollen from the herbs they ate. With great trouble they arrived at a small ancón which was twelve leagues ahead. This ancón was not very wide and seemed like a river in width, and there they stopped the day they arrived.

The following day an Indian came from the other side of the ancón, but although they called him, he did not want to come and went away. He came back in the afternoon and brought with him a Christian whose name was Figueroa, and he was one of the four they had sent the preceding winter to see if he could reach the land of Christians, as it has already been told. Then the Indian and the Christian [Figueroa] passed [crossed] to where the other nine were.

There he [Figueroa] told them how the other three companions had died, two from hunger, and the other [whom] the Indians had killed. And he told them how he [Figueroa] had met a Christian who was called Esquivel, who alone had escaped from the two barges of the governor and Alonso Enriquez, eating the flesh of those who died. And [Esquivel told Figueroa][5] that the rest of them had died from hunger, and some of them had eaten one another; and that the barge of Alonso Enriquez had turned over at the place where those others [Dorantes' party] had found it, as it was said. And that following along the coast, the governor met them, who was still in his barge at sea.[6] And when he [the governor] saw them he decided to land all his people to bring them together at the coast, so as to make the barge lighter, because they were very fatigued from the sea and did not have a thing to eat. And that he had remained in the barge, within sight of them so that when there would be a bay or river he would get them all across in the barge. And that thus they [the people from the two barges] arrived at the bay which it is said that they believed was that of Espíritu Santo. And there the governor had crossed all the people from the other part of the bay, and he stayed in

---

5. Editor's note: All that follows in this long paragraph is what Esquivel told Figueroa and Figueroa later recounted to the Dorantes party.
6. The barge of Alonso Enriquez appears to have been wrecked at some point *east* of the supposed bay of Espíritu Santo as the Dorantes party followed the coast some distance toward Pánuco before they reached this bay. The barge of Narváez had not been wrecked. He happened to come close to shore where the Enriquez barge had overturned.

the barge, and did not want to land, and only a pilot whose name was Antón Pérez, and a servant of his who was called Campo stayed with him. When night came a very strong north wind came and took them out to sea, and never again were they [Narváez, Pérez, and Campo] heard from. And that the governor was very weak and ill and covered with leprosy, and those who were with him were not very strong either, on account of which it is to be believed that they were devoured by the sea. And that all of the other people [from the two barges] who had been left there had entered through [went past] certain lakes and overflowed places which were there, and went inland, as people without resources, where all of them died that preceding winter from hunger and cold,[7] eating one another as has been said.

He [Figueroa] did not know what else to say, except that Esquivel was somewhere along there, prisoner of some Indians, and that it could happen that they would see him very soon. But a month later, a little more or less, it was learned [by Dorantes and his men] that the Indians with whom he [Esquivel] was had killed him because he had escaped from them; and that they went after him and killed him.

There they [the Dorantes party] stayed with this Christian [Figueroa] for a while, hearing from him this bad news which is said [here]. Because the Indian with whom he came did not want to leave him, he was forced to go back with him. And because the others did not know how to swim, [only] two of these Christians were able to go with them, one of whom was a clergyman, and the other one was a young swimmer, because none of the other ones left knew how to swim.[8] These two went with the intention of bringing [back] some fish which they [the Indians] told them they had, and that they would return to cross them over the *ancón*. The Indians saw them [the clergyman and the young swimmer] there at their houses, [but] did not want to come back with them or let them return.

Instead they moved their houses on their canoes and took the other two [the same two] Christians along with them, telling them that they would come back later and that they were going nearby for a certain leaf which they used to gather, of which they make a certain beverage, which they drink as hot as they can. And one of

7. This was the same winter of 1528–29 that the people from the barges of Cabeza de Vaca and Dorantes had remained at Malhado. It was during the spring of 1529 that the Dorantes party went along the coast, reached the bay of Espíritu Santo, and heard this account from Figueroa, who had heard it from Esquivel, the last survivor of the Narváez and Enríquez barges.
8. Figueroa was obliged to go back with his Indian, the Asturian priest and the "young swimmer" going with him. Much later, when the last four survivors were among the Avavares Indians, they heard that the Asturian and Figueroa were among the Indians called "of the figs" farther along the coast. The "young swimmer" must have died after these three left Dorantes and his companions, and there is no record of the other two having reached Spanish settlements.

the two Christians turned back the next day to tell them [the other Spaniards] this, and to bring to the other seven Christians a little fish they [the Indians] had given him.[9] And they [the seven Christians] stayed there that day on account of the great need they had.

Next day in the morning they saw two Indians from the other side who were from a settlement and [who] came there to eat blackberries, of which there were some along that coast. [They] came for these for a season, as long as these [blackberries] last, which are very tasty and which is the food which sustains them when there are some. They [the Christians] called them [the Indians], and they came to where these Christians were, [acting] as if they [the Christians] were inferior people, and even took some of their things from them, almost by force. They [the Christians] begged them to get them across and thus they did in a canoe, and took them to their houses which were there nearby, and that night gave them a little [bit of] fish. And the next day [the Indians] went fishing and returned at night with [more] fish and gave them part of it. Then the following day they [the Indians] moved and took them along, so that they never again could see the other two Christians that the other Indians had taken away.[1]

Great God, such excessive hardship for such a short time as that of the life of man is! Such unheard of torments for the human body! Such intolerable hungers for people so weak! Such extreme misfortune for such sensitive flesh! Such desperate death for such a reasonable intellect! With what did the captain and ministers of these voyages pay, when so blinded and deceived they took so many poor people to die such death? It could be answered that they paid with their own greed, which gave credit to their words.

We know already that Pámphilo de Narváez was never [before] in that land, to where he thought of bringing these people, dreaming of being their governor and lord, and it seems to me that he did not [even] know how to govern himself. Could there be greater imprudence than to listen [to] and follow such commanders? And consider how skilled his pilots were, that they neither knew where they were going nor where they were, when they passed to that land! And thus, both men of sea and men of land [ended up] in such terrible death, without understanding one another!

For many to die in a battle, or drown in a voyage, because the ship was lost, on account of the weather or for any other accident in which many others perished, or because of a plague, terrible and

9. This Spaniard must then have returned to his companion and the Indians, as the next paragraph indicates that the Dorantes party never saw the two again.
1. Editor's note: Oviedo's account is very confused as to who and how many went where. Since *Los naufragios* and presumably the original report to the Audiencia are much clearer, the confusion seems to have been Oviedo's.

quick, are things of great terror and unfortunate and rigorous for those who suffer them. But even in all of these maladies there is some part which is good, because he who dies in battle or goes to war, if he is a Christian, he goes already confessed and leaves his testament done and his soul secured, and continues in war serving his prince. And he can die in this state and road to salvation since he follows orders of his king and lord, to whom he neither can nor should disobey without falling into shame or deserving blame for being a bad subject or servant. He who drowns, as it is said, before his trip begins or before he goes to sea, goes to confession and communion and secures his soul, as a Catholic, and then proceeds on his way, if he is commanded in order to fulfill what he must do. Or if he goes for his own motives, being a merchant or because it is convenient to him for other just reasons which are honestly excused, or for making a living [buscar de comer] without detriment to a third person, [there is no real harm done] though death might meet him. And if, as it has been said, death was pestilential and sudden, in this case God also gives, because of His mercy, time for the reparation of the souls who die thus. But these unfortunate ones, who suffered so many and so diverse kinds of deaths, what could be compared to them when their misfortune and sins brought them to eat each other, or to die ravenously from hunger and thirst, and other maladies and hardships, never suffered by men nor so continuously?

I say to you impoverished gentleman or nobleman in need, or artisan with bad repose, or badly advised villain, that you and all who have these qualifications and who come together in this fleet, that you have received just payment according to your bad intentions. Because the impoverished gentleman had been safer in his former state, serving his superior. And the shield-bearer [had been better off] training himself in such a way that if his fortune was not enough for him, he should be enough for it. And the artisan [also had been better off] not leaving his trade, or the villain his plow, because in digging and in the other labors and agriculture which he left [in order] to come to the Indies, there was more security and peace for the body and the soul, than in choosing such notorious and dangerous imprudence as you did in following Pámphilo de Narváez.

In Cuba he knew very well what to tell you about what there is in it [Cuba] and where he had been. But where he took you to, he did not know and he did not know where he thought he was to go. And once he left, he had not seen it either nor did he know what it was that he was looking for; but he wanted to abandon his rest in order to command. And had he not included anyone else but himself, the damage had not been so great; but of his artifice and wrong advice you are as much responsible as he was, because neither did he escape death, nor did he avoid giving it [death] to all.

Let me know, those of you who have read [this], if you have heard of or known about other people as unfortunate or as overworked, or as wrongly advised. Search for that peregrination of Ulysses, or the navigation of Jason, or the hardships of Hercules, all of these being fiction and metaphors. And if you understand them as you should interpret them you will find neither anything to be marveled at, nor are their works comparable to those of these sinners who followed such an unhappy road and miserable end. And any of these [Spaniards] suffered more than any of the three captains [Ulysses, Jason, Hercules] already mentioned, though together with them you might mention Perseus with his Medusa, if they experienced what these others experienced.

Oh, cursed gold! Oh, treasures and profits involving such dangers! Oh, the [furs of] marten sable! I well believe that if at the price they [the men of Narváez] paid for that cloak of sable fur (which the story says was left to Narváez in exchange for a blow from a rock), the princes and lords in Europe had to obtain the daily coats they used in winter, they would appreciate them [the coats] more. But those who bought with money, and the others with blood and lives, and even thus they could not take them out and bring them back from among those savage people.

Let us turn back to our story, which we have not finished, though of the people of Narváez there are left but a few of the many he took, as it has been said above, and as you will hear in the next chapter, following the same narrative of that gentleman Álvar Núñez Cabeza de Vaca and his companions.

*   *   *

DON ANTONIO de MENDOZA

Letter from the Viceroy of New Spain to the Emperor (1539)[†]

In the ships that went last from hence (whereof Michael de Usnago was Admiral) I wrote into your maiestie, how I had sent two Franciscan Friers to discover the end of this firme land, which stretcheth to the North. And because their iourney fell out to greater purpose than was looked for, I will declare the whole matter from the beginning. It may please your Maiestie to call to mind how often I wrote unto your Highnesse, that I desired to know the ende of this Province of Nueva Espanna, because it is so great a countrey, and that we have

† Translated by Fanny Bandelier (1904).

yet no knowledge thereof. Neither had I onely this desire; for Nunno de Guzman departed out of this city of Mexico with 400 horsemen, and 14,000 Indians footemen borne in these Indias, being the best men and the best furnished, which have bene seene in these parts; and he did so little with them, that the most part of them were consumed in the enterprize and could not enter nor discover any more then already was discovered. After this the saide Nunno Guzman beeing Governour of Nueva Galicia, sent Captaines and Horsemen foorth divers times, which sped no better then he had done. Likewise the Marques de valle Hernando Cortez sent a captaine with 2 ships to discover the coast: which 2 ships and the captaine perished. After that he sent again 2 other ships, one of the which was divided from her consort, and the master and certaine mariners slue the captaine and usurped over the ship.

After this they came to an Island, where the Master with certaine mariners going on land, the Indians of the Country slew them, and tooke their boat: and the ship with those that were in it, returned to the coast of Nueva Galicia, where it ran on ground. By the men which came home in this ship, the Marques had knowledge of the countrey which they had discovered: and then, either for the discontentment which hee had with the bishop of Saint Domingo and with the Judges of this royal audience in Mexico, or rather because of his so prosperous successe in all things here in Nueva Espanna, without seeking any farther intelligence of the state of that Island, he set forward on that voyage with 3 ships, and with certaine foote-men and horsemen, not throughly furnished with things necessary; which fell out so contrary to his expectations that the most part of the people which he carried with him, dyed of hunger. And although he had ships, and a Countrey very neere him abounding with victuals, yet could hee never finde meanes to conquer it, but rather it seemed, that God miraculously did hide it from him: and so he returned home without achieving ought else of moment. After this, having heere in my company Andrew Dorantez, which is one of those who were in the voyage of Panphilo Naruaez, I often was in hand with him, supposing that he was able to doe Your Maiestie great service, to imploy him with fortie or fiftie horses, to search out the secret of those parts: and having provided all things necessary for his iourney, and spent much money in that behalfe, the matter was broken off, I wot not how, and that enterprise was given over. Yet of the things which were provided for that purpose, I had left mee a negro, which returned from the foresayde voyage of Naruaez with Dorantez, and certaine slaves which I had bought, and certaine Indians which I had gathered together who were borne in those North partes, whome I sent with Frier Marco de Nica, and his companion a Franciscan Frier, because they had bene long travelled, and exercised in those

partes, and had great experience in the affaires of the Indies, and
were men of good life and conscience, for whom I obtained leave of
their superiours: and so they went with Frances Vazquez de Coronado, governour of Nueva Galicia unto the Citie of Saint Michael of
Culiacan, which is the last Province subdued by the Spaniards
towarde that quarter, being two hundred leagues distant from this
Citie of Mexico. As soone as the governour, and the Friers were
come unto that Citie, hee sent certaine of those Indians which I had
given him, home into their Countrey, to signifie, and declare to the
people of the same, That they were to vnderstand, that your Maiestie had commanded they should not hereafter bee made slaves, and
that they should not be afrayd any more, but might returne
unto their houses, and live peaceably in them, (for before that time
they had bin greatly troubled by the evill dealings which were used
toward them) and that your maiestie would cause them to be chas-
tened, which were the causes of their vexation. With these Indians
about twentie dayes after returned about 400 men; which coming
before the governour said unto him, that they came on the behalfe of
al their countrey-men, to tell him, that they desired to see and know
those men which did them so great a pleasure as to suffer them to
returne to their houses, and to sow maiz for their sustenance, for by
the space of many yeres they were driven to flee into the mountaines, hiding themselves like wild beasts, for feare lest they should
be made slaves, and that they and all the rest of their people were
ready to doe whatsoever should bee commanded them: whom the
governour comforted with good wordes, and gave them victuals, and
stayed them with him three or foure dayes wherein the Friars taught
them to make the signe of the crosse, and to learne the name of our
Lorde Jesus Christ, and they with great diligence sought to learne
the same. After these dayes hee sent them home againe, willing
them not to be afraid, but to be quiet, giving them apparel, beades,
knives, and other such like things, which I had given him for such
purposes. The sayde Indians departed very well pleased, and said,
that whensoever hee would send for them, they and many others
would come to doe whatsoever he would command them. The
entrance being thus prepared, Frier Marco and his companion, with
the Negro and other slaves, and Indians which I had given him, went
forward on their voyage 10 or 12 dayes after. And because I had likewise advertisement of a certaine Province called Topira situate in the
mountaines and had appointed the governour Vazquez de Coronado,
that he should use meanes to learne the state thereof: he supposing
this to be a matter of great moment determined himselfe to goe and
search it, having agreed with the said Frier, that he should returne
by that part of the mountaine, to meete with him in a certaine valley called Valle de los Coraçones, being 120 leagues distant from

Culiacan. The Governour travelling into this province (as I have
written in my former letters) found great scarcity of victuals there,
and the mountaines so craggy that he could finde no way to passe
forward, and was inforced to returne home to Saint Michael: so that
as well in chusing of the entrance, as in not being able to finde the
way, it seemeth onto all men that God would shut up the gate to all
those, which by strength of humane force have gone about to attempt
this enterprise, and hath reveiled it to a poore and bare-footed Frier.
And so the Frier beganne to enter into the Land, who because he
found his entrance so well prepared, was very well received; and
because he wrote the whole successe of his voyage, according to the
instruction which I had given him to ondertake the same, I wil not
write any more at large, but send your Maiestie this copy of all such
things as he observed in the same.

FRAY MARCOS DE NIZA

From Relación on the Discovery
of the Kingdom of Cibola (1539)†

Chapter I

I Frier Marco de Nica of the order of S. Francis, for the execution
of the instruction of the right honourable lord Don Antonio de Mendoça, Vice-roy and captaine Generall for the Emperors Maiestie in
New Spaine, departed from the towne of S. Michael in the province
of Culiacan on Friday the 7. of March, in the yeere 1539. having for
my companion Frier Honoratus, and carying with me Stephan a
Negro, belonging to Andrew Dorantez, and certaine of those Indians
which the sayde lord Vice-roy had made free, and bought for this
purpose: whom Frances Vazquez de Coronado governour of Nueva
Galicia delivered me, and with many other Indians of Petatlan, and
of the towne called Cuchillo, which is some 50. leagues from Petatlan, who came to the valley of Culiacan, shewing themselves to bee
exceeding glad, because they were certified by the Indians which had
bin set free, whom the said governour had sent before to advertise
them of their libertie, that none of them from thenceforth should be
made slaves, and that no man should invade them, nor use them
badly; signifying onto them, that the Emperors Maiesty had willed
and commanded that it should be so. With the foresaid company I
went on my voyage vntil I came to the towne of Petatlan, finding all
the way great intertainment, and provision of victuals, with roses,

† Translated by Fanny Bandelier (1904).

flowers, and other such things, and bowers which they made for me of chalke and boughs platted together in all places where there were no houses. In this towne of Petatlan I rested 3. dayes, because my companion Honoratus fell so sicke, that I was constrained to leave him there behinde.

Then, according to my said instruction, I followed my iourney as the holy Ghost did leade me, without any merit of mine, having in my company the said Stephan the Negro, Dorantez, and certaine of the Indians which had bin set at liberty, and many of the people of the countrey, which gave me great intertainment and welcome in all places where I came, and made mee bowers of trees, giving me such victuals as they had, although they were but small: because (as they said) it had not rained there in 3 yeres, and because the Indians of this countrey sought means rather to hide themselves, then to sowe corne, for feare of the Christians of the Towne of S. Michael, which were wont to make in-roades even to that place, and to warre upon them, and to carry them away captives. In all this way, which may be about 25 or 30. leagues from that part of Petatlan, I saw nothing worthy the noting, save that there came to seeke me certaine Indians from the Island, where Fernando Cortez the Marques of the valley had bin, of whom I was informed, that it was an Island, and not firme land, as some suppose it to be. They came to the firme land upon certaine rafts of wood: and from the maine to the island is but halfe a league by sea, little more or lesse. Likewise certaine Indians of another island greater then this came to visit me, which island is farther off, of whom I was informed that there were 30. other small islands, which were inhabited, but had smal store of victuals, saving 2. which have maiz or corne of the countrey. These Indians had about their necks many great shels which were mother of Pearle. I shewed them pearles which I carryed with me for a shew, and they told me that there were in the Islands great store of them, and those very great: howbeit I saw none of them. I followed my voyage through a desert of 4 dayes iourney, having in my company both the Indians of the islands and those of the mountaines which I had passed, and at the end of this desert I found other indians which marvelled to see me, because they had no knowledge of any Christians, having no traffike nor conversation with those Indians which I had passed, in regard of the great desert which was between them. These Indians intertained me exceeding courteously, and gave me great store of victuals and sought to touch my garments and called me Hagota, which in their language signifieth A man come from heaven. These Indians I advertised by my interpreter, according to my instructions, in the Knowledge of our Lord God in heaven, and of the Emperor. In these countries and in all places els by all wayes and meanes possible, I sought information where any Countreys were of more Cities and people of civilitie and onderstanding, then those which I had found: and I could heare no newes of any such: howbeit they tolde mee, that foure or five dayes iourney within the Country, at the foote of the mountaines, there is a large and mightie plaine, wherein they tolde mee, that there were many great Townes, and people clad in Cotton: and when I shewed them certaine metals which I carryed with mee, to learne what riche metals were in the Lande, they tooke the minerall of Golde and tolde mee, that thereof were vesselles among the people of that plaine, and that they carryed certaine round greene stones hanging at their nostrilles, and at their eares, and that they have certaine thinne plates of that Golde, wherewith they scrape off their sweat, and that the walles of their Temples are covered therewith, and that they use it in all their household vessels. And because this Valley is distant from the Sea-coast, and my instruction was not to leave the Coast, I determined to leave the discovery thereof ontill my returne; at which time I might doe it more commodiously.

Thus I travelled three dayes iourney through Townes inhabited by the sayde people, of whome I was received as I was of those which I had passed, and came onto a Towne of reasonable bignesse, called Vacupa, where they shewed mee great courtesies, and gave mee great store of good victuals, because the soyle is very fruitful, and may bee watered. This Towne is fortie leagues distant from the Sea.

And because I was so farre from the Sea, it being two dayes before Passion Sunday, I determined to stay there until Easter, to informe myselfe of the Islandes, whereof I sayde before that I had informa- tion. And so I sent certaine Indians to the Sea by three severall wayes whom I commaunded to bring mee some Indians of the Sea-coast and of some of those Islandes that I might receive information of them: And I sent Stephan Dorantez the Negro another way, whom I commaunded to goe directly northward fiftie or threescore leagues, to see if by that way hee might learne any newes of any notable thing which wee sought to discover, and I agreed with him, that if hee found any knowledge of any peopled and riche countrey which were of great importance, that hee should goe no further but should returne in person, or should sende mee certaine Indians with that token which wee were agreed upon, to wit, that if it were but a meane thing, hee should sende mee a White Crosse of one handfull long; and if it were any great matter, one of two handfuls long; and if it were a Countrey greater and better then Nueva Espanna, hee should send mee a great crosse. So the sayde Stephan departed from mee on Passion-sunday after dinner: and within foure dayes after the messengers of Stephan returned vnto me with a great Crosse as high as a man, and they brought me word from Stephan, that I should forthwith come away after him, for hee had found people which gave him information of a very mighty Province, and that he had certaine Indians in his company, which had bene in the sayd Province, and that he had sent me one of the said Indians. This Indian told me, that it was thirtie dayes iourney from the Towne where Stephan was, vnto the first Citie of the sayde Province, which is called Ceuola. Hee affirmed also that there are seven great Cities in this Province, all vnder one Lord, the houses whereof are made of Lyme & Stone, and are very great, and the least of them with one lofte above head, and some two and of three loftes, and the house of the Lorde of the Province of foure, and that all of them ioyne one onto the other in good order, and that in the gates of the principall houses there are many Turques-stones cunningly wrought, whereof hee sayth they have there great plentie: also that the people of this Citie goe very well apparelled: and that beyond this there are other Provinces, all which (hee sayth) are much greater then these seven cities. I gave credite to his speach because I found him to bee a man of good vnderstanding: but I deferred my departure to follow Stephan Dorantez, both because I thought hee would stay for mee, and also to attend the returne of my messengers which I had sent vnto the Sea, who returned vnto me upon Easter day, bringing with them certaine inhabitants of the Seacoast, and of two of the Islands. Of whom I vnderstoode, that the Islandes above mentioned were scarce of victuals, as I had learned before, and that they are inhabited by people, which weare shelles of Pearles upon their foreheads, and they say that they have great Pearles, and much Golde. They informed mee of foure and thirtie Islandes, lying one neere vnto another: they say that the people on the sea-coast have small store of victuals, as also those of the Islandes, and that they trafficke one with the other upon raftes. This coast stretcheth northward as is to bee seene. These Indians of the Coast brought me certaine Targets made of Cow-hydes very well dressed, which were so large, that they covered them from the head to the very foote, with a hole in the toppe of the same to looke out before: they are so strong, that a Crossebow (as I suppose) will not pierce them.

Chapter II

The same day came three Indians of those which I called Pintados, because I saw their faces, breasts and armes painted. These dwel farther up into the countrey towards the East, and some of them border upon the seven cities, which sayd they came to see mee, because they had heard of mee: and among other things they gave me information of the seven cities, and of the other Provinces, which the Indian that Stephan sent me had tolde mee of, almost in the very same manner that Stephan had sent mee worde; and so I sent backe the people of the sea-coast: and two Indians of the Islands sayde they would goe with mee seven or eight dayes.

So with these and with the three Pintados above mentioned, I departed from Vacupa upon Easter Tuesday, the same way that Stephan went, from whom I received new messengers with a crosse of the bignesse of the first which he sent me: which hastened me forward, and assured me that the land which I sought for, was the greatest and best countrey in all those partes. The sayd messengers told mee particularly without fayling in any one poynt, all that which the first messenger had tolde mee, and much more, and gave mee more plaine information thereof. So I travelled that day being Easter Tuesday, and two dayes more, the very same way that Stephan had gone: at the end of which 3 dayes they tolde mee that from that place a man might travell in thirtie dayes to the citie of Ceuola, which is the first of the seven. Neither did one onely tell me thus much, but very many; who tolde me very particularly of the greatnesse of the houses, and of the fashion of them, as the first messengers had informed me. Also they told me, that besides these seven Cities, there are 3 other Kingdomes which are called Marata, Acus and Tontonteac. I enquired of them wherefore they travelled so farre from their houses: They said that they went for Turqueses, and Hides of Kine, and other things; and that of all these there was great abundance in this Countrey. Likewise I enquired how, and by what meanes they obtained these things: They tolde me, by their service and by the sweat of their browes, and that they went unto the first citie of the province which is called Ceuola, and that they served them in tilling their ground, and in other businesses, and that they give them Hydes of oxen, which they have in those places, and turqueses for their service, and that the people of this city weare very fine and excellent turqueses hanging at their eares and at their nostrils. They say also, that of these turqueses they make fine workes upon the principall gates of the houses of this citie. They tolde mee, that the apparell which the inhabitants of Ceuola weare, is a gowne of cotten downe to the foote, with a button at the necke, and a long string hanging downe at the same, and that the sleeves of these gownes are as broad beneath as above. They say, they gyrded themselves with gyrdles of turqueses, and that over these coates some weare good apparel, others hides of Kine very well dressed, which they take to bee the best apparell of that countrey, whereof they have there great quantitie. Likewise the women goe apparelled, and covered downe to the foote. These Indians gave me very good intertainment, and curiously enquired the day of my departure from Vacupa, that at my returne they might provide me of foode and lodging. They brought certaine sicke folkes before mee, that I might heale them, and sought to touch my apparell, and gave mee certaine cow-hydes so well trimmed and dressed, that by them a man might coniecture that they were wrought by civile people, and all of them affirmed, that they came from Ceuola.

The next day I followed my iourney, and carrying with mee the Pintados, I came to another Village where I was well received by the people of the same: who likewise sought to touch my garments, and gave mee as particular knowledge of the Lande afore-saide, as I had received of those which mette mee before: and also tolde mee, that from that place certaine people were gone with Stephan Dorantez, foure or five dayes iourney. And here I found a great crosse, which Stephan had left mee for a signe, that the newes of the good Countrey increased, and left worde, that with all haste they should send mee away, and that hee would stay for me at the ende of the first Desert that he mette with. Heere I set up two Crosses, and tooke possession according to mine instruction, because that the Countrey seemed better unto mee then that which I had passed, and that I thought it meete to make an acte of possession as farre as that place.

In this maner I travailed five dayes, always finding inhabited places with great hospitalitie and intertainments, and many Turqueses, and Oxe-hides, and the like report concerning the countrey. Heere I understood, that after two dayes iourney I should finde a desert where there is no foode, but that there were certaine gone before to build mee lodgings, and to carrie foode for me: whereupon I hastened my way, hoping to finde Stephan at the ende thereof, because in that place hee had left worde that hee would stay for mee. Before I came to the desert, I mette with a very pleasant Towne, by reason of great store of waters conveighed thither to water the same. Heere I mette with many people both men & women clothed in Cotton, and some covered with oxe-hydes, which generally they take for better apparell then that of cotton.

All the people in this village go in caconados, that is to say, Turquesses hanging at their nostrilles and eares, which Turquesses they call Cacona. Amongst others, the Lord of this Village came unto me; and two of his brethern, very well apparrelled in cotton, who also were in Caconados, each of them having his collar of Turquesses about his necke; and they presented unto mee many wild beastes, as conies, quailes, Maiz nuttes of Pine trees, and all in great abundance, and offered me many Turqueses, and dressed Oxe-hydes, and very fayre vessels to drinke in, and other things; whereof I would receive no whit. And having my garment of gray cloth, which in Spaine is called çaragoça, the Lord of this Village and the other Indians touched my gowne with their handes, and tolde mee, that of such cloth there was great store in Tontonteac, and that the people of that Countrey wore the same. Whereat I laughed, and sayde that it was nothing else but such apparell of Cotton as they wore. And they replyed: We would have thee thinke that we vnderstand, that that apparell which thou wearest, and that which we weare are of divers sortes. Understand thou, that in Ceulo all the houses are full of that apparrell which we weare, but in Totonteac there are certaine litle beasts, from whom they take that thing wherewith such apparell as thou wearest is made. I prayed them to informe mee more playnely of this matter. And they tolde mee that the sayde beastes were about the bignesses of the two braches or spaniels which Stephan caryed with him, and they say that there is great store of that cattell in Totonteac.

Chapter III

The next day I entered into the Desert, and where I was to dine, I found bowers made, and victuals in abundance by a rivers side: and at night I found bowers and victuals in like sort, and after that maner I found for 4 dayes travell: all which time the wildernesse continueth.

At the ende of these foure dayes, I entred into a valley very well inhabited with people. At the first village there mette me many men and women with victuals and all of them had Turqueses hanging at their nostrils and eares, and some had collars of turqueses like those which the Lord of the Village before I came to the Desert, and his two brethern wore: saving that they ware them but single about their neckes, and these people weare them three or foure times double, and goe in good apparrell, and skinnes of Oxen: and the women weare of the said Turqueses at their nostrils and eares, and very good wast-coates and other garments. Heere there was as great Knowledge of Ceula, as in Nueva Espanna of Temistitan, and in Peru of Cuzco; and they tolde us particularly the maner of their houses, lodgings, streetes and market-places, as men that had bene oftentimes there, and as those which were furnished from thence with things necessary for the service of their householde, as those also had done, which I already had passed. I told them it was impossible that the houses should be made in such sort as they informed mee, and they for my better vnderstanding tooke earth or ashes, and poured water thereupon, and shewed me how they layd stones upon it, and how the buylding grewe up, as they continued laying stones thereon, vntill it mounted aloft. I asked them whether the men of that countrey had wings to mount up unto those loftes; whereat they laughed, and showed mee a Ladder in as good sort as I myselfe was able to describe it. Then they tooke a Staffe and helde it over their

heads, and said that the lofts were so high one above another. Likewise heere I had information of the woollen cloth of Totonteac,
where they say are houses like those of Ceuola, and better and more
in number, and that it is a great Province, and hath no governour.
Here I onderstood that the coast of the sea trended much toward the
West; for vnto the entrance of this first desert which I passed, the
coast still stretched Northward; and because the trending of the coast
is a thing of great importance, I was desirous to Knowe and see it; and
I saw plainely, that in 35. degrees the coast stretcheth to the West,
whereat I reioyced no lesse, then of the good newes within land, and
so I returned back to proceede on my iourney.

Through the foresayd valley I travailed five dayes iourney, which
is inhabited with goodly people, and so aboundeth with victuals,
that it sufficieth to feede above three thousand horsemen: it is all
well watered and like a garden: the burroughs and townes are halfe
and a quarter of a league long, and in all these villages, I found very
ample report of Ceuola, whereof they made such particular relation
onto me, as people which go yeerely thither to earne their living.
Here I found a man borne in Ceuola, who told me that he came
thither, having escaped from the governour or Lieutenant of the
towne; for the Lord of these seven Cities liveth and abideth in one
of those townes called Ahacus, and in the rest he appoynteth lieu-
tenants under him. This townesman of Ceuola is a white man of a
good complexion, somewhat well in yeeres, and of fame greater
capacitie then the inhabitants of this valley, or then those which I
had left behind me. Hee sayde that hee would goe with mee, that I
might begge his pardon: and of him I learned many particulars: he
tolde me that Ceuola was a great Citie, inhabited with great store of
people, and having many streetes and marketplaces: and that in
some parts of this Citie there are certaine very great houses of five
stories high, wherein the chiefe of the Citie assemble themselves at
certaine dayes of the yeere. He sayeth that the houses are of Lyme
and Stone, according as others had tolde mee before, and that the
gates, and small piliars of the principall houses are of Turqueses,
and all the vessels wherein they are served, and the other ornaments
of their houses were of golde: and that the other sixe Cities are built
like onto this, whereof some are bigger: and that Ahacus is the
chiefest of them. Hee sayth that toward the Southeast there is a
Kingdome called Marata, and that there were woont to be many,
and those great Cities, which were all built of houses of Stone, with
divers lofts: and that these have and doe wage warre with the Lord
of the seven Cities, through which warre this Kingdome of Marata
is for the most part wasted, although it yet continueth and main-
taineth warre against the other.

Likewise he saith, that the Kingdome called Totonteac lyeth toward the West, which he saith is a very mightie Province, replenished with infinite store of people and riches. And that in the sayde Kingdome they weare woollen cloth like that which I weare, and other finer sorts of woollen cloth made of the fleeces of those beastes which they described before onto me: and that they are a very civile people. Moreover hee tolde me, that there is another great Province and Kingdome called Acus; for there is Acus, and Ahacus with an aspiration, which is the principall of the seven cities: and Acus without an aspiration is a Kingdome and Province of it selfe. He told me also, that the apparrel which they weare in Ceuola is after the same maner as they before had certified me, and that all the inhabitants of the Citie lie upon beddes raysed a good height from the ground, with quilts and canopies over them, which cover the sayde Beds: and hee tolde mee that hee would goe with me to Ceuola and farther also, if I would take him with me. The like relation was given vnto me in this towne by many others, but not so particularly. I travelled three dayes iourney through this valley: the inhabitants whereof made me exceeding great cheere and intertainment. In this valley I saw above a thousand Oxe-hides most excellently trimmed and dressed. And here also I saw farre greater store of Turqueses and chaines made thereof, then in all places which I had passed; and they say, that all commeth from the city of Ceuola whereof they have great Knowledge, as also of the Kingdome of Marata and of the Kingdomes of Acus and Totonteac.

Chapter IV

Here they shewed me an hide halfe as bigge againe as the hide of a great oxe, and tolde me that it was the skin of a beast which had but one horne upon his forehead, and that this horne bendeth toward his breast, and that out of the same goeth a point right forward, wherein he hath so great strength, that it will breake any thing how strong so ever it be, if he runne against it, and that there are great store of these beasts in that Countrey. The colour of the hide is of the colour of a great Goat-skin, and the haire is a finger thicke. Here I had messengers from Stephan which brought me word, that by this time he was come to the farthest part of the desert, and that he was very ioyful, because the farther he went, the more perfect Knowledge he had of the greatnesse of the countrey, and sent me word, that since his departure from me, hee never had found the Indians in any lye; for even vnto that very place he had found al in such maner as they had informed him and hoped that he should find the like at his arrivall in the valley which he was going vnto, as he had found in the villages before passed. I set up crosses and used those acts and ceremonies, which were to be done according to my instructions. The inhabitants requested me to stay here three or foure days, because that from this place there were four days iourney vnto the desert, and from the first entrance into the same desert vnto the citie of Ceuola are 15 great dayes iourney more; also that they would provide victuals, for me and other necessaries for that voyage. Likewise they told me, that with Stephan the Negro were gone above 300 men to beare him company, and to carry victuals after him, and that in like sort many of them would go with me to serve me, because they hoped to returne home rich. I thanked them, and willed them to set things in order with speede, and so I rested there three dayes, wherein I always informed my selfe of Ceuola, and of as many other things as I could learne, and called many Indians vnto mee, and examined them severally and all of them agreed in one tale, and told me of the great multitude of people, and of the order of the streetes, of the greatnesse of the houses, and of the strength of the gates, agreeing altogether with that which the rest before had told me. After three dayes many assembled themselves to go with me, 30 of the principal of whom I tooke, being very well apparrelled, and with chaines of turqueses, which some of them weare five or sixe times double, and other people to cary things necessary for them and me, and so set forward on my voyage.

Thus I entred into the second desert on the 9 of May, and travelled the first day by a very broad and beaten way, and we came to diner vnto a water, where the Indians had made provision for me: and at night we came to another water, where I found a house which they had fully made up for me, and another house stood made where Stephan lodged when he passed that way, and many old cottages and many signes of fire which the people had made that travelled to Ceuola by this way. In this sort. I travelled 12 dayes iourney being alway well provided of victuals, of wild beasts, Hares, and Partridges of the same colour and tast with those of Spaine although they are not as big, for they be somewhat lesse. Here met us an Indian the sonne of the chiefe man that accompanied mee, which had gone before with Stephan, who came in a great fright, having his face and body all covered with sweat, and shewing exceeding sadnesse in his countenance and he told mee that a dayes iourney before Stephan came to Ceuola he sent his great mace made of a gourd by his messenges, as he was always woont to sent them before him, that hee might knowe in what sort hee came onto them, which gourd has a string of belles upon it and two feathers one white and another red, in token that he demanded safe conduct, and that he came peaceably. And when they came to Ceuola before the magistrate which the Lord of the citie had placed there for his Lieutenant, they delivered him the sayde great gourd, who tooke the same in his hands, and after he spyed the belles, in a great rage and fury he cast it to the ground, and willed messengers to get them packing with speed, for he knew well ynough what people they were, and that they should will them in no case to enter into the citie, for if they did hee would put them all to death. The messengers returned and tolde Stephan how things had passed, who answered them that it made no great matter, and would needes proceed on his voyage till he came to the citie of Ceuola: where he found men that would not let him enter into the towne, but shut him into a great house which stoode without the citie, and straightway tooke all things from him which hee carried to truck and barter with them, and certain turqueses, and other things which he had received of the Indians by the way, and they kept him there all that night without giving him meate or drinke, and the next day in the morning this Indian was a thirst, and went out of the house to drinke at a river that was neere at hand, and within a little while after he saw Stephan running away, and the people followed him, and slewe certain of the Indians which went in his company. And when this Indian saw these things, he hid himselfe on the banks of the river, and afterward crossed the high way of the desert. The Indians that went with me bearing these newes began incontinently to lament, and I thought these heavie and bad news would cost mee my life, neither did I feare so much the losse of mine owne life, as that I should not bee able to returne to give information of the greatnesses of that Countrey, where our Lord God might be glorified: and streight way I cut the cords of my budgets which I carried with me ful of merchandise for traffique, which I would not doe till then, nor give anything to any man, and began to divide all that I carried with mee among the principall men, willing them not to be afraid, but to goe forward with me, and so they did. And going on our way, within a dayes iourney of Ceuola wee met two other Indians of those which went with Stephan, which were bloody and wounded in many places: and as soone as they came to us, they which were with me began to make great lamentation. These wounded Indians I asked for Stephan, and they agreeing in all poynts with the first Indian sayd, that after they had put him into the foresayd great house without giving him meat or drinke all that day and all that night, they tooke from Stephan all the things which hee carried with him. The next day when the Sunne was a lance high, Stephan went out of the house, and some of the chiefe men with him, and suddenly came store of people from the citie, whom as soone as hee sawe he began to run away and we likewise, and foorthwith they shot at us and wounded us, and certaine dead men fell upon us, and so we lay till night and durst not stirre, and we heard great rumours in the citie, and saw many men and women keeping

watch and ward upon the walles thereof, and after this we could
not see Stephan any more, and wee thinke they have shot him to
death, as they have done all the rest which went with him, so that
none are escaped but we onely.

Chapter V

Having considered the former report of the Indians, and the evill
meanes which I had to prosecute my voyage as I desired, I thought
it not good wilfully to loose my life as Stephan did; and so tolde
them, that God would punish those of Ceuola, and that the Viceroy
when he should understand what had happened, would send many
christians to chastise them: but they would not believe me, for they
sayde that no man was able to withstand the power of Ceuola. And
herewith I left them, and went aside two or three stones cast, and
when I returned I found an Indian of mine which I had brought
from Mexico called Marcus, who wept and sayde unto me: Father,
these men have consulted to kill us, for they say, that through your
and Stephans meanes their fathers are slaine, and that neither man
nor woman of them shall remaine unslaine. Then againe I divided
among them certaine other things which I had, to appease them,
whereupon they were somewhat pacified, albeit they still shewed
great griefe for the people which were slaine. I requested some of
them to goe to Ceuola, to see if any other Indian were escaped, with
intent that they might learne some newes of Stephan; which I could
not obtaine at their handes. When I saw this, I sayd unto them, that
I purposed to see the citie of Ceuola, whatsoever came of it. They
sayde that none of them would goe with me. At the last when they
sawe mee resolute, two of the chiefe of them sayde they would goe
with me; with whome and with mine Indians and interpreters I followed my way, till I came within sight of Ceuola, which is situate on
a plaine at the foote of a round hill, and maketh shew to bee a faire
citie, and is better seated then any that I have seene in these partes.
The houses are builded in order, according as the Indians told me,
all made of stone with divers stories, and flatte roofes, as farre as I
could discerne from a mountaine, whither I ascended to viewe the
citie. The people are somewhat white, they weare apparell, and lie in
beds, their weapons are bowes, they have Emeralds and other iewels,
although they esteeme none so much as turqueses wherewith they
adorne the walles of the porches of their houses, and their apparell and vessels, and they use them instead of money through all the
Countrey. Their apparell is of cotton and Oxe hides, and this is their
most commendable and honourable apparell. They use vessels of
gold and silver, for they have no other mettall, whereof there is
greater use and more abundance then in Peru, and they buy the

same for turqueses in the province of the Pintados, where there are
sayd to be mines of great abundance. Of other Kingdomes I could
not obtaine so particular instruction. Divers times I was tempted to
goe thither, because I knewe I could but hazard my life, and that I
had offered unto God the first day that I began my iourney: in the
ende I began to bee afraid, considering in what danger I should put
my selfe, and that if I should dye, the knowledge of this countrey
should be lost, which in my iudgement is the greatest and the best
that hitherto hath beene discovered: and when I tolde the chief
men, what a goodly citie Ceuola seemed unto mee, they answered
me that it was the least of the seven cities, and that Totonteac is the
greatest and best of them all, because it hath so many houses and
people, and there is no ende of them. Having seene the disposition
and situation of the place, I thought good to name that countrey El
Nueva reyno de San Francisco: in which place I made a great heape
of stones by the helpe of the Indians, and on the toppe thereof I
set up a small slender crosse because I wanted meanes to make a
greater, and sayd that I set up that crosse and heape in the name of
the most honourable Lord Don Antonio de Mendoça Viceroy and
Captaine generall of Nueva Espanna, for the Emperour our Lord,
in token of possession, according to mine instruction. Which possession I sayd that I tooke in that place of all the seven cities, and of
the Kingdomes of Totonteac, of Acus, and of Marata. Thus I returned
with much more feare then victuals, and went untill I found the
people which I had left behind mee, with all the speede that I could
make, whome I overtooke in two dayes travell, and went in their
company till I had passed the desert, where I was not made so much
of as before: for both men and women made great lamentation for
the people which were slaine at Ceuola, and with feare I hastened
from the people of this valley, and travelled tenne leagues the first
day, and so I went daily eight or ten leagues, without staying until
I had passed the second desert. And though I were in feare, yet I
determined to go to the great plaine, whereof I said before, that I
had information, being situate at the foote of the mountaines, and
in that place I vnderstoode, that this plaine is inhabited for many
dayes iourney toward the East, but I durst not enter into it, considering, that if hereafter wee shoulde inhabite this other countrey of the
seven cities, and the kingdomes before mentioned, that then I might
better discover the same, without putting my selfe in hazard, and
leaue it for this time, that I might give relation of the things which
I had now seene. At the entrance of this plaine I sawe but seven
Townes onely of a reasonable bignesse, which were a farre off in a
lowe valley beeing very greene and a most fruitfull soyle, out of
which ranne many Rivers. I was informed that there was much golde
in this valley, and that the inhabitants worke it into vessels and

thinne plates, wherewith they strike and take off their sweat, and that they are people that will not suffer those of the other side of the plaine to traffique with them, and they could not tell me the cause thereof. Here I set up two crosses, and tooke possession of the plaine and valley in like sort and order, as I did at other places before mentioned. And from thence I returned on my voyage with as much haste as I coulde make, untill I came to the citie of Saint Michael in the province of Culiacan, thinking there to have found Francis Vazquez de Coronado governour of Nueva Galicia, and finding him not there, I proceeded on my iourney till I came to the citie of Compostella, where I found him. I write not here many other particularities, because they are impertinent to this matter: I only report that which I have seene, and which was tolde me concerning the countreys through which I travelled, and of those which I had information of.

Other Contemporary Accounts of the New World

MIGUEL LEÓN-PORTILLA

From The Broken Spears[†]

Chapter 1. Omens Foretelling the Arrival of the Spaniards

INTRODUCTION

The documents presented in the first thirteen chapters relate the events that began a few years before the arrival of the Spaniards on the east coast of Mexico and ended with the fall of Tenochtitlan to the conquistadors. The last two chapters offer, by way of conclusion, a somewhat different account of the Conquest written in 1528 by the anonymous informants of Tlatelolco, and three of the *icnocuicatl* (threnodies, or songs of sorrow) lamenting the defeat and destruction of the Aztec capital.

The texts have been arranged to give a chronological narrative of the Conquest, and they contain a number of obvious discrepancies and contradictions. We have not attempted to solve all of the problems which these discrepancies pose for the historian. Our fundamental concern is with the human interest of the accounts, which reveal how the Nahuas interpreted the downfall of their civilization.

This first chapter begins with a passage from the *Codex Florentino;* the original text is in the Nahuatl of Sahagun's native informants. It is followed by two selections from the *Historia de Tlaxcala* by Diego Munoz Camargo, who married into the nobility of Tlaxcala. The Tlaxcaltecas allied themselves with Cortes, and Munoz Camargo wrote from their point of view, but his description of the omens which appeared in Mexico agrees quite closely with that of Sahagun's informants.

[†] From *The Broken Spears. The Aztec Account of the Conquest of Mexico,* edited by Miguel León-Portilla and translated by Lysander Kemp (Boston: Beacon Press, 1962), pp. 1–12. Reprinted by permission of Beacon Press, Boston. Copyright © 1962, 1990 by Miguel León-Portilla. Expanded and updated edition © 1992 by Miguel León-Portilla.

THE OMENS AS DESCRIBED BY SAHAGUN'S INFORMANTS

The first bad omen: Ten years before the Spaniards first came here, a bad omen appeared in the sky. It was like a flaming ear of corn, or a fiery signal, or the blaze of daybreak; it seemed to bleed fire, drop by drop, like a wound in the sky. It was wide at the base and narrow at the peak, and it shone in the very heart of the heavens.

This is how it appeared: it shone in the eastern sky in the middle of the night. It appeared at midnight and burned till the break of day, but it vanished at the rising of the sun. The time during which it appeared to us was a full year, beginning in the year 12-House.

When it first appeared, there was great outcry and confusion. The people clapped their hands against their mouths; they were amazed and frightened, and asked themselves what it could mean.

The second bad omen: The temple of Huitzilopochtli[1] burst into flames. It is thought that no one set it afire, that it burned down of its own accord. The name of its divine site was Tlacateccan [House of Authority].

And now it is burning, the wooden columns are burning! The flames, the tongues of fire shoot out, the bursts of fire shoot up into the sky!

The flames swiftly destroyed all the woodwork of the temple. When the fire was first seen, the people shouted: "Mexicanos, come running! We can put it out! Bring your water jars . . . !" But when they threw water on the blaze it only flamed higher. They could not put it out, and the temple burned to the ground.

The third bad omen: A temple was damaged by a lightning-bolt. This was the temple of Xiuhtecuhtli,[2] which was built of straw, in the place known as Tzonmolco.[3] It was raining that day, but it was only a light rain or a drizzle, and no thunder was heard. Therefore the lightning-bolt was taken as an omen. The people said: "The temple was struck by a blow from the sun."

The fourth bad omen: Fire streamed through the sky while the sun was still shining. It was divided into three parts. It flashed out from where the sun sets and raced straight to where the sun rises, giving off a shower of sparks like a red-hot coal. When the people saw its long train streaming through the heavens, there was a great outcry and confusion, as if they were shaking a thousand little bells.

The fifth bad omen: The wind lashed the water until it boiled. It was as if it were boiling with rage, as if it were shattering itself in its frenzy. It began from far off, rose high in the air and dashed against

1. Sun god and god of war.
2. Fire god.
3. Part of the main temple of Tenochtitlan.

the walls of the houses. The flooded houses collapsed into the water. This was in the lake that is next to us.

The sixth bad omen: The people heard a weeping woman night after night. She passed by in the middle of the night, wailing and crying out in a loud voice: "My children, we must flee far away from this city!" At other times she cried: "My children, where shall I take you?"[4]

The seventh bad omen: A strange creature was captured in the nets. The men who fish the lakes caught a bird the color of ashes, a bird resembling a crane. They brought it to Motecuhzoma in the Black House.[5]

This bird wore a strange mirror in the crown of its head. The mirror was pierced in the center like a spindle whorl, and the night sky could be seen in its face. The hour was noon, but the stars and the *mamalhuaztli*[6] could be seen in the face of that mirror. Motecuhzoma took it as a great and bad omen when he saw the stars and the *mamalhuaztli.*

But when he looked at the mirror a second time, he saw a distant plain. People were moving across it, spread out in ranks and coming forward in great haste. They made war against each other and rode on the backs of animals resembling deer.

Motecuhzoma called for his magicians and wise men and asked them: "Can you explain what I have seen? Creatures like human beings, running and fighting . . . !" But when they looked into the mirror to answer him, all had vanished away, and they saw nothing.

The eighth bad omen: Monstrous beings appeared in the streets of the city: deformed men with two heads but only one body. They were taken to the Black House and shown to Motecuhzoma; but the moment he saw them, they all vanished away.

THE OMENS AS DESCRIBED BY MUÑOZ CAMARGO[7]

Ten years before the Spaniards came to this land, the people saw a strange wonder and took it to be an evil sign and portent. This wonder was a great column of flame which burned in the night, shooting out such brilliant sparks and flashes that it seemed to rain fire on the earth and to blaze like daybreak. It seemed to be fastened against the

---

4. Apparently a reference to Cihuacoatl, an ancient earth goddess, who wept and cried out in the night. She is one of the antecedents of the *llorona* (weeping woman), who is still heard in rural Mexico.
5. The house of magical studies. Motecuhzoma, the king, was a devoted amateur wizard.
6. Three stars in the constellation Taurus. They were extremely important in the Nahuatl religion: the Nahuas performed various ceremonies in their honor and offered them copal incense three times each night.
7. This selection from the *Historia de Tlaxcala* obviously is based on the account by Sahagun's informants.

sky in the shape of a pyramid, its base set against the ground, where it was of vast width, and its bulk narrowing to a peak that reached up and touched the heavens. It appeared at midnight and could still be seen at dawn, but in the daytime it was quelled by the force and brilliance of the sun. This portent burned for a year, beginning in the year which the natives called 12-House—that is, 1517 in our Spanish reckoning.

When this sign and portent was first seen, the natives were overcome with terror, weeping and shouting and crying out, and beating the palms of their hands against their mouths, as is their custom. These shouts and cries were accompanied by sacrifices of blood and of human beings, for this was their practice whenever they thought they were endangered by some calamity.

This great marvel caused so much dread and wonder that they spoke of it constantly, trying to imagine what such a strange novelty could signify. They begged the seers and magicians to interpret its meaning, because no such thing had ever been seen or reported anywhere in the world. It should be noted that these signs began to appear ten years before the coming of the Spaniards, but that the year called 12-House in their reckoning was the year 1517, two years before the Spaniards reached this land.

The second wonder, sign or omen which the natives beheld was this: the temple of the demon Huitzilopochtli, in the sector named Tlacateco, caught fire and burned, though no one had set it afire. The blaze was so great and sudden that wings of flame rushed out of the doors and seemed to touch the sky. When this occurred, there was great confusion and much loud shouting and wailing. The people cried: "Mexicanos! Come as quickly as you can! Bring your water jars to put it out!" Everyone within hearing ran to help, but when they threw water on the fire, it leaped up with even greater violence, and thus the whole temple burned down.

The third wonder and sign was this: a lightning-bolt fell on a temple of idolatry whose roof was made of straw. The name of this temple was Tzonmolco, and it was dedicated to their idol Xiuhtecuhtli. The bolt fell on the temple with neither flash nor thunder, when there was only a light rain, like a dew. It was taken as an omen and miracle which boded evil, and all burned down.

The fourth wonder was this: comets flashed through the sky in the daytime while the sun was shining. They raced by threes from the west to the east with great haste and violence, shooting off bright coals and sparks of fire, and trailing such long tails that their splendor filled the sky. When these portents were seen, the people were terrified, wailing and crying aloud.

The fifth wonder was this: the Lake of Mexico rose when there was no wind. It boiled, and boiled again, and foamed until it reached a great height, until it washed against half the houses in the city. House after house collapsed and was destroyed by the waters.

The sixth wonder was this: the people heard in the night the voice of a weeping woman, who sobbed and sighed and drowned herself in her tears. This woman cried: "O my sons, we are lost . . . !" Or she cried: "O my sons, where can I hide you . . . ?"

The seventh Wonder was this: the men whose work is in the Lake of Mexico—the fishermen and other boatmen, or the fowlers in their canoes–trapped a dark-feathered bird resembling a crane and took it to Motecuhzoma so that he might see it. He was in the palace of the Black Hall; the sun was already in the west. This bird was so unique and marvelous that no one could exaggerate its strangeness or describe it well. A round diadem was set in its head in the form of a clear and transparent mirror, in which could be seen the heavens, the three stars in Taurus and the stars in the sign of the Gemini. When Motecuhzoma saw this, he was filled with dread and wonder, for he believed it was a bad omen to see the stars of heaven in the diadem of that bird.

When Motecuhzoma looked into the mirror a second time, he saw a host of people, all armed like warriors, coming forward in well-ordered ranks. They skirmished and fought with each other, and were accompanied by strange deer and other creatures.

Therefore, he called for his magicians and fortune-tellers, whose wisdom he trusted, and asked them what these unnatural visions meant: "My dear and learned friends, I have witnessed great signs in the diadem of a bird, which was brought to me as something new and marvelous that had never been seen before. What I witnessed in that diadem, which is pellucid like a mirror, was a strange host of people rushing toward me across a plain. Now look yourselves, and see what I have seen."

But when they wished to advise their lord on what seemed to them so wondrous a thing, and to give him their judgments, divinations and predictions, the bird suddenly disappeared; and thus they could not offer him any sure opinion.

The eighth wonder and sign that appeared in Mexico: the natives saw two men merged into one body—these they called *tlacantzolli* ("men-squeezed-together")—and others who had two heads but only one body. They were brought to the palace of the Black Hall to be shown to the great Motecuhzoma, but they vanished as soon as he had seen them, and all these signs and others became invisible. To the natives, these marvels augured their death and ruin, signifying that the end of the world was coming and that other peoples would be created to inhabit the earth. They were so frightened and grief-stricken that they could form no judgment about these things, so new and strange and never before seen or reported.

THE WONDERS AND SIGNS OBSERVED IN TLAXCALA

Other signs appeared here in this province of Tlaxcala, a little before the arrival of the Spaniards. The first sign was a radiance that shone in the east every morning three hours before sunrise. This radiance was in the form of a brilliant white cloud which rose to the sky, and the people were filled with dread and wonder, not knowing what it could be.

They also saw another marvelous sign: a whirlwind of dust that rose like a sleeve from the top of the Matlalcueye, now called the Sierra de Tlaxcala.[8] This sleeve rose so high that it seemed to touch the sky. The sign appeared many times throughout a whole year and caused the people great dread and wonder, emotions which are contrary to their bent and to that of their nation. They could only believe that the gods had descended from heaven, and the news flew through the province to the smallest villages. But however this may have been, the arrival of a strange new people was at last reported and confirmed, especially in Mexico, the head of this empire and monarchy.

CHRISTOPHER COLUMBUS

Letter to the Chief Treasurer of Aragón about the Islands Found in India (1493)[†]

My lord, because I know that you will be pleased by the great victory that Our Lord has given me in my journey, I write you this letter through which you will know that in thirty-three days I traveled to India[1] with the fleet given me by the most illustrious King and Queen our lords. There I found many islands populated by innumerable people, and I took possession of them all in the name of their highnesses, with proclamation and royal flag unfurled, and was not contradicted.[2] To the first one I found I gave the name San Salvador [Holy Savior] in commemoration of His High Majesty [Christ], Who has most marvelously given us all this; the Indians call it Guanahani.

---

8. Its present name is La Malinche.
† A new translation by David Frye. The letter was published in Barcelona in 1493, almost immediately after Columbus's arrival and was quickly translated and republished across Europe. The translation is based on Carlos Sanz's facsimile of the first edition (Madrid, 1956).
1. Or The Indies (*Las indias*); i.e., East Asia, which Columbus always insisted he had reached, threatening to jail anyone who contradicted him.
2. A standard legal phrase used to indicate that, with their silence, the locals had accepted this transfer of jurisdiction to the Spanish Crown.

To the second island I gave the name Santa María de Concepción; to the third, Fernandina; to the fourth, Isabela; to the fifth island, Juana, and thus to each island a new name.[3]

When I reached Juana, I followed its coastline eastward and found it so large that I thought it was the mainland province of Cathay [China]. As I did not find towns and villages on the seacoast, but only small hamlets whose people I could not talk with because they fled right away, I continued along the same route, thinking I would not miss any great cities or towns. After many leagues, seeing that there was no change and that the coast was taking me northward, which went against my wishes because winter had already taken form and I had planned to spend it going south, and also that the wind was coming head-on, I decided not to wait any longer and returned to an excellent harbor from where I sent two men inland to learn whether there was a king or any great cities.[4] They walked for three days and found an infinite number of small hamlets and countless people, but no sort of administration, for which reason they returned.

I amply understood from other Indians I had already taken that this land was most certainly an island; thus I followed its coastline eastward for one hundred seven leagues to where it ended.[5] From which cape I saw another island to the east, eighteen leagues distant from this one, which I named the Spanish Island.[6] I went there and followed its northern coast, as I had with Juana, one hundred eighty-eight long leagues east in a straight line as I had with Juana, which island and all the others are most robust in the highest degree, and this one extremely so. It has many harbors on its seacoast beyond compare to those I know in Christian lands, and ample rivers so good and broad it is a marvel. Its fields are high and it has many tall mountains and ranges beyond compare to those of Tenerife, all very handsome, of a thousand forms, and all walkable and full of a

---

3. The first four islands are in the Bahamas. Juana was later renamed Cuba after its indigenous name.
4. From Las Casas's summary of Columbus's lost ship's log: "Friday, November 2. The Admiral [Columbus] decided to send two Spanish men: one was named Rodrigo de Xerez who used to live in Ayamonte, and the other was a Luis de Torres who had been in the entourage of the Adelantado of Murcia and had been a Jew, and they say that he knew Hebrew and Chaldean and a little Arabic; and with them he sent two Indians, one of the ones he had brought with him from Guanahani and one from those houses that lined the rivers." The emphasis on using interpreters to communicate with local people (Columbus thought a speaker of Hebrew and Arabic might be understood in East Asia) became the standard method of exploration and conquest in the early colonial period, and is reflected in Cabeza de Vaca's text.
5. Columbus's measurements are fairly accurate, but when he errs it is on the side of exaggeration. He followed the coast of Cuba for 220 to 250 miles, not 107 nautical leagues (370 miles); the northern coast of Hispaniola, mentioned next, measures 350 miles, not 188 leagues (650 miles).
6. *La Spañola*; still called Hispaniola in English but renamed Santo Domingo by Spain; the island is now shared by Haiti and the Dominican Republic. Its indigenous name according to Las Casas was Haiti, but Columbus recorded it as "Bohío," which means "house."

thousand kinds of trees so tall they seem to reach the sky, and I have heard that they never lose their leaves from what I could understand, for I saw them as green and as handsome as the trees are around May in Spain. Some of them were in flower, others bore fruit, and others in different stages, each according to its type; and the nightingale and a thousand other kinds of little birds sang there where I went during the month of November. There are six or eight kinds of palm trees, and it is a wonder to see them for their handsome variety, much as with the other trees and fruits and plants. There are marvelous pine forests there, and great open fields, and honey, and many kinds of birds and a great diversity of fruits. In these lands there are many mines of precious metals and there are inestimable numbers of people.

The Spanish Island is a marvel: its ranges and mountains and lowlands and open fields, its soil so handsome and deep for sowing and planting, for raising all sorts of cattle, for founding towns and villages. The sea harbors are not to be believed without seeing, and the rivers are many and broad and of good water, and most of them bear gold.[7] Among its trees and fruits and plants there are many differences from those of Juana: here there are many spice-bearing plants, and great mines of gold and other metals.

The people of this island, and of all the other islands I have found, those of which I have learned and have not learned, go about entirely naked, both men and women, just as their mothers bore them, though a few women would cover up a single spot with a plant leaf or a piece of cotton that they make for that purpose. They have no iron nor steel nor weapons, nor are they made for that—not because they are not well-built people of handsome stature, but because they are marvelously timid. They have no other weapons but the reeds that they cut in seed, into which they fit a sharp little stick; and even those they do not dare use. For many times it befell me to send two or three men ashore to some town to hold a talk, and countless people came out, and as soon as they saw them arrive they fled, parent not even waiting for child; and this not because they would have done them any harm (rather, at every cape where I have landed and have been able to hold talks I have given to them from everything I have, both cloth and many other things, without receiving anything in return), but because they are hopelessly timid. The truth is that after they are reassured and lose that fear, they are so guileless and so liberal with what they have that no one would believe it but one

---

7. The river gold of Hispaniola, though not very abundant, proved enough to finance the next stages of Spanish conquest in the Caribbean. Las Casas writes of the enslavement of Indians forced to pan for gold on the Spanish settlers' behalf.

who has seen it. Whatever they have, ask for it and they will never say no. Rather, they offer it to one and show one so much love that they would give their hearts, whether it is something of value or something of little worth; and then they are happy with any little thing that one gives them in return.

I prohibited people from giving them such shabby things as bits of broken bowls and bits of broken glass and ends of bootlaces, although when they could carry off one of those it seemed to them that they had gotten the best gem in the world. For one sailor managed to get, for one lace, two and a half *castellanos*' weight of gold; and other sailors for other things worth much less got much more: for new *blancas* they would give all they had, even if it were two or three *castellanos* of gold, or an *arroba*[8] or two or spun cotton. They would even accept the broken barrel hoops, and would give what they had like brutes; this seemed wrong to me, and I prohibited it. And I freely gave away a thousand good things so that they would take love, and beyond that, would become Christians and inclined toward the love and service of their highnesses and of the whole Castilian nation, and would try to gather and give to us of all the things that they have in abundance and that are necessary to us.

And they know no sect nor idolatry; rather, all believe that power and good reside in the heavens, and they firmly believed that I and these ships and these people came from the heavens, and they received me with this observance in every cape, once they had lost their fear. And this does not come from their being ignorant, for they are of very subtle wit and are men who navigate all those seas, and it is a marvel how well they account for everything; rather, it is because they have never seen people clothed, nor such ships.

And as soon as I arrived in India, in the first island that I found, I took some of them by force so that they could learn [Spanish] and give me news of what there was in those parts. And so it was that they soon understood, and we understood them, be it by tongue or by signs; and these people have been very useful. Even today I find them insistent that I have come from the heavens, for all the conversation they might have with me; and they were the first to announce it, wherever I arrived, and the others would run about from house to house and to the nearby towns shouting, "Come, come, see the people from the heavens." So everyone, men and women alike, after they were reassured in their hearts about us, would come out so that not one stayed behind, big or small, and all brought us something to eat and drink and gave it with a marvelous love.

---

8. Twenty-five pounds. "*Castellanos*": gold coins that weighed 4.6 grams. "*Blancas*": the smallest copper-silver coins of the era.

In all the islands they have a great many *canoes*,[9] which are like rowboats, some bigger, some smaller. Many of them are bigger than an eighteen-seat rowboat. They are less broad, because they are made from a single piece of wood, yet a boat could not hold its own against them in rowing, for they go faster than one can believe; and with these they navigate all those islands, which are countless, and they carry their merchandise. I have seen some of these canoes with seventy or eighty men aboard, each with his oar.

Among all the islands I did not see much diversity in the form of the people, nor in their customs, nor in their language; rather they all understand each other, which is a very singular thing. For which, I await what their highnesses will decide regarding their conversion to our holy faith, toward which they are very disposed.

I have already said that I went one hundred seven leagues along the seacoast in a straight line from west to east off the island of Juana. According to this path, I can say that this island is bigger than England and Scotland together, because, apart from these hundred seven leagues, I still have on the western side two provinces that I did not pass, one of which is called Auau, where the people with tails are born. These two provinces cannot be less than fifty or sixty leagues long, from what I could understand from these Indians that I have, who know all the islands. This other Spanish Island is larger in circumference than all Spain from Colibre [at the eastern border with France] by seacoast around to Fuente Rabia in Viscaya [at the western border], for along one side of the square I went one hundred eighty-eight leagues in a straight line from west to east.[1] This island is to be desired and, having seen it, never to be let go; and this, of all the islands of which I have taken possession for their highnesses, and all of them better supplied than I know and can tell, and I have taken them all for their highnesses, this is the one they can make use of most correctly as King and Queen of Castile.

In this Spanish Island, in the most convenient place and the best district for gold mines and for all sorts of trading—both from this mainland over here and from the mainland of the Great Khan over there, where there will be much trade and profit—I have taken possession of a large town to which I have given the name Navidad, and in it I have made a fortress and a stronghold which by this time should be completely finished; and I have left enough people in it to

9. *Canoa*; this marks the first appearance of a Native American (Taino) word in print in Europe.
1. These are miscalculations that exaggerate the area of the islands. Hispaniola has a north coast about as long as Spain's but less than one sixth of Spain's land area. Cuba is roughly as long as Great Britain but half its area.

accomplish that deed,[2] with weapons and artillery and provisions for more than a year, and a rowboat and a master shipbuilder for making more; and great friendship with the King of that land, to the degree that he boasted of calling me and thinking of me as his brother. And even if his will should change toward attacking these people, neither he nor his people know of weapons and they go about naked; as I have said, they are the most timid in the world. Thus the [Spanish] people who remained there are, alone, enough to destroy that entire land, and it is an island without danger to their persons if they know how to govern themselves.[3]

In all these islands it seems to me that all the men are happy with one woman, and to their chief or King they give up to twenty. The women, it seems to me, work more than the men. Nor have I been able to understand whether they have private property, for it seemed to me that whatever one had, all took part of, especially in the case of edible things. In these island I have up to now not found monstrous men as many thought; instead, they are all people of quite lovely observance. Nor are they black, as in Guinea; rather, they have flowing hair, and they do not raise their children where the solar rays have too much impetus. For it is true that the sun has a great force there, for it is only twenty six degrees from the equatorial line. On these islands, where there are great mountains the cold was strong this winter, but they endure it by custom and with the help of their food: they eat with many spices, and excessively hot ones.

Thus I have found no monsters, nor news of any, except in the island of Quarives, the second one at the entrance to India, which is populated with a people held to be very fierce in all the other islands, who eat human flesh.[4] These people have many canoes, with which they roam all the islands of India stealing and taking as much as they can. They are no more deformed than the others, except that they have the custom of wearing their hair long, like women; and they use bows and arrows made of the same reeds, with a little stick at the end for lack of iron, which they do not have. They are fierce among these other peoples who are all too cowardly, but I

2. Columbus does not mention that he left sailors behind at Navidad because his largest ship, the *Santa María*, was shipwrecked. The fortress was built from its broken timbers. "The mainland of the Great Khan"; i.e., China, which was ruled by Genghis Khan in the time of Marco Polo. Columbus insisted that his India was near China, and he spent much time searching for the Khan.
3. Before Columbus's return in 1494, the Spanish settlers at Navidad provoked a rebellion and all died.
4. From Las Casas's extract of the log, January 13, 1493: "The Admiral also says that in the islands visited everyone greatly feared those of Carib—in some islands they call it Caniba, but in the Spanish Island, Carib—and they must be a bold people, for they go about all these islands and eat all the people they find." The words *cannibal* and *Caribbean* both derive from the name of this imagined island and its rumored people.

do not esteem them any greater than the others. They are the ones who have relations with the women of Matinino, which is the first island one finds when leaving Spain for India, in which there is not a single man. Those women do not follow feminine occupations, but rather use bows and arrows (like the above-mentioned, of reeds), and they arm themselves and cover themselves with plates of copper, which they have much of. There is another island, they assure me, bigger than the Spanish Island, in which the people have no hair. In this island there is gold beyond count; and of these and of the other islands I bring Indians with me as witnesses.

In conclusion, speaking only of what has been done on this journey that was all in a rush, their highnesses can see that I will give them as much gold as they are in need of, with the very little aid that their highnesses will give me; and then spices and cotton, as much as their highnesses order shipped; and mastic, as much as they order shipped, such as has never been found but in Greece on the island of Chios, where the Dominion [of Genoa] sell it at whatever price they wish; and lignum aloe, as much as they order shipped; and slaves, as many as they order shipped, and they will be from among the idolators; and I believe I have found rhubarb and cinnamon, and I will find a thousand other things of substance, which the people I left behind there will find.[5] Because I have not stopped at any cape, I have navigated onward as soon as there was wind; only in the town of Navidad, until I had left it sure and well established. And the truth is that I would have done much more if the ships were as useful to me as reason demanded.

This is enough, and eternal God Our Lord Who gives to all those who follow His path victory in things that seem impossible—and this was notably one of them, for although these lands may have been talked about or written of, it was all by conjecture without adding any eyewitness, but understanding to the point that the audience, for the most part, listened and judged more through talk than through things[6]—so that Our Redeemer gave this victory to our most illustrious king and queen, and [has made] their kingdoms famous for such a high thing, for which all Christianity should rejoice and make great festivities and give solemn thanks to the Holy Trinity with many solemn prayers, for all the exaltation there will be when so many peoples turn to our Holy Faith, and then, for the temporal good,

5. The letter returns from the realm of fabulous rumors to matters of commerce. Columbus has scouted out possible sources of profit: gold; spices and cotton (which grew well in Europe, so that no Asian-style spice trade developed); plants he optimistically misidentifies as mastic (fragrant resin), lignum aloe (fragrant wood), rhubarb (used medicinally and as dye), and cinnamon, all staples of the East–West trade; and non-Christians, who could be legally enslaved.
6. This phrase is not very clear.

because not only Spain but all Christians will here find relief and profit, according to what has now been briefly done.

Written on the caravel, at the island of Grand Canary, on 15 February of the year 1493.[7]

To serve as you command,

The Admiral

Postscript that came with the Letter.

After this was written, and on entering the sea of Castile, so much wind came upon me south and southeast that I was made to unload the ships. But I ran into this port of Lisbon today, which was the greatest marvel in the world, and I resolved to write to your majesties. Throughout India I have always found the weather to be as in May; I traveled there in 33 days, and returned in 28, except that these storms have detained me 14 days.

All the men of the sea hereabouts say that there has never been so bad a winter, nor so many ships lost.

Written on 4 March.

HERNÁN CORTÉS

From The First Letter from Mexico (1520)[†]

＊　＊　＊

It seemed to us, Most Excellent Princes, that in order to preserve peace and concord amongst ourselves and to govern us well it was necessary to elect someone for Your Royal service who might act in Your Majesties' name, in the aforementioned town and in these parts, as chief justice, captain and our leader, whom we might all respect, until an account of these events had been sent to Your Royal Highnesses so that You might provide for what is best suited to Your service. And seeing that no person was better fitted for such a responsibility than Fernando Cortés, for in addition to being the person most suited, he is most zealous in the service of Your Majesties, and also has much experience in these lands through the Royal offices and commands he has held from Your Majesties in the islands, in which he has always given good account of himself: moreover he spent all he had to come with this fleet in Your Majesties' service and held of small account, as we have already related, all he might have gained if he had continued to trade as had been agreed, we appointed

7. The island turned out to be one of the Azores, not the Canaries.
† From Hernán Cortés: Letters from Mexico, translated and edited by Anthony Pagden (New Haven: Yale University Press, 1987), pp. 27–30, 35–37. Reprinted by permission.

him therefore, in the name of Your Royal Highnesses, chief justice and *alcalde mayor* and received from him the oath required in such cases. When this was done, as is appropriate to Your Majesties' service, we received him in Your Royal name, into our council and chamber, as chief justice and captain of Your Royal armies, and so he is and shall remain until Your Majesties provide whatever is more suitable to Your service. We desire to relate all this to Your Royal Highnesses so that You may be acquainted with all that has passed here and our present position and circumstances.

Having thus completed our business and being all together in our council, we decided to write to Your Majesties and send You all the gold, silver and jewels which we have obtained in the land, over and above the fifth which belongs to Your Royal revenues by law, for we decided that by sending You all the first spoils from these lands, and in keeping nothing for ourselves, we should serve Your Royal Highnesses and demonstrate the very great satisfaction we have in Your service, as we have shown before by venturing our persons and our possessions. When this had been agreed upon we elected as our representatives Alonso Fernández Puerto Carrero and Francisco de Montejo, whom we send to Your Majesties with all that we mention above that they may kiss Your Royal hands on our behalf and in our name, and in the name of this town and council beg Your Royal Highnesses to favor us with certain things necessary for the service of God and Your Majesties and for the common and public good of this town, as is set down at greater length in the instructions which we have given them. Which representatives we do most humbly beseech Your Majesties, with all the reverence which we owe You, to receive, and give Your Royal hands for them to kiss on our behalf, and to grant us all the favors which they, in the name of this council and ourselves, shall request of You, for besides doing a great service to Our Lord thereby, this town and council would reckon it a most singular grace such as we daily hope Your Royal Highnesses may see fit to bestow upon us.

In a previous section of this letter we said that we were sending Your Royal Highnesses an account of this land so that Your Highnesses might be better acquainted with its customs and riches, of the people who inhabit it, and of the laws and beliefs, rites and ceremonies by which they live. Most Powerful Lords, this land which we have now settled in Your Majesties' name extends for fifty leagues along the coast on either side of this town: the coast is completely flat with sandy beaches which in some places stretch for two leagues or more. The country inland is likewise very flat with most beautiful meadows and streams; and among these are some so beautiful that in all Spain there can be none better, for they are both pleasing to the eye and rich in crops, and well cared for and well situated; and there are places to walk and to graze all kinds of herds.

In this land there is every kind of game, and animals and birds similar to those of our acquaintance, such as deer, and fallow deer, wolves, foxes, partridges, pigeons, several kinds of turtledove, quails, hares and rabbits: so that in the kinds of birds and animals there is no difference between this land and Spain, and there are lions and tigers as well.

Some five leagues inland from the sea, and in certain places less, runs a great range of the most beautiful mountains, and some of these are exceedingly high, but there is one which is much higher than all the others from which one may see a great part of the sea and land; indeed it is so high that if the day is not fine one cannot even see the summit, for the top half of it is all covered by cloud. At other times, however, when the day is very fine one can see the peak rising above the cloud, and it is so white we think it to be covered in snow, and even the natives say it is snow, but as we have not seen it very clearly, although we have come very close to it, and because this region is so hot, we cannot be certain that it is.

We shall endeavor to see and learn the secret of this and other things of which we have heard so that we may render Your Royal Highnesses a true account, as of the wealth in gold and silver and precious stones which Your Majesties may judge according to the samples we are sending. In our view it cannot be doubted that there must be in this land as much as in that from which Solomon is said to have taken the gold for the temple. But so little time has passed since we first landed that we have been unable to explore more than five leagues inland and some ten or twelve leagues along the coast on either side of the place where we landed, although from the sea there appears to be much more, and indeed we saw more while sailing hither.

The people who inhabit this land, from the island of Cozume[1] and the cape of Yucatan to the place where we are now, are of medium height and of well-proportioned bodies and features, save that in each province their customs are different; some pierce their ears and put very large and ugly objects into them; others pierce their nostrils down to the lip and put in them large round stones which look like mirrors; and others still split their lower lips as far as the gums and hang there some large stones or gold ornaments so heavy that they drag the lips down, giving a most deformed appearance. The clothes they wear are like large, highly colored yashmaks; the men cover their shameful parts, and on the top half of their bodies wear thin mantles which are decorated in a Moorish fashion. The common women wear highly colored mantles from the waist to the feet, and others which cover their breasts, leaving the rest uncovered.

The women of rank wear skirts of very thin cotton, which are very loose-fitting and decorated and cut in the manner of a rochet.

The food they eat is maize and some chili peppers, as on the other islands, and *patata yuca,* just the same as is eaten in Cuba, and they eat it roast, for they do not make bread of it; and they both hunt and fish and breed many chickens such as those found on *Tierra Firme,* which are as big as peacocks.

There are some large towns and well laid out. The houses in those parts where there is stone are of masonry and mortar and the rooms are small and low in the Moorish fashion. In those parts where there is no stone they make their houses of adobes, which are white-washed and the roofs covered with straw. There are houses belonging to certain men of rank which are very cool and have many rooms, for we have seen as many as five courtyards in a single house, and the rooms around them very well laid out, each man having a private room. Inside there are also wells and water tanks and rooms for slaves and servants of which they have many. Each of these chieftains has in front of the entrance to his house a very large courtyard and some two or three or four of them raised very high with steps up to them and all very well built. Likewise they have their shrines and temples with raised walks which run all around the outside and are very wide: there they keep the idols which they worship, some of stone, some of clay and some of wood, which they honor and serve with such customs and so many ceremonies that many sheets of paper would not suffice to give Your Royal Highnesses a true and detailed account of them all. And the temples where they are kept are the largest and the best and the finest built of all the buildings found in the towns; and they are much adorned with rich hanging cloths and featherwork and other fineries.

Each day before beginning any sort of work they burn incense in these temples and sometimes sacrifice their own persons, some cutting their tongues, others their ears, while there are some who stab their bodies with knives. All the blood which flows from them they offer to those idols, sprinkling it in all parts of the temple, or sometimes throwing it into the air or performing many other ceremonies, so that nothing is begun without sacrifice having first been made. They have a most horrid and abominable custom which truly ought to be punished and which until now we have seen in no other part, and this is that, whenever they wish to ask something of the idols, in order that their plea may find more acceptance, they take many girls and boys and even adults, and in the presence of the idols they open their chests while they are still alive and take out their hearts and entrails and burn them before the idols, offering the smoke as sacrifice. Some of us have seen this, and they say it is the most terrible and frightful thing they have ever witnessed.

This these Indians do so frequently that, as we have been informed, and, in part, have seen from our own experience during the short while we have been here, not one year passes in which they do not kill and sacrifice some fifty persons in each temple; and this is done and held as customary from the island of Cozumel to this land where we now have settled. Your Majesties may be most certain that, as this land seems to us to be very large, and to have many temples in it, not one year has passed, as far as we have been able to discover, in which three or four thousand souls have not been sacrificed in this manner. Let Your Royal Highnesses consider, therefore, whether they should not put an end to such evil practices, for certainly Our Lord God would be well pleased if by the hand of Your Royal Highnesses these people were initiated and instructed in our Holy Catholic Faith, and the devotion, trust and hope which they have in these their idols were transferred to the divine power of God; for it is certain that if they were to worship the true God with such fervor, faith and diligence, they would perform many miracles. And we believe that it is not without cause that Our Lord God has been pleased that these parts be discovered in the name of Your Royal Highnesses so that Your Majesties may gain much merit and reward in the sight of God by commanding that these barbarous people be instructed and by Your hands be brought to the True Faith. For, as far as we have been able to learn, we believe that had we interpreters and other people to explain to them the error of their ways and the nature of the True Faith, many of them, and perhaps even all, would soon renounce their false beliefs and come to the true knowledge of God; for they live in a more civilized and reasonable manner than any other people we have seen in these parts up to the present.

To attempt to give Your Majesties all the details about this land and its people might lead us to make some mistakes in our account, for there is much we have not seen but only heard from the natives, and therefore we venture only to render account of those things which Your Majesties may hold to be most true and certain. Your Majesties may, if You see fit, send a report to the Holy Father, so that diligence and good order may be applied to the work of converting these people, for it is hoped that much may be gained thereby; also that His Holiness may permit and approve that the wicked and the rebellious, after having first been admonished, may be punished as enemies of our Holy Catholic Faith. This will be the occasion of a fearsome warning and example to those who are obstinate in coming to the knowledge of the truth; and the great evils which they practice in the service of the Devil may be prevented. For in addition to those which we list above, of the children and men and women which they kill and offer in their sacrifices, we have been informed, and are most certain it is true, that they are all sodomites and practice that abominable sin. In all of which we entreat Your Majesties to provide as You judge most fitting to the service of God and Your Royal Highnesses and that we who are here in Your service be favored and rewarded.

* * *

FRAY BARTOLOMÉ DE LAS CASAS

From A Brief Account of the Destruction of the Indies (1542)[†]

The Indies were discovered in the year 1492. The following year Christian Spaniards went to settle them, so that it has been forty-nine years since a large number of Spaniards went there. The first land they went to settle in was the great and fortunate island of Hispaniola, which is six hundred leagues in circumference.[1] There are endless other large islands around it in every direction, all of which, as we witnessed, were as settled and filled with native people—the local Indians—as any land on earth could be. The Mainland,[2] which is two hundred fifty leagues or more from this island at its closest, has had more than ten thousand leagues of seacoast discovered, and every day more is discovered; and all of it as full of people as a beehive, for it seems that God put the greater part of human kind into those lands.

All these endless peoples were created utterly simple by God, with no guile or duplicity, completely obedient, faithful to their natural lords and to the Christians whom they serve. They are the most humble, patient, peaceful, and tranquil, the least quarrelsome and contentious, the most lacking in quarrels, bickering, anger, hatred, or desire for vengeance of all the peoples in the world. They are likewise the most delicate, feeble, and tender in constitution, who are least able to withstand hard labor, and who die most easily of any illness. Not even the children of princes and lords among us, raised in a delicate life of luxury, are more delicate than these people, even those among them who come from a line of peasants. They are also the poorest of peoples, those who possess the least and who have the least desire to possess earthly goods, and thus they are neither proud nor ambitious nor avaricious. Their food is like what the saintly

---

[†] Translation and notes by David Frye.
1. Like Columbus, whose log book served as his main source, Las Casas tends to exaggerate distances and areas by a factor of about two.
2. *Tierra Firme*; specifically Panama, the first part of continental America to be colonized; more broadly, all of North and South America.

fathers in the desert must have eaten; it is just as scanty, meager, and unappetizing. Their normal clothing is nakedness, covering only their shameful parts; at most, they cover themselves with a cotton cloth, which would be something like a yard and a half or two yards of cloth square. Their beds are mats, or at most they sleep in something like a net that they hang up, which in the language of Hispaniola they call *hamacas*.[3]

Their intellects are likewise clear, unworried, and lively, very capable and docile for any good doctrine; they are quite ready to receive our holy Catholic faith and to be endowed with virtuous habits, and are the people who have the fewest impediments in this regard of any that God created on earth. And once they begin to find out about the matters of faith, they are so insistent on learning and exercising the sacraments of the Church and divine worship that, to tell the truth, priests need to be endowed by God with a sizable portion of patience in order to bear them. And, finally, many times over many years I have heard many lay Spaniards, unable to deny the goodness that they see in them, say: "These people were surely the most blessed in the world, if only they had known God."

Among these tame sheep, who had been endowed by their Maker and Creator with all the qualities just mentioned, the Spaniards entered just as soon as they learned of them, like cruel and starving wolves and tigers and lions. They have done nothing else for the past forty years—and they still do this today—but tear them to pieces, kill them, distress them, afflict them, torment them and destroy them with strange and new and varied and never before seen nor read about nor heard of manners of cruelty, just a few of which will be mentioned below, to such a degree that in Hispaniola, where we saw more than three million souls living, today no more than two hundred native individuals remain. The island of Cuba is almost as long as from Valladolid to Rome; today it is all but depopulated. The great, fortunate and pleasant islands of San Juan [Puerto Rico] and Jamaica are both laid waste. In the Lucayos [Bahamas]—the northern neighbors of Hispaniola and Cuba, more than seventy islands including those they call the Giant Isles and other islands great and small, the poorest of which are as fertile and pleasant as the King's Garden in Seville, and which are the healthiest lands on earth— where there had been more than half a million souls, today there is not a single being. They killed them all by bringing them to Hispaniola once they saw that they were running out of natives there. A ship spent three years roving through these islands to search for whatever people were left after they had been harvested, because a good Christian was moved by pity for those who might be found to

3. I.e., hammocks, a Taino word.

convert them and win them for Christ. Only eleven people were found; I saw them. More than thirty other islands near the island of San Juan have been depopulated and lost for the same cause. All these islands must cover more than two thousand leagues of land, and all are depopulated and deserted of people.

On the great Mainland we are sure that our Spaniards, with their cruelties and abominable deeds, have depopulated and desolated and left deserted—when before they were filled with rational men—more than ten kingdoms larger than all Spain, even including Aragon and Portugal, and more land than there is from Seville to Jerusalem twice over, which is more than two thousand leagues.

We will set down as a true and certain account that in these forty years, the tyrannies and infernal deeds of the Christians have unjustly and tyrannically killed more than twelve million souls—men, women, and children; indeed I believe, and I do not think I am deceiving myself, that the number is more than fifteen million.

Those who have gone over there and who call themselves Christians have had two main, general methods of annihilating and wiping off the face of the earth those pitiful nations. First, through unjust, cruel, bloody and tyrannical wars. Second, after killing all those who might yearn or sigh or dream of freedom, or of escaping from the torments that befall them, such as the natural lords and the grown men (because in these wars they normally only spare the lives of the young men and the women), by oppressing them with the harshest, most horrible, hardest servitude that any man or beast has ever been forced into. All the infinite other various and sundry ways of desolating these people can be reduced or subordinated to variations on these two types of infernal tyranny.

The cause for which the Christians have killed and destroyed so many infinite numbers of souls has been solely to obtain, as their ultimate end, gold; and to swell with wealth in just a few days; and to rise to high stations, out of proportion to their persons. Let it be known: it is because of their insatiable avarice and ambition, which is as great as could ever be in the world; because those lands are so fortunate and so rich, and their peoples so humble, so patient and so easy to subjugate that they have respected them less and have held them in less account or esteem (I am telling the truth because I know it and have seen it all this time) than, I won't even say beasts (because God grant they might have treated them as well as beasts!), but the dung in the city square. And this is how they have cared for their lives and their souls, and this is why all those numbers and millions that I have mentioned have died without the faith and without the sacraments. And this is a well known and tested truth, which everyone, including the tyrants and killers, knows and will confess: that no Indians anywhere in the Indies have ever done any evil to the

Christians; rather, they took them to have come from heaven, until they or their neighbors had first received many evils, robberies, murders, rapes, and grievances from them themselves.

Hispaniola

In Hispaniola—which, as we have said, was the first island the Christians entered, where they began the ravages and ruin of these peoples; the one they first destroyed and depopulated; where the Christians began to take the women and children of the Indians so as to make use of and to abuse them, and to eat up the food that they had raised by their labor and the sweat of their brows, not being content with what they Indians willingly gave them, according to the ability of each, which was always too little, since normally they keep only what they need and can grow with little labor; and what might suffice for three households of ten persons each for a whole month, a single Christian can eat and destroy in a day; and all the other shows of force and violence and grievances that they did to them—the Indians began to understand that those men must not have come from heaven. Some of them hid their food; others, their women and children; others escaped to the forest to get away from people with such hard and terrible dealings. The Christians slapped and punched them and beat them with sticks, even laying hands on the lords of their towns. Their audacity and shamelessness reached the point that one Christian captain forcibly raped the wife of the greatest king and lord of the whole island. Hence the Indians began to look for ways to expel the Christians from their lands: they took up arms, which were all too feeble and offered little offense and less defense (which is why all their wars are little more than what over here are sports or even child's play); the Christians, with their horses and swords and spears, began to slaughter them with unwonted cruelty.

They entered the towns and did not spare children nor the aged, pregnant women nor those who had just given birth, but disemboweled them and tore them to pieces, as if they had fallen on some lambs hiding in a sheepfold. They made bets on who could split a man in half with the slash of a blade, or cut off his head with a thrust, or spill his entrails. They took babies from their mothers' breasts by the legs, and smashed their heads against the rocks. Others, laughing and joking, hurled them into the rivers, and when they fell in the water they would say: "Look at you kicking!" They would put other babies to the sword together with their mothers and anyone else who got in front of them. They built gallows just tall enough so the feet could not quite reach the ground, and taking them thirteen at a time (in honor of Our Redeemer and the twelve apostles) they would set fire and burn them alive. Others they would tie up from head to foot in dry grass, set it on fire, and burn them that way. With others—all those that they wanted to take alive—they would cut off both their hands and hang them around their necks, saying "Carry these letters," that is, bring the news to the people who had fled into the forests.

Normally they killed the lords and nobles in this way: they would make grills out of poles propped on forked sticks, tie them up on them, and set a slow fire beneath them, so that little by little, screaming, desperate, and in torment, they would give up their souls. One time I saw they had four or five nobles and lords burning on these grills (and I think they even had two or three pairs of grills where they were burning more); and because they were screaming very loudly and shaming the captain, or interrupting his sleep, he ordered them drowned. And the bailiff who was burning them, who was worse than an executioner (and I know his name, and even met his relatives in Seville), did not want to drown them; instead, with his own hands he put sticks in their mouths so that they could not shout, and stirred the flames until they roasted as slowly as he liked.

I saw all the things described above, and endless others as well. And because all the people who were able to do so would hole up in the forests and climb the mountains to escape from such inhuman men, such ruthless and ferocious beasts, annihilators and mortal enemies of human kind, they trained hounds, savage dogs that would tear an Indian to pieces on sight in no time, and would rather go after and eat an Indian than a pig. These dogs wreaked havoc and butchery. And because on a few rare occasions the Indians killed some Christians, with perfect right and saintly justice, the Christians made it a law among themselves that for every Christian the Indians killed, they would kill a hundred Indians.

The Former Kingdoms of Hispaniola

On this island of Hispaniola there were five main, large kingdoms, and five powerful kings who were obeyed by almost all the innumerable other lords, given that a few lords of a few remote provinces recognized no superiors.

The first kingdom was called Maguá (with the accent on the last syllable), which means Kingdom of the Meadow.[4] This meadow is one of the most remarkable and wonderful things in the world, because it stretches for eighty leagues from the Southern Sea to the

---

4. *La Vega*; meaning a well-watered plain with scattered trees. The plain that Las Casas describes crosses Hispaniola from northwest to southeast; the town of La Vega lies at its center, just south of Santiago, Dominican Republic.

Northern Sea.[5] It is five, eight, even ten leagues wide, and has very high land on either side. More than thirty thousand streams and rivers empty into it, the twelve largest of which are as big as the Ebro, Duero, and Guadalquivir.[6] All the rivers that flow from the mountain range on one side (twenty-five thousand of them) are very rich in gold. This mountain range contains the province of Cibao, which is the source of the well-known gold, so high in carats, that has gained such fame over here.

The king and lord of this kingdom was named Guarionex. He had such great lords as vassals that one of them gathered sixteen thousand fighting men to serve Guarionex; I knew some of them. This King Guarionex was very obedient and virtuous, naturally peaceful and devoted to the kings of Castile. Some years, at his command, every householder among his people gave as much gold as fit in the hollow of a bell; later, when they could no longer fill them, they cut the bells in half and they gave that half filled, because the Indians of that island had almost no facility for mining gold. This cacique[7] offered to serve the king of Castile by making a farm that would stretch from Isabela, which was the first settlement of the Christians, to the city of Santo Domingo, which is fifty long leagues, so that they would not demand gold of him, because he truthfully said that his vassals did not know how to obtain it. I know that he could have made the farm that he said he would make, and he would have done so happily, and it would have been worth more than thirty million *castellanos*[8] a year to the king, and this farm would even have caused there to be on the island today more than fifty cities as large as Seville.

The way they repaid this lord and king, who was so good and so great, was to dishonor him through his wife, a bad Christian captain raping her for him. He, who could have bided his time and raised his people to take vengeance, resolved to go away, himself alone, to hide and die, in exile from his kingdom and status, to a province called Los Ciguayos where a great lord was his vassal. As soon as the Spaniards noticed he was missing, there was no sheltering him from them. They went and made war on the lord who was keeping him and committed great massacres there, until at last they found him and arrested him, and put him imprisoned in chains and shackles on a ship to bring him to Castile. The ship was lost at sea, and with

5. The Atlantic. "Southern Sea": usually refers to the Pacific, but here Las Casas means the Caribbean.
6. The largest rivers in Spain.
7. A Taino word for "lord" or "ruler." This became the standard Spanish word for "Indian chief" all over the Americas.
8. A gold coin of the era, weighing approximately one sixth of a troy ounce.

it many Christians were drowned and a large quantity of gold perished, among it the great nugget that was like a bread loaf and weighed three thousand six hundred *castellanos*: Thus God took vengeance on these great injustices.

The next kingdom was called El Marién, where Puerto Real[9] is today, at the northern end of the Meadow. It was larger than the kingdom of Portugal, though a good deal more pleasant and worthy of being populated, and had many great mountain ranges and rich mines of gold and copper; its king was named Guacanagarí (accent on the last syllable), under whom were many great lords, many of whom I saw and knew. This king's land was the first landing place of the former Admiral who discovered the Indies; he was received that first time by Guacanagarí, when he discovered the island, with such humaneness and charity, together with all the Christians who went with him, and he gave them such a gentle and gracious reception, assisting in their resupply (the Admiral having even lost there the ship in which he had been traveling) that they could not have received better in their own country or from their own parents. I know this from the account and words of the Admiral himself. This king died escaping from the massacres and cruelties of the Christians, destroyed and deprived of his status, lost in the forests. All the other lords who were his subjects died in the tyranny and servitude that will be spoken of below.

The third kingdom and domain was La Maguana, another wonderful, healthy and fertile land, where today the best sugar on that island is produced. Its king was named Caonabó. In courage, status, and dignity, and in ceremonies in his service, he exceeded all the others. He was arrested with great subtlety and evil one day when he was safe at home. They later put him on a ship to bring him to Castile, and when six ships were in the port ready to leave, God wished to show the great iniquity and injustice of this and other deeds. That night He sent a storm that sank all the ships and drowned all the Christians in them; Caonabó died there, weighed down by chains and shackles.

This lord had three or four brothers who were as manly and courageous as he. Seeing how unjustly their lord and brother had been imprisoned, and the devastation and massacres that the Christians had committed in other kingdoms, especially after they found out that the king their brother had died, they rose up in arms against the Christians to take their vengeance. The Christians went out against them, some on horse (which is the most pernicious weapon there could be against the Indians), and wreaked so much havoc and so

---

9. One of the first Spanish towns founded on Hispaniola (1503). Abandoned in 1578, its ruins were discovered in 1975 near modern Cap-Haïtien, Haiti.

many massacres that they desolated and depopulated half of that entire kingdom.

The fourth kingdom is the one they called Xaraguá. This was like the core or the brains or the court of that entire island. It surpassed the others in having the most polished language and speech, the most well-ordered and composed etiquette and breeding, the amount of nobility and generosity, because it had such a great number of lords and nobles, and the beauty and loveliness of all its people. The king and lord here was named Behechio; he had a sister named Anacaona. These two siblings performed great services for the kings of Castile and immense benefits for the Christians, freeing them many times from the threat of death. After the death of King Behechio the kingdom went to Lady Anacaona. One time the governor who governed this island [Nicolás de Ovando] went here with sixty men on horse and more than three hundred infantrymen, the horsemen alone being enough to desolate the entire island and the Mainland as well. More than three hundred trusting lords came there at his calling, and he had most of them put into a large straw house by trickery. Once they were inside, he ordered it set afire and burned them alive. All the others were speared and put to the sword with an infinite number of people; to honor Anacaona, they hanged her. It occurred to some Christians, whether out of pity or out of avarice, to take some children and save them from the slaughter, putting them on their horses' croups; another Spaniard would then come up behind and spear them. Another, if the child was on the ground, would cut off his legs with his sword. A few people who were able to flee from this inhumane cruelty went over to a small island nearby, eight leagues offshore, and the same governor condemned all who had gone there to slavery, because they had fled the butchery.

The fifth kingdom was called Higüey, and it was ruled by an old queen named Higuanama. She was hanged, and I saw an endless number of people burned alive and torn to pieces and tortured in various new methods of death and torture, and all those who were taken alive were made slaves.

There are so many details about the massacres and injuries of these peoples that they could never all be written down, because I truly believe that, no matter how much is said about it, only the thousandth part could be explained. Therefore, regarding these wars, I want only to conclude by saying and declaring that, by God and my conscience, I hold it to be certain that, for all the injustices and evils mentioned here, and yet more that might be mentioned, the Indians gave no more cause nor had more guilt than a monastery full of good and obedient monks might have, that they should be robbed and murdered, and that those who might be left alive should be placed in perpetual captivity and servitude as slaves. I also declare that, before all the multitudes of peoples on that island were killed and desolated, I cannot imagine nor believe that they had committed a single mortal sin against the Christians that was punishable by men. As for those sins reserved for God's punishment, such as desires for vengeance, hatred, and wrath, which those peoples may have felt against such mortal enemies as were the Christians, I believe that very few of the Indians fell into these, and they were little more impetuous or violent, from my experience with them, than children of ten or twelve years of age. And I know with absolute certainty that the Indians always had the most just causes for war against the Christians, and that the Christians never fought a just war against the Indians; rather, theirs were always unjust and diabolical, and much worse than could be said of any tyrant in the world. And I declare the same of all the wars fought throughout the Indies.

After the wars had ended and all the men had been killed in them, so that generally only young men, women, and children were left, these were divided among [the Christians, who] gave thirty to one, forty to another, one hundred or two hundred to another, depending on the favor each held with the head tyrant who was called governor. They were divided up like this and doled out to the Christians under the pretext that they would teach them the matters of the Catholic faith, making them pastors of souls even though they were generally all idiots and cruel, miserly, and depraved men. And the care or concern that they showed was to send the men to the mines to gather gold, which is intolerable labor, and they put the women on their *estancias*, which means farms, to plow fields and cultivate the land—work for strong and hardy men.

They gave neither the men nor the women anything to eat but plants and things without any substance. The milk dried up in the breast of the women who gave birth, and so all their babies quickly died. Since their husbands were kept apart and never saw their wives, their progeny came to an end. The men died in the mines from hard labor and hunger, and the women died in the *estancias* or farms from the same causes, and thus so many masses of peoples on that island died that you would have thought all the peoples on earth had expired. To mention only the burdens: they were burdened with three or four *arrobas*, which they carried one hundred or two hundred leagues, and the Christians had themselves carried in hammocks, which are like nets, on the Indians' backs, as if the Indians were beasts of burden.[1] They had sores on their shoulders and backs

---

1. The Dominican report of 1519, on which Las Casas bases this denunciation, stated that Indian porters were forced to carry burdens of two *arrobas* (fifty pounds) for distances of sixty to seventy leagues. Human portage was common throughout the Americas, which had no beasts of burden (other than llamas in the Andes, which could carry no more than a man) before horses and donkeys were brought from Europe.

from these burdens, like over-burdened beasts. To say the same of the whippings, beatings, punches, kicks, curses, and thousand other forms of torture that they gave them at labor, in truth there could never be time nor paper enough to describe it all, which would horrify men.

And it is noteworthy that the ruin and destruction of these islands and lands began after they learned of the death of the most serene Queen Isabel, which was in the year 1504, because up until then on this island alone they had destroyed only a few provinces through unjust war, but not the whole island, and most of the provinces were sheltered by the queen. Because the queen, may she rest in holy glory, took the greatest care and wonderful zeal in the salvation and prosperity of those peoples, as those of us know who saw these examples with our own eyes and felt them with our own hands.

CRITICISM

MORRIS BISHOP

From The Odyssey of Cabeza de Vaca[†]

Chapter XI. Mexico

For an hour, perhaps for a day, the joy in Cabeza de Vaca's breast was unmixed. Then gradually his vision cleared; he began to perceive the Spaniards, not as symbols of rescue, of home-coming, of the happy issue out of all affliction, but as human individuals with qualities of their own. The bright light of bliss faded, and out of the dazzle emerged mental topographies which the wanderer could recognize only too well. During the long captivity, he had dreamed of the white men as all kind, all virtuous; he had dreamed away their pettiness and cruelty. Now, as memory stirred, he remembered the old outlines of the pitiless, heavy-handed conquistador. He remembered, even, himself.

He was conscious, too, that his joy, religious in essence, made up of gratitude to his kind Savior, was met only by surprise, which changed gradually to the satisfaction of heartless self-interest. The captain, Diego de Alcaraz,[1] soon disclosed that all the wonder of Cabeza de Vaca's great journey was nothing to him beside the failure of his slave-hunting foray. And a certain greedy smile showed the forming of his sordid purpose, to use the Child of the Sun as a slave-decoy.

His expedition, which had begun with success, was now in a sorry state. Not only had the natives fled their villages to take refuge in the mountains; they had destroyed or hidden their crops of corn and beans. The Spaniards, too inexpert to live off the country, found themselves wandering through a hungry solitude.

From this pass they were relieved by the arrival of Dorantes and Castillo and six hundred Indian followers, "men and women, some with nursing babies in their arns, and with their mouths besmeared with corn pudding."[2] "Since you are so powerful," said Alcaraz, "send forth word to all the natives of this region to return to their villages. Tell the pigs we won't touch them. And tell them to bring food."

"This last was unnecessary," says Cabeza de Vaca's record, "the Indians being ever diligent to bring us all they could. Directly we

† From The Odyssey of Cabeza de Vaca, by Morris Bishop (New York: The Century Co., 1933), pp. 145–163.

1. "A man unfitted to have people under his command," Pedro de Castañeda, "Expedition of Coronado," in Spanish Explorers in the Southern United States, 1528–1543, edited by Frederick W. Hodge. New York: Charles Scribner's Sons, 1907, 303.
2. Fernández de Oviedo y Valdés, Gonzalo "The Expedition of Pánfilo de Narváez," trans. ed. by Harbert Davenport, Southwestern Historical Quarterly, xxvii–xxviii (Oct. 1923–Oct. 1924): 612.

sent our messengers to call them, when there came six hundred souls, bringing us all the maize in their possession. They fetched it in certain pots, closed with clay, which they had concealed in the earth. They brought us whatever else they had; but we, wishing only to have the provision, gave the rest to the Christians, that they might divide among themselves. After this we had many high words with them; for they wished to make slaves of the Indians we brought."

It was a conflict of irreconcilable minds. Captain Diego de Alcaraz was a familiar type of colonial subjugator, and a worthy subordinate of the infamous Nuño de Guzmán, governor of Nueva Galicia, who had inaugurated the export of natives to the Antillean gold-mines, Indian graves. It was Governor Nuño de Guzmán who caused several natives to be hung for failing to sweep the roads before him. Although, to be sure, the enslavement of Indians was illegal, interest found definitions which permitted the fact of slavery under improved names. The encomienda system, by which each settler was rendered responsible for "the spiritual welfare" of even hundreds of natives, flourished in Mexico. By the carrier system, officials could impress any needed number of Indians to act as burden-bearers. With such legal resources, an unscrupulous governor, like Nuño de Guzmán, and his fortune-hunters in the far northwest could laugh at the pious regulations of the authorities in the City of Mexico.

A curious feature of the formal code of gentlemanliness is that the obligations of honor are enforced toward gentlemen alone. To Diego de Alcaraz the capture of slaves by false promises was a war-like stratagem, as justifiable toward Indians as toward the Moors of Spain. Cabeza de Vaca had learned, in his wanderings, so many codes that he had a little forgotten, perhaps, the old formula of the gentlemen. So high words followed, and much anger, with no possibility of compromise. The Indians stood by, gaping; they understood no words, but they comprehended well that the Children of the Sun were very angry with the bad white men who carried off their wives and brothers.

Cabeza de Vaca turned to his followers, and in their own tongue bade them begone to their homes. At this they protested.

> They were willing to do nothing until they had gone with us and delivered us into the hands of other Indians, as had been the custom; for, if they returned without doing so, they were afraid they should die, and, going with us, they feared neither Christians nor lances. Our countrymen became jealous at this, and caused their interpreter to tell the Indians that we were of them, and for a long time we had been lost; that they were the lords of the land who must be obeyed and served, while we were persons of mean condition and small force. The Indians cared little or

nothing for what was told them; and conversing among themselves said the Christians lied: that we had come whence the
sun rises, and they whence it goes down; we healed the sick,
they killed the sound; that we had come naked and barefooted,
while they had arrived in clothing and on horses with lances;
that we were not covetous of anything, but all that was given to
us we directly turned to give, remaining with nothing; that the
others had the only purpose to rob whomsoever they found,
bestowing nothing on any one.

Cabeza de Vaca spoke to his Indians, these comely and kindly
people, as he calls them, and told them that they must obey and not
question; that the Children of the Sun had come to the end of their
journey, and their work was done; that the faithful servants of
the Children of the Sun must now leave their masters and return
home in peace and till their fields. For the Children of the Sun too
were going to their home. And once there, they would not forget their
friends, but would think of them often, and bless them, and pray for
them, as they too had learned to pray. So he would bless them now,
in the name of the Father, and the Son, and the Holy Ghost. . . .

He drew the sign of the cross in the air; the Indians, as they had
been taught, spread their arms wide, to make of their bodies the
holy crucifix.

> The Indians, at taking their leave, told us they would do what we
> commanded, and would settle in their towns, if the Christians
> would suffer them; and this I say and affirm most positively,
> that, if they have not done so, it is the fault of the Christians.

Alcaraz and his men seemed strangely quieted and polite. They
were impressed, perhaps, by the moving scene of leave-taking.
Alcaraz detailed a lieutenant, Cebreros, and a guard of honor, to
lead the four on the back trail south to the frontier outpost of Culiacan. The way was curiously difficult, mountainous, and solitary. No
Indian was encountered in that desert. They were lost; they could
find no stream, no waterhole. They passed two days in the burning
country, without water. Seven men died. The steadfast reached at
last a village of friendly Indians, near Culiacan, the present capital
of Sinaloa.

There the four learned that they had been brought south by a
crazy roundabout mountain route, only in order that they should
meet no tale-bearing native. And in that time gained, Alcaraz had
fallen upon the six hundred Indian companions and had taken them
for slaves.

Perhaps it was at this moment that Cabeza de Vaca, sick with
man's treachery, undoing God's blessing, vowed to make reparation
for the enslaved six hundred, and for all the misery of the subject

race. In the midst of anger, grief, and bewildered prayer, he may now have sworn to spend his life in the service of these simple people, to act as a mediator between the strong and the weak. For this, he felt, the Lord had given him his experience of the most abject weakness. "Who is weak, and I am not weak? Who is offended, and I burn not?"

He was aware of evil, drowning in it. He knew that he must not sink gently in that sea, and sinking exclaim that evil had disappeared, because it was universal. If he should breathe in that universal evil his soul would die.

Through some such spiritual passion Las Casas had passed when, a priest in Cuba, he found for his Pentecost sermon of 1514 the text of Ecclesiasticus: "The bread of the needy is their life; he that defraudeth him thereof is a man of blood. He that taketh away his neighbor's living slayeth him; and he that defraudeth the laborer of his hire is a shedder of blood." From that day of revelation until his death in 1566 Las Casas had no other purpose but to comfort and succor the desolate millions of the new world.

In the face of Cabeza de Vaca's anger, Cebreros fled by night to put his case before Melchior Díaz, the alcalde mayor in charge of the garrison and at the same time the vice-governor of the district. Unfortunately for Cebreros and Alcaraz, fortunately for Cabeza de Vaca, Melchior Díaz was an honorable man, with bowels of mercy.[3] He came in all haste to the village where the four Christians lay. "He wept with us, giving praises to God our Lord for having extended over us so great care. He comforted and entertained us hospitably. In behalf of the governor, Nuño de Guzmán, and himself, he tendered all that he had, and the service in his power. He showed much regret for the seizure, and the injustice we had received from Alcaraz and others. We were sure, had he been present, what was done to the Indians and to us would never have occurred."

Melchior Díaz could ease somewhat Cabeza de Vaca's dismal apprehensions as to the lot of the natives. The slave-hunters were acting on very questionable orders. The second Mexican Audiencia, in 1530, had issued stringent regulations against slavery, which, though much disregarded, could be enforced by a willing vice-governor. Don Diego Fernández de Proaño, Melchior Díaz's predecessor at Culiacan, had about two years before been tried, and condemned to death—though later pardoned—for branding, chaining, and selling gangs of Indians. But just recently, in the current year of 1536, Governor Nuño de Guzmán in Compostela had sanc-

---

3. He was destined to die grotesquely, while with Coronado's expedition in 1541. Riding at a gallop, he cast his lance at a marauding dog. The lance bounded, caught with butt in earth, and pierced him through the body, rupturing his bladder. Castañeda, in *Spanish Explorers in the Southern United States*, 325.

tioned the enslavement of rebels, conspirators, and disturbers of the peace. This was taken by his agents as a license for general slave-taking. Well, the conscienceless govenor's provincial decree could not invalidate the king's laws for all of Mexico. In fact, as the event proved, Nuño de Guzmán paid dear for his greedy temerity. "There was so much cruelty in making these slaves," says a chronicler, "that the clamor of the innocent reached the pious and Christian ears of the King our Lord, who provided an efficient remedy," to wit, a judicial examination of Nuño de Guzmán, resulting in degradation, imprisonment, and confiscation of property.[4]

Melchior Díaz, a newcomer to the province, recognized all too well the results of Governor Guzmán's countenancing of slave-making. Count pity and humanity but womanish weakness; still it must be recognized that an uninhabited country is valueless to any conqueror. The only salvation of the land lay in the suppression of slavery and the tempting back of the people from their mountain refuges.

> The alcalde mayor besought us to tarry there, since by so doing we could be of eminent service to God and your Majesty; the deserted land was without tillage and everywhere badly wasted, the Indians were fleeing and concealing themselves in the thickets, unwilling to occupy their towns; we were to send and call them, commanding them in behalf of God and the king, to return to live in the vales and cultivate the soil.

Cabeza de Vaca, Dorantes, and Castillo shook their heads doubtfully. All their escort had been dismissed, and with the escort had vanished, perhaps, the tradition of miracle and authority. These Indians spoke an unfamiliar language. But still—the purpose of Díaz was their own. They had succeeded already in many a more unlikely venture.

They chose two native captives who had accompanied them as carriers and who had seen the arrival of the six hundred faithful from the north. They had heard of the god-like origin of the Children of the Sun, and had had direct testimony of wonders worked, of ailments cured, and of the kind bounties of the strangers. These two had their fetters struck off; they were ordered to go, with others of the town, to the hostile tribes in the mountains, and to bring summons from the men of God. The tribesmen must come to the feet of the men of God, who wished to speak with them. The messengers bore, as a symbol and as a guarantee, one of the holy orbs of the Children of the Sun, a rattling gourd filled with stones, carried reverently in the white men's hands from the lower Río Grande.

---

4. Coopwood, Bethel. "The Route of Cabeza de Vaca," *Texas State History Quarterly* 3 (1899–1900): 257.

For seven days no word came, and the Christians were turning to the belief that the envoys, having once found safety, had chosen to preserve it. But on the eighth day they returned, with three chiefs and fifteen retainers, bearing gifts of beads, turquoises, and feathers.

> The messengers said they had not found the people of the river where we appeared [the Sinaloa], the Christians having again made them run away into the mountains. Melchior Díaz told the interpreter to speak to the natives for us; to say to them we came in the name of the Lord, who is in heaven; that we had traveled about the world many years, telling all the people we found that they should believe in God and serve him; for he was the Master of all things on the earth, benefiting and rewarding the virtuous, and to the bad giving perpetual punishment of fire; that, when the good die, he takes them to heaven, where none ever die, nor feel cold, nor hunger, nor thirst, nor any inconvenience whatsoever, but the greatest enjoyment possible to conceive; that those who will not believe in him, nor obey his commands, he casts beneath the earth into the company of demons, and into a great fire which is never to go out, but always torment; that, over this, if they desired to be Christians and serve God in the way we required, the Christians would cherish them as brothers and behave toward them very kindly; that we would command they give no offense nor take them from their territories, but be their great friends. If the Indians did not do this, the Christians would treat them very hardly, carrying them away as slaves into other lands.
>
> They answered through the interpreter that they would be true Christians and serve God. Being asked to whom they sacrifice and offer worship, from whom they ask rain for their corn-fields and health for themselves, they answered of a man that is in heaven. We inquired of them his name, and they told us Aguar; and they believe he created the whole world, and the things in it. We returned to question them as to how they knew this; they answered their fathers and grandfathers had told them, that from distant time had come their knowledge, and they knew the rain and all good things were sent to them by him. We told them that the name of him of whom they spoke we called Dios; and if they would call him so, and would worship him as we directed, they would find their welfare. They responded that they well understood, and would do as we said. We ordered them to come down from the mountains in confidence and peace, inhabit the whole country and construct their houses: among these they should build one for God, at its entrance place a cross like that which we had there present; and, when Christians came among them, they should

go out to receive them with crosses in their dwellings, giving of what they have to eat, and the Christians would do them no injury, but be their friends; and the Indians told us they would do as we had commanded.

The captain having given them shawls and entertained them, they returned, taking the two captives who had been used as emissaries. This occurrence took place before the notary, in the presence of many witnesses.

The power of the white man's revelation had not diminished. The natives came flooding into the village, fearless and eager, with gifts of beads and feathers. They promised to build churches and put crosses on them. The priest baptized the tribal chiefs and the children. And Captain Melchior Díaz "made a covenant with God, not to invade nor consent to invasion, nor to enslave any of that country and people, to whom we had guaranteed safety."

When, therefore, Cabeza de Vaca could feel that his friends had found some sort of safety for their bodies in this world and their souls in the next, he was willing to take another step toward his own happiness. He and his companions went the little distance to Culiacan. They arrived there on April 1, 1536, and were obliged to remain until May 15. They dared not advance southward without a considerable guard, for all this country was wasted and in rebellion, only because of Spanish slave-hunts.

During the long delay, good news came from the north. Diego de Alcaraz returned, much mystified. He had received peremptory orders from Melchior Díaz to release his captives; and he had seen, throughout that country, the natives coming down, fearless, from the hills, each with a cross in his hand. In return for the Spaniards' lashes, they brought food; in return for banishment from their homes to the unkindly mountains, they invited the Spaniards to sleep as honored guests in their villages. "The Christians had slept among them over night. They were surprised at a thing so novel; but as the natives said they had been assured of safety, it was ordered that they should not be harmed, and the Christians took friendly leave of them."

The six hundred Indians who had accompanied the four from the north, and who had been so treacherously captured by Alcaraz, were settled on the Rio Fuerte. They were Pima Indians, probably from Ures, the village of the deer hearts. And still to-day, in their village of La Concepción de Bamoa, their descendants speak the Pima tongue in their linguistic island.[5]

---

5. Bandelier, Adolph F. "Contributions to the History of the Southwestern Portion of the United States," Archaeological Institute of America (1890): 650.

On the fifteenth of May, a guard of twenty mounted men being assembled, the four set off for the subjugated regions to the south. On the way they were joined by six Christians with five hundred slaves. It seemed vain to persuade the six Christians to part with all their wealth; but as the procession advanced, the groans of the captives, their bewildered misery, the whipping of the sick to keep up the step in the long chain, the halts to unfetter a laggard to die by the wayside,[6] left unhealing wounds in Cabeza de Vaca's mind. And gradually a bold purpose formed within him, as he walked. When he should come to the Court of King Charles, he would ask the privilege of returning as governor to the land of his slavery, and there give an example of rule by honor and justice. It was a pretty dream, which dispossessed little by little the familiar dreams of beds with sheets, of Spanish hams, of the wines of Jerez.

At the end of a hundred leagues of travel, the convoy arrived at Compostela, hard by the present Tepic. The three hidalgos were most graciously received by Governor Nuño de Guzmán himself. All testimonies concur in recognition of the governor's charming manners and evident culture. It was no doubt with humorous grace that he had personally supervised the burning of his interpreters' feet until the toes dropped off, and had dragged King Tangaxoan at the tail of a horse before burning him at the stake.[7] The govenor's politeness toward the wanderers was due not alone to his gentlemanly instincts. He recognized that, after having witnessed the operations of his slave-gatherers, they were on their way to the court of Mexico, and perhaps to the presence of His Majesty himself. He put his own clothing on the refugees' backs, and showed them to soft and downy beds. This was agony! The persistent softness of cotton tickled their hard bodies, and woolen shirts bit them like insects. For some time, Cabeza de Vaca confesses, he could sleep nowhere but on the ground.

All Nuño de Guzmán's winning courtesy could not distract the merciful conquistador from his purpose. Secretly, Cabeza de Vaca obtained from a notary a *testimonio*, or certified copy of Nuño de Guzmán's protocol, authorizing his agents to take slaves. Having this safe, he dared to remonstrate with the governor, telling him "that he had let his hand slip."[8] All the governor's courtesy fell away; fearing, no doubt, to resort to violence, he sent the four on their way, after forwarding to the viceroy the best proofs he could contrive of their sun-crazed irresponsibility.

The journey along the old Camino Real, up over the mountains to Mexico, took the form of a triumph. "Many came out on the roads to

6. Bancroft, Hubert Howe. *History of Mexico*, vol. II, San Francisco: A. L. Bancroft, 1883–1888: 332.
7. Bancroft, *History of Mexico*, II, 345–6.
8. Coopwood, 261.

gaze at us, giving thanks to God for saving us from so many calamities." Arriving in Mexico on July 23, they were most handsomely received by the viceroy Antonio de Mendoza, and by Hernán Cortés, Marqués del Valle, who was leading an irritable existence as subordinate in the land he had conquered. The viceregal wardrobe was put at the gentlemen's disposal; they sighed and shuddered as they donned gold-laced brocades, but a Spanish hidalgo might not walk the streets of Mexico in a breech-clout. However, Spanish foods and wines made a happy change from Aztec diet, the everlasting tamales and tortillas, with such delicacies as frog spawn and stewed ants peppered with chile. On St. James's Day, July 25, a bull-fight and a joust with canes was held in the newcomers' honor. Meanwhile Estebanico swaggered among the Spanish negroes who filled the capital.[9]

At the first opportunity Cabeza de Vaca sought a private interview with Viceroy Antonio de Mendoza. This gentleman, commonly referred to as "el bueno," was an honest and intelligent administrator. Austere and ascetic in physical habit and in character, he had been chosen to suppress the abuses of the colony. After the conqueror, fearless and bold, and also lawless, thievish, brutal, and reckless of any permanent good, comes the organizer, the legalist. Mendoza received grimly the news from the northwest. He noted down a reprimand for Captains Alcaraz and Cebreros.[1] He accepted Cabeza's *testimonio* and added it to a bulging dossier marked "Nuño de Guzmán." "Have no fear on that score," he said. "I have just had word from Spain that His Majesty is sending out a special judge to investigate and try his case, and I warrant you there shall be no slackness." He was indeed imprisoned, tried, and condemned about the end of the year.

Mendoza showed particular interest in the travelers' tales of the north country which, the first of any Christians, they had explored. How much gold had they seen? Only traces and indications, they admitted, but there were circumstantial stories of great cities to the north, beyond a desert. They had received a gift of emeralds, with a veracious account of their origin. Don Antonio's eyes gleamed with satisfaction. This news fitted with another report, each certified the other. Had they heard of the Isle of the Amazons, where the fierce, rich, man-hating women dwelt? No, to be sure; but as they had traveled south in the lee of the western mountains they had heard that the coast of the South Sea abounded with pearls and riches. It was not conclusive, but there was enough in the story to tempt further

9. The number of negroes was regarded as a menace as early as 1523, and their numbers were restricted. In 1537 a negro plot to massacre the Spanish and seize the country was bloodily suppressed. Bancroft, *History of Mexico*, II, 384–5.
1. Bandelier, "Southwestern Historical Contributions," 75.

exploration. He ordered the refugees to make a map of their wanderings, and this they did.

If some researcher will discover that map in the Archives of
Mexico or Spain, he will settle many a dispute.

Cabeza de Vaca had, in his turn, a diffident question to ask. Had
news come from Spain of the grant to any man of the rights once
issued to Narváez—the right to explore and colonize "Florida," the
present Florida and all the gulf region to Pánuco? No, said Mendoza;
since the disappearance of Narváez none had shown any desire to
visit those ill-omened shores. The field was free; Cabeza de Vaca
could ask the privilege as well as another.

That summer and autumn of 1536 and the following winter were
spent in Mexico. Cabeza de Vaca was eager to return to Spain; but
a ship in which he spoke for passage in October foundered; and all
through the winter no vessels braved the winter gales. Time passed
agreeably in the diversions of the capital. And a task which provided the three gentlemen with much occupation was the redaction
of a report on the great journey. When finished, it was forwarded to
the Audiencia of Hispaniola, which was the General Headquarters
of the Spanish colonies. Although the report itself has disappeared,
Oviedo, the contemporary historian, consulted it, and made an
ample summary in his History of the Indies. Dorantes's share in the
work is evident; the episodes of the long captivity on the Texas coast
are told from his point of view. Oviedo's abstract enlightens many
difficult passages of Cabeza de Vaca's personal narrative.

During the winter in Mexico, Don Antonio the viceroy sought to
persuade the three gentlemen to remain with him. With all secrecy,
for fear of his ambitious rival Cortés, he outlined a scheme of exploration and conquest to the seven golden cities of Cíbola, beyond the
northern deserts. It was notorious that Nuño de Guzmán owned a
Tejos (Texas) Indian who was the son of a trader, long deceased,
whose business had been the transport of feathered plumes for head
dresses. These he had carried across the desert to beautiful cities,
and bartered for great weight of gold and silver, base metals of that
country.

This Tejos slave, when a boy, said the viceroy, had once or twice
accompanied his father, and he had seen with his own eyes cities as
large as Mexico and its suburbs. There were seven of these cities,
and in them whole rows of streets inhabited by gold and silver work-
ers. To reach them it was necessary to cross a desert for forty days,
barren of any growth except a dry grass five inches high. What other
proof was needed than the emeralds that Cabeza and his companions had brought home from the north? Very well; let them remember that in the eighth century, when the Arabs invaded Portugal, the
Bishop of Lisbon took his flock and sailed west into the ocean until

he came to a land he called Antillia, and there he founded seven noble cities, perhaps in the same region as the lost continent of Atlantis. Some of the first discoverers thought they had found this country, wherefor the islands are still called the Antilles. Clearly they were mistaken; the old story must point to the Seven Cities of Cíbola.

Now, continued the viceroy, would not the gentlemen remain and lead an expedition which he would raise and equip? With their knowledge of the country and their prestige among the natives they could find their way where all others would fail. They would be well rewarded; as a guarantee, in case of failure or success, he would marry them to certain rich widows and give them fine estates and large encomiendas of docile natives. And in case of success the rewards would be illimitable and unimaginable!

Cabeza de Vaca resolutely put away the temptation. He had other purposes, the first of which was to see His Majesty the King and Emperor. Whatever power he might win must come from the fountainhead itself. He would be the agent of no subordinate, not even a viceroy. He had his own plans of government, which might prove most unacceptable to a viceroy, Mendoza or his successor; he could not risk the checkmating of all his purpose by a peremptory order from his superior. Probably also he regarded the dreams of golden cities as mere chimeras. What tangible proof had he seen of these legends? Only a copper rattle with a crudely indicated face, and a handful of emeralds; perhaps not genuine emeralds at all!

Dorantes, as well as Cabeza de Vaca, refused the bait. Dorantes had had his bellyful of adventure; his chief desire was to see again his home in Béjar and the serene patios beside the Seville streets. He made only one concession to Mendoza's purpose; he gave or sold to him his Estebanico, who, no longer Deity's steward, had unquestioningly resumed his status, under civilization, as a slave. Alonso del Castillo, who seems never to have deeply impressed his superiors, remained in Mexico, but to him no captaincies were offered.

Dorantes and Cabeza de Vaca went to Vera Cruz in Lent of 1537, to take ship for home. Three vessels lay in harbor, waiting a fair wind. The two veterans boarded one of the craft; while idling at anchor Cabeza de Vaca was alarmed by the constant rattle of the pumps. Although Dorantes ridiculed his fears, Cabeza de Vaca insisted on transferring to another ship. Dorantes vowed that no peril of the sea could affright one who had cruised the length of the Gulf of Mexico in a crazy barge calked with palmetto fibre; the two would race to Spain. But prudent Cabeza de Vaca would not be robbed of his home-coming for lack of a little care.

The three ships left port on the tenth of April, and sailed together for a hundred and fifty leagues. One morning Cabeza de Vaca looked in vain for his companions. As he afterward learned, the two vessels leaked so badly that the captains turned back in apprehension to Mexico.

Let us return to Mexico with Andrés Dorantes. When Mendoza heard of his return to Vera Cruz, he bade him return to Mexico City. There the viceroy repeated his suggestion of a northern reconnoissance. Dorantes acceded, perhaps fearing further adventures on the sea, perhaps tempted by the prospect of sole command. Mendoza raised some troops, with accompanying clerics, forty or fifty horses, and a baggage train of Indians. He set aside the considerable sum of 3,500 or 4,000 pesos for expenses. "I spent much money for the expedition," he reported to the king,[2] "but I don't know how it happened that the matter came to nothing."

Dorantes continued in official favor. Mendoza married him to a rich widow, María de la Torre, the owner of the wealthy towns of Asala and Jalazintzo, and bestowed another wealthy widow, as the most perfect recompense for long adversity, upon Alonso del Castillo. Sufferings in the wilderness had not sapped Dorantes's stamina. He served gallantly in the subjection of Jalisco and other regions, and begat eleven children, whose line, no doubt, still flourishes in the Republic of Mexico. Castillo's children were all girls; Andrés Dorantes's son was unable to trace them.[3]

Estebanico was destined for a more spectacular end. In 1539 the viceroy, disappointed by the failure of his military expedition to the north, proposed to the Order of St. Francis that they send some monks on an exploring journey in the interests of religion and His Majesty. Brother Marcos of Nice, vice-commissioner of the order, and a companion, answered the call. The governor instructed them to push northward as far as possible, and to reassure the Indians along the way, promising them that they should not be enslaved, "that therefore they shall lose all fear." The monks should take Estebanico as a guide, "and I command him to obey you in all and everything you order him to do, as if you were my own self; and in case of disobedience he will be severely punished, according to the penalties imposed upon those who disobey persons holding from His Majesty power to command them."[4]

The little band left Culiacan on March 7, 1539, and proceeded northwest through country which Estebanico remembered well, as far as Matape, forty miles south of Ures, the village of the deer hearts. Along the way Indians came humbly forth to greet him,

2. Winship, George P. "The Coronado Expedition," *Fourth Report of Bureau of Ethnology*, Washington, 1896: 349.
3. Dorantes de Carranza, Baltasar. *Sumaria Relación de la Nueva España*. Mexico: Imprenta del Museo Nacional, 1902.
4. Bandelier, 110.

recalling old acquaintance, begging for the healing touch of his hands. Arrogantly he swaggered before his Franciscan masters; he alone knew the road; he bore a magic rattling gourd in hand; he alone could speak and understand, and if words failed he possessed the Esperanto of the wilderness, the rich idiom of the sign manual. His authority, by which he could king it over the Indians and loftily belittle a vice-commissioner of the Franciscan order, induced him to the misdeeds of intolerable pride.

At Matape, Fray Marcos despatched Estebanico on a reconnoitering journey. The negro's instructions were to proceed north forty or fifty leagues, and if he found any knowledge of any rich and peopled country to go no further but to return in person, or to send Indian messengers with a token, which should be "a white cross of one handful long; and if it were any great matter, one of two handfuls long; and if it were a country greater and better than Nueva España [Mexico], he should send me a great cross. So the said Stephen departed from me on Passion Sunday after dinner; and within four days the messengers of Stephen returned unto me with a great cross as high as a man."[5] The messengers reported that Fray Marcos must come at once to join Estebanico, for he had learned that it was only thirty days' journey to the city of Cíbola.

> He affirmed also that there are seven great cities in this province, all under one Lord, the houses whereof are made of lime and stone, and are very great, and the least of them with one loft above head, and some of two and of three lofts, and the house of the Lord of the Province of four, and that all of them join one onto the other in good order, and that in the gates of the principal houses there are many turquoise-stones cunningly wrought, whereof he saith they have there a great plenty; also that the people of this city go very well apparelled; and that beyond this there are other provinces, all of which (he saith) are much greater than these seven cities.

No more was necessary to send Fray Marcos—his brother-monk had fallen sick—hastening after Estebanico, tense with excitement. But his forerunner would not wait. He enjoyed his sole authority; he had a taste for Indian women, and not content with accepting their hospitality for the night he would carry away with him those who especially pleased him. He was also making a collection of turquoises. He feared, certainly, the Franciscan's interference with these godlike impositions on the simple people.

5. Hakluyt, Richard. *The Principal Navigations: Voyages, Traffiques and Discoveries of the English Nation.* Glasgow: James MacLehose and Sons, 1903–1905. vol. ix, 128.

Estebanico, the bearded negro Moor from Azamor, felt himself dangerously akin to Deity. In his hand he carried with majesty the sacred gourd. He wore feathers on his arms and legs, and belled anklets and bracelets that chimed nobly with his holy rattle. At his heels followed two adoring Spanish greyhounds. He carried green dinner plates for the proper service of his food.[6]

Estebanico passed through Ures, the village of the deer hearts. There his course diverged from the way he had previously followed. Instead of taking the mountain path to the northeast he headed directly up the valley of the Sonora. Every day he would send back word to Fray Marcos, or would leave a large cross planted on a hillock; but he took good care not to be overtaken. Emerging from the Sonora Valley, he crossed the uninhabited height of land and was guided to the northward-flowing San Pedro. He descended the river, near Tombstone, perhaps as far as its junction with the Gila. He then turned northeast across the desert, hurrying toward the pueblo of Zuñi. He was careful to mark his passage; Fray Marcos found shelters constructed for his nightly rest.

Coming within a day's journey of Zuñi, Estebanico halted, with his three hundred companions from the south. He then sent messengers to the lord of the place, carrying as a holy symbol of authority the master's great gourd, hung with bells and feathers; the envoys announced that a Child of the Sun was at hand, bringing good fortune and offering to heal the sick. The style of Cabeza de Vaca is easily to be recognized. In this circumstance, however, was some confusion of the symbols. The lord of the place took the gourd in his hands, and threw it angrily on the floor, crying: "I know these people, for these rattles are not the make of our own! Tell them to return at once, else not one of them will remain alive!"

When the trembling ambassadors brought this word to Estebanico, he only laughed, saying that they need not fear, for those who gave him evil words at the outset always received him most devoutly in the end. He led his band forward to the city; but when he reached the walls, uttering promises and threats, he found no entry. Some citizens met him, and showed the troop courteously enough to an outlying house.

That night, as Castañeda, the recorder of Coronado's expedition, was informed by the Zuñis, the elders met in council. They were offended by Estebanico's demand that they surrender to him their treasure and their women, and alarmed at his proclamation that he foreran two white men, sent by a mighty prince to teach them a better religion. What chiefly distressed and disturbed them was that a

---

6. Hernando de Alarcón heard these stories in the following year, as far away as the mouth of the Colorado. (Hakluyt, *Principal Navigations*, IX, 300, 305.)

black man should come as agent and annunciator of a people whom he asserted, and they knew, to be white! Might this not be a demon's masquerade? They puzzled long over this baffling problem, and finally concluded that the wisest judgment was death.

In the morning, when the sun rose a lance-length high, Estebanico stood forth in the manner of Joshua and called on the city to surrender. He was answered only by a shower of arrows and a sudden sortie. Estebanico's companions turned to flee, and after a moment he joined them, all his godhood dropping away. He fell pierced by an arrow; all the Indian escort were killed but three, who escaped to bring the news to Fray Marcos. Estebanico's body was cut in pieces and distributed to various chiefs as a proof of death and as an interesting curiosity. The chief of Cíbola kept his dogs and the four green dinner plates.

Toward the end of the last century, Mr. Frank H. Cushing went to live among the Zuñi Indians for anthropological purposes. One of the ancient legends he recorded tells how, before the first coming of the Mexicans, a black stranger appeared at the village of Kia-ki-ma. He was very greedy, voracious, and bold, and so they killed him. After his death the Mexicans appeared in great numbers, finally subduing the Zuñis.[7]

Time, at its graveyard work, moves slow in those still altitudes. It has not yet interred the memory of a solitary black slave's death, by the arrows of savages, in the desert.

When the refugees brought to Fray Marcos word of the calamity, he was hard put to it to restrain his escort from immediate flight. He was a hardy friar, and having come so close to his goal, he would not yet turn back. He undid the bundle of presents prepared for the Lord of Cíbola, and offered them to any willing guide. At last two "principal men" offered to take him to a spot whence he might see Cíbola from afar. They made their way cautiously to a summit, from which he looked down on the populous town, and imagined the riches of gold and silver, "for they have no other metal," behind the adobe walls. "I was tempted to go thither, because I knew I could but hazard my life, and that I had offered unto God the first day that I began my journey; in the end I began to be afraid, considering in what danger I should put myself, and that if I should die, the knowledge of this country should be lost, which in my judgment is the greatest and the best that hitherto hath been discovered." Having then looked on Canaan from his Nebo, he turned about and fled back to Mexico, "with much more fear than victuals," bringing news that was to send Coronado and his men hunting gold over all the plains of the west.

7. Bandelier, 154.

Let us now return to Cabeza de Vaca, beating across the Gulf of
Mexico on his voyage to Spain. Leaving Vera Cruz on April 10,
1537, he reached Havana on May 4, a two days' journey to-day.
Entering the harbor, he crossed his outward track. He set sail
again on June 2, much in fear of French corsairs. "Having arrived
near the island of Bermuda, we were struck by one of those storms
that overtake those who pass there, according to what they state
who sail thither." Twenty-nine days out from Havana, they were off
Corvo in the Azores, the spectrum-bright cloud-pedestal that New
York-Mediterranean liners pass, for their passengers' delight. Here
a French corsair, with an accompanying prize, gave chase. By dusk
he was only a cannon-shot distant. All that night the Spanish captain tried to give his pursuer the slip, and all night the Frenchman
foiled the maneuvers, and hung close, firing an occasional shot,
and waiting for morning.

What were their contrary emotions when, with the dawn, the
three ships were found to be close to nine other sail, Portuguese
men-of-war! The French captain was a man of ready wit. He brought
up from his ship's prison the master and the pilot of his prize, a Portuguese slaver with a cargo of negroes, and informed them that his
quarry, the Spanish freighter, was in fact a French companion. The
master and the pilot believed the tale. The Frenchman then put the
two in a boat to join the Portuguese men-of-war, and thrusting sixty
oars overside, fled away with oar and sail, "moving so fast it was
hardly credible." The slaver informed the fleet that the Spaniard was
a French corsair, and Cabeza de Vaca and his mates came near to
being sunk on suspicion. The admiral asked their name and freight;
the Spanish captain answered simply that they were loaded with silver and gold. "And how much silver and gold might that be?" "Three
thousand pounds." The commander's reply Cabeza de Vaca humor-
ously transcribes in Portuguese: "In honest truth you come very rich,
although you bring a very sorry ship and a still poorer artillery. By
God, that renegade whoreson French bastard has lost a good mouth-
ful ¡o fi de puta! can, a renegado frances, y ¡que bon bocado perdio,
vota Deus!"

The Frenchman got clean away; the Spanish treasure ship joined
the Portuguese fleet, which was convoying three spice-ships from
the Orient. They waited two weeks at Terceira in the Azores for a
strayed Indian spice-carrier, then left with the whole armada for Lisbon, arriving there on August 9, four months out from Vera Cruz.

Álvar Núñez Cabeza de Vaca, writing the report of his adventures,
here came to his conclusion. He attested all he had written by his
name and his honor as a gentleman. "That what I have stated in my
foregoing narrative is true, I subscribe with my name. Cabeza de
Vaca." Thereto he added the symbol of his arms.

This was the end of half his life. By the fortitude of his great heart, by readiness of wit and strength of body, and by the grace of God, he had emerged whole out of the deepest pit of disaster. But these did not preserve him in a later day of success.

ROLENA ADORNO AND PATRICK CHARLES PAUTZ

[From Conquest and Settlement to Journey of Escape]†

When Thomas Jefferson remarked in a letter to a friend in 1787 that citizens of the new United States should study the Spanish language, he gave as one of the reasons the fact that "the ancient part of American history is written chiefly in Spanish" (Jefferson 11:558). Jefferson had in mind the accounts of the earliest European exploration, conquest, and settlement in the Americas that are found in narrative texts that extend from Columbus's letters from the Antilles through the reports, chronicles, and histories of the conquests of Mexico and Peru. His notion of American history was a hemispheric one, one which embraced the Circum-Caribbean area and North and South America, and the authors of that early history were Spanish. Most of those firsthand accounts of the cycles of European and Amerindian contact, as well as the great synthetic histories of Spain's intervention in the Americas, narrated the Spanish wars of conquest in which the European triumphed over the Amerindian. The firsthand reporters and learned historians wrote about Amerindian cultures and customs only secondarily.

Within this larger context of Spanish New World writings, Álvar Núñez Cabeza de Vaca's 1542 *Relación* is unique as the tale of the first Europeans and the first African to confront and survive the peopled wilderness of North America. Among captivity narratives Cabeza de Vaca's account tells a unique story of survival against the highest odds. It offers the repeated spectacle of first encounters between inhabitants of the Old World and those of New World lands unknown to them, and it foregrounds native Amerindian peoples, their customs, and their interactions with the newcomers in a manner seldom seen in expeditionary writings. The work fires the reader's imagination as it simultaneously documents historical occurrences

† Reprinted from *The Narrative of Cabeza de Vaca* by Álvar Núñez Cabeza de Vaca, edited, translated, and with an introduction by Rolena Adorno and Patrick Charles Pautz, by permission of the University of Nebraska Press. Copyright 2003 by the University of Nebraska Press.

of the actual Spanish expedition and describes the peoples, flora, and fauna of pre-Columbian North America. For these reasons contemporary history, ethnohistory, and archaeology have examined it for fresh clues about the North American past, contemporary fiction and film have recreated its timeless characters and plot, and current literary and cultural readings strive to suggest its myriad and ultimate meanings.

Cabeza de Vaca's vivid account offers the earliest European depiction of the vast expanse of continental North America. The events narrated by Cabeza de Vaca occurred not long after the conquest of Mexico. The year was 1527: Juan Ponce de León and other Spanish explorers and conquerors had already chanced upon the Florida Peninsula in their search for gold and slaves, but it would be nearly a century later that the English would found Jamestown (1607) and land at Plymouth Rock (1620). Cabeza de Vaca and three other expeditionary survivors thus experienced areas of the future United States as no natives of Europe or Africa previously had done. They explored the lands of the Florida Peninsula, coasted the northern shore of the Gulf of Mexico on rafts, lived for six and a half years among the native groups of eastern coastal Texas, traversed northern Mexico and southwestern Texas on foot, and ultimately encountered their countrymen in Spanish Nueva Galicia in northwestern Mexico before proceeding on to the ancient city of México-Tenochtitlán, the capital of New Spain.

Cabeza de Vaca's account starts as a typical conquest narrative. He tells how the Pánfilo de Narváez expedition, on which he served as one of the king's treasury officials, gathered supplies in the Caribbean for war and settlement on the mainland in *Florida* (the area named in Narváez's grant that consisted of the vast unexplored territories that lay beyond the northern frontier of New Spain from the Florida Peninsula to the unexplored Pacific Coast). Things went wrong, and it soon became a drama of survival without the force of arms amidst the variously hostile and friendly native groups of North America. The tables had turned: what had begun as the saga of some six hundred men (and ten women) bound for conquest and settlement along the northern rim of the Gulf of Mexico became the fascinating tale of four men, told from the perspective of one of them, living separated and in captivity before being reunited and beginning, nearly a year after that, their dramatic journey of escape.

The Cabeza de Vaca account brings us the Atlantic world not only along its Spain–North America axis but also along that of Portugal in relation to Africa and India. The Portugal–West Africa nexus is epitomized in the figure of Estevanico, the black Arabic-speaking African slave from Portuguese-held Azemmour in coastal northwestern Africa, one of the four survivors of the overland North

American trek. Cabeza de Vaca's journey home opens out on to the horizons of the sixteenth-century Iberian world: the Spanish treasure ship on which he traveled was accosted by French privateers in the Azores and saved by a nine-ship Portuguese armada that included in its convoy several vessels returning to Europe from Africa and India. One was a slave ship inbound from West Africa; three others came from India bearing the magnificent, fragrant bounty of the Portuguese spice trade. In short, the Atlantic and global perspectives of his times are explicit in Cabeza de Vaca's *relación*.

The Mediterranean and Atlantic Worlds of Cabeza de Vaca

Álvar Núñez Cabeza de Vaca's personal experience (1485–92 to ca. 1559) and ancestral lineage offer similarly broad perspectives, reminding us that life in provincial Andalusia for a man of military tradition and vocation was likely to be anything but confined to local affairs. At the end of his account he lauded his paternal grandfather, Pedro de Vera Mendoza, by identifying him as the conqueror of the island of Gran Canaria in the Canary Islands. His maternal lineage, whose name of Cabeza de Vaca he bore, dated back at least as far as the early thirteenth century. *Caballeros*, or members of the untitled middle-ranking nobility, of the Cabeza de Vaca line had participated in the "reconquest" of Spain from the Muslims. Fernán Ruiz Cabeza de Vaca's chronicled participation in the Christian conquest of Córdoba in 1236, which took place under the leadership of one of the most celebrated Christian monarchs of medieval Spain—Fernando III of Castile and León—links the Cabeza de Vaca name with one of the major military offensives of its era. (The popular legend that the Cabeza de Vaca name was created when bestowed on a humble shepherd for his role in the battle of Las Navas de Tolosa in 1212 is apocryphal.)

Cabeza de Vaca's life story is cartographically projected onto the map that traces his journeys in Europe and to the Americas. Like many Andalusians of his regional and familial traditions and other men of his generation, this native of Jerez de la Frontera was oriented first to the Mediterranean and then, fully, to the Atlantic. While his forebears had occupied themselves on the frontiers of Muslim Spain in Andalusia and on the seacoasts of southern Spain and northern Africa, Cabeza de Vaca and his contemporaries were involved in even broader international domains. National and international conflicts during the reigns of King Ferdinand of Aragon and his grandson, King Charles I of Spain, were part of Cabeza de Vaca's military experience before he set sail, for the first time, to the Indies.

Serving the house of the dukes of Medina Sidonia from his youth until his departure for America (1503–27), Cabeza de Vaca's career at arms spanned the period of King Ferdinand's North African campaigns and the defense and expansion of his Aragonese territories in Italy (1511–13). In Italy, under Ferdinand's banner, Cabeza de Vaca participated in the 1512 battles of Ravenna and Bologna and the siege of the lands of the duke of Ferrara. As a reward he was appointed royal standard bearer (*alférez*) of the city of Gaeta, near Naples. The *relación* (f42v) contains an occasional, fleeting reference to these earlier military experiences. When Cabeza de Vaca recalled the warlike character of the natives of eastern coastal Texas, he remarked, "they have as much cunning to protect themselves from their enemies as they would have if they had been raised in Italy and in continuous war."

In 1520–21 Cabeza de Vaca again supported the crown while in the employ of the dukes of Medina Sidonia during the early years of the reign of Charles I of Spain (Charles V of the Holy Roman Empire). In Spain in 1521 Cabeza de Vaca participated in the final defeat of the year-long Comunero uprising that threatened the stability of the Castilian state by reasserting local needs and interests against Charles's new centralized royal power and the threat of his treasury-draining wars abroad. In the same year Cabeza de Vaca participated in the battle of Puente de la Reina, in Navarre, in which Charles's forces repelled those of Francis I of France in the first of the series of wars between those monarchs.

Cabeza de Vaca's easy familiarity with European and Mediterranean reference points reveals the breadth of his personal horizons as a military man and as a mariner. His Indies career was remarkable for its geographical range over North and South America, first to *Florida* as royal treasurer and later to Río de la Plata as governor of the province centered at Asunción, in today's Paraguay. His governorship lasted from March 1541 until April 1544, when he was arrested and imprisoned for eleven months before being sent home in chains, arriving back in Spain in September 1545. He was tried by the Royal Council of the Indies on criminal charges that included misconduct in office, mistreating the Indians, and raising his own heraldic standard when he should have raised the king's. In 1551 he was found guilty and sentenced to be stripped of all titles conferred on him, banned in perpetuity from the Indies, and banished to the penal colony of Oran on the North African coast for five years of service to the emperor at his own expense. Cabeza de Vaca appealed the sentence, and in 1552 it was reduced: his banishment from the Indies henceforth pertained only to Río de la Plata, and he was relieved from the obligation of five years of service in Oran. The perpetual loss of his titles was still apparently in effect, as was his liability for court costs and any civil suits that might be brought against him. Nevertheless, the royal license to print the

1555 edition of his work, which was signed by the Infanta Juana on behalf of her brother, Prince Philip (the future Philip II), identified Cabeza de Vaca by his Río de la Plata title of governor. Ironically, by apparent bureaucratic error the phrase "el governador Álvar Núñez Cabeza de Vaca" in the royal license mistakenly referred to the Narváez expedition to North America.

Even in his last days, when back home in Jerez de la Frontera, Andalusia, Cabeza de Vaca looked outward: the last known, documented public act of his life was his 1559 ransom of a distant relative, Hernán Ruiz Cabeza de Vaca, who was being held captive by the king of Algiers after being captured in an expedition against the Ottoman Turk. As a member of the *caballero* class of the Jerez de la Frontera house of Cabeza de Vaca, our Álvar Núñez (often synonymously referred to as an "hidalgo") almost certainly ended his days in Jerez de la Frontera, and is probably interred in the Dominican convent of Santo Domingo el Real where his paternal grandfather, Pedro de Vera Mendoza, had been buried. (The popular notion that Cabeza de Vaca died "penniless, old, and broken-hearted" in Valladolid is another bit of oft-repeated but unsubstantiated apocrypha.)

The Geography of the Relación and Consideration of the Route

Charles V and, by extension, his ministers who oversaw the affairs of the Indies, were the original intended readers of Cabeza de Vaca's *relación*. By the time a version of Cabeza de Vaca's account reached them in 1537, Spanish officials had spent almost half a century watching the Spanish American empire unfold from its center in the Caribbean. These men were intimately familiar with the physical and political geography of the Americas, and Cabeza de Vaca's geographical references in the *relación* appropriately assume that knowledge. Cabeza de Vaca's account represented a fundamental contribution to this continuously evolving corpus of information, even as he sought to influence its development through his own report. From a remove of almost five hundred years, a modern-day comprehension of Cabeza de Vaca's account naturally requires the definition of geographical terminology and identification of geographical locators whose significance was obvious to its intended readers in the 1530s and 1540s.

Spanish exploration of the southern Gulf of Mexico originated from Cuba and followed along the Gulf's southern rim, from the tip of the Yucatán Peninsula to the region of modern-day Cabo Rojo (north of Veracruz) between 1517 and 1519. This exploration led ultimately to Cortés's discovery and conquest of Tenochtitlán, and in the ensuing years he expanded his control over central Mexico, which came to be known as New Spain, in all directions. One outcome of this expansion was the conquest of Pánuco and the establishment in 1523 of Santisteban del Puerto near the mouth of the Río Pánuco in present-day central Tamaulipas, Mexico. Cortés's impulse for founding this settlement was to push the frontier of his conquests as far north and east along the coast as possible in response to competing exploration moving west along the northern coast of the Gulf of Mexico at that time.

This westward-moving exploration of the northern coast of the Gulf of Mexico had its precursor in Juan Ponce de León's discovery of the Florida Peninsula in 1513. Apparently incited by the promising discoveries along the southern coast of the Gulf of Mexico, Francisco de Garay, the governor of the island of Jamaica (known then as Santiago), sent exploratory expeditions from Jamaica along the entire expanse of the northern Gulf Coast in 1518 and 1519. In the summer of 1519 Garay's men confronted Cortés's men briefly at a location north of Cabo Rojo on the western Gulf Coast. Garay's subsequent activities in the region along the northern Gulf of Mexico did not receive the detailed historical treatment that Cortés's conquests in New Spain did, largely because the attempts failed miserably. Nevertheless, primary sources and all of the early histories point to Garay's attempt to establish a settlement on the northwestern Gulf Coast, most likely at the mouth of the Río Pánuco, during the summer of 1519 or earlier.

Garay launched a final failed attempt to found a settlement at Pánuco in the summer of 1523, only to find upon his arrival that Cortés had already founded Santisteban del Puerto there. Cortés's officials at Santisteban del Puerto suggested to Garay that he take his men back to either the Río de las Palmas or the Río del Espíritu Santo to found a settlement. Both rivers were known to be in the direction of the Florida Peninsula with respect to Santisteban del Puerto; the mouth of the latter river was assumed to be approximately 200 leagues distant along the coast from the Spanish enclave. From 1523 onward Santisteban del Puerto, located slightly inland on the Río Pánuco, came to be known as the farthest northeastern outpost of Spanish settlement in New Spain along the coast of the Gulf of Mexico.

By the time the Narváez expedition departed from Spain in 1527 it had been largely agreed that the Florida Peninsula was not an island, but rather a protrusion of a large northern land mass connected ultimately to the territories of New Spain. On 4 November 1525 Nuño Beltrán de Guzmán was named governor of the newly defined province of Pánuco, an area comprised of the northeastern territories conquered by Cortés with Santisteban del Puerto as its capital. The Spanish government separated Pánuco from New Spain in an attempt to limit Hernán Cortés's growing monopolistic influence on the mainland. Whereas the term *Florida* referred originally and specifically to the Florida Peninsula, by 1527 it had come to represent a legal jurisdiction representing the entire northern mass of land that extended from the tip of the peninsula to the vast territories north of the jurisdictions of New Spain and Pánuco. Knowing *Florida* to be attached to an ever-expanding landmass, Cabeza de Vaca likewise referred in the proem of his account (f1v) to the area as *tierra firme*, the mainland, distinguishing it from the Caribbean Islands.

When the Spanish monarch granted Pánfilo de Narváez his right to explore and conquer in this region on 11 December 1526, he specifically gave Narváez authority to "discover and conquer and settle the said territories that are from the Río de las Palmas to the cape of what is called *La Florida*."[1] The concession makes reference to Narváez's earlier petition to explore and conquer *Florida* "from one sea to the other," with specific reference to the Río de las Palmas and the coastline between the mouth of that river and "the island of *La Florida*" (in other words, the Florida Peninsula). The two seas referenced were the North Sea, made up of the Atlantic Ocean and the Gulf of Mexico, and the South Sea, the Spaniards' name for the Pacific Ocean and Gulf of California. In Seville, on 30 August 1527 (only forty-five days after Narváez had set out from Sanlúcar de Barrameda for the Caribbean), a former Cortés expeditionary, Luis de Cárdenas, gave a formal opinion (*parecer*) regarding the jurisdictional divisions of New Spain. Cárdenas described the fourth section of New Spain as extending from the Río de las Palmas west to the opposite sea (the South Sea), and said that Pánfilo de Narváez was now going to conquer that region. Cárdenas believed that the distance from the Río de las Palmas west to the South Sea was 650 leagues and that from the river east to the Florida Peninsula was another 300. According to Cárdenas, not even three governors would be sufficient to bring under Spanish control the region that the crown had granted to Narváez.

The Río de las Palmas is today believed to be the Río Soto la Marina in the state of Tamaulipas in northeastern Mexico. As both the concession granted to Narváez and Luis de Cárdenas's testimony show, this river was the focal point for defining the province of *Florida* in 1527 and was the obvious intended destination of the Narváez expedition. Once the Narváez expedition struck land on the Gulf Coast in April 1528, the motivation to identify a port at the mouth of a river along the coastline was driven initially by the intention of locating the Río de las Palmas in order to establish a settlement there. The frequent references to harboring the ships in a safe

---

1. Vas Mingo, Milagros del. *Las capitulaciones de las Indías en el siglo XVI*. Madrid: Instituto de Cooperación Iberoamericana, 1986: 234.

and populated port were clear references to the expedition's expectation of locating Santisteban del Puerto on the Río Pánuco nearby. The importance of these two rivers in Cabeza de Vaca's text gave rise to the directional references "the way of Palms" (*la vía de Palmas*) and "the way of Pánuco" (*la vía de Pánuco*), both of which signified travel along the coast in the direction of these rivers, and "the way of *Florida*" (*la vía de la Florida*), which signified travel along the coast toward the Florida Peninsula. Over time Cabeza de Vaca came to refer to travel toward the Río de las Palmas and the Río Pánuco as traveling ahead (*adelante*) and to locations in the opposite direction as behind or back (*atrás*).

In light of the Narváez expedition's geographic knowledge and the obvious intended destination of the Río de las Palmas to the north of Santisteban del Puerto on the west side of the Gulf of Mexico, the expedition's actual landfall on the east side of the Gulf of Mexico, on the west coast of the Florida Peninsula, is disorienting, and it persists as one of two geographical conundrums regarding the Narváez expedition and Cabeza de Vaca's account. In his *relación* Cabeza de Vaca never explicitly states the expedition's intended destination nor does he explicitly address the magnitude of the error at any time. The spectacular outcome of the expedition made it impossible to conceal the fact that the expedition did not reach its intended destination. Yet in his writing Cabeza de Vaca never confronts the issue directly. Instead, at the end of his text, in a most matter-of-fact way, he observes that the bay the Narváez expedition discovered lies 100 leagues north of the port of Havana. The subtlety of the comment and the silence on the scope of the expedition's error are such that some readers come away from the text with the false understanding that the west coast of the Florida Peninsula was the expedition's originally intended destination, and that the Narváez men were simply unable to locate a known port on that coast which Spaniards such as Ponce de León and the men of Francisco de Garay's expedition had previously visited.

In his account Cabeza de Vaca repeats over and over the expeditionaries' goal of reaching Pánuco, and it appears to have persisted as the objective of the final four survivors, at least through the summer of 1535. The importance of reaching the river and the Spanish settlement of Santisteban del Puerto has significant implications regarding Cabeza de Vaca's silence on the second unanswered geography question of the *relación*—the four survivors' ultimate abandonment of their coastal search for Santisteban del Puerto and their unexpected crossing of the entire expanse of northern Mexico to reach the Gulf of California and the Pacific Ocean. When we consider the state of Spanish exploration of the Pacific coast and of western New Spain prior to 1528 when the Narváez expeditionaries entered *Florida*, the fact that the Narváez expedition survivors ended up following the path they did takes on an even more astounding dimension.

Vasco Nuñez de Balboa's discovery of the Pacific Ocean (known to the Spaniards as the South Sea) in 1513 was preceded by nearly a decade of speculation about the existence of a southern sea that would offer great wealth through direct access to Cathay and Great India. On 16 September 1522 Sebastián del Cano, Magellan's Spanish navigator, arrived in Spain following his circumnavigation of the globe, and the existence of the vast Pacific Ocean became widely known. Certainly most directly influential on the Narváez expedition survivors, however, would have been the publication in 1523 and 1525 of Cortés's third and fourth letters of relation. In the third letter of relation, dated 15 May 1522, Cortés announced his men's arrival at the South Sea from México-Tenochtitlán. The title page to the published edition of this letter announced how Cortés "relates how he discovered the South Sea and many more great provinces, very rich in gold and pearls and precious stones; and how he has even heard tell that there are spices."[2] In his third letter Cortés placed the South Sea at twelve to fourteen days' journey from México-Tenochtitlán, and spoke of plans to construct ships for the purpose of exploration in the South Sea and along the coast. Whereas Cortés's third letter of relation spoke of riches in connection with New Spain's potential proximity to Asia, Cortés's fourth letter of relation, dated 15 October 1524, was the source of considerable expectations about the wealth of the South Sea in its own right. Specifically, Cortés detailed in his fourth letter that his men had traveled from Zacatula to Colima, where they had founded a settlement, and that pearls and a good harbor had been discovered there.

Cortés's letters alone suffice to explain the expectations the Narváez expeditionaries would have had about the wealth of the South Sea; the constant undercurrent and frequent direct references in Cabeza de Vaca's account to the possibility of discovering great wealth along the whole course of the Narváez expedition were undoubtedly inspired by Cortés's discovery and conquest of México-Tenochtitlán. The information emanating from Cortés's conquests likewise may have been the source of the Narváez expeditionaries' significantly understated notion of the distance to be traveled in crossing New Spain if they equated it with the well-known route between Veracruz and México-Tenochtitlán plus some additional fourteen days to travel from México-Tenochtitlán to the coast of the South Sea. In contrast to their thinking, however, stands Luis de

2. Pagden, Anthony, trans. and ed. *Letters from Mexico* by Hernán Cortés. Introd. by J. H. Elliot. New Haven: Yale University Press, 1986: 310.

Cárdenas's testimony from 1527 (mentioned earlier) that the distance from the Río de las Palmas to the South Sea was 650 leagues (nearly two thousand miles). Whatever the Narváez expeditionaries' expectations about this distance were, those expectations would have been a direct influence on the men's decision to follow the overland course.

The most perplexing aspect of the Narváez expeditionaries' crossing of northern Mexico and southwestern Texas between late summer 1535 and April 1536 is the complete absence in Cabeza de Vaca's account of any explicit reference to the great risk the men took in abandoning their much more certain coastal search for Santisteban del Puerto on the Río Pánuco in exchange for the unknown overland route. Cabeza de Vaca (f49v, f54r–v) acknowledges the men's motivation—the discovery of material wealth—for seeking the South Sea; he does not acknowledge directly, however, that they set out across lands whose extent and harshness were completely unknown to his countrymen at the time.

The absence of a clear declaration and turning point in the narrative was a strong influence on modern readers' hypotheses about the route that the men followed, with the general effect being an assumed abandonment by the men of their coastal route at a point much earlier in the account than the narrative's contents can support. It is important to note that the statement Cabeza de Vaca made in the *relación* just after he narrated the men's sighting of mountains near the North Sea (Gulf of Mexico) for the first time on their journey along the coast, can easily be misinterpreted as an explicit declaration of the men's intention to leave their coastal route and cross over to the Pacific coast:

> All the people of the coast are very bad, and we considered it preferable to go through the land because the people farther inland are of a better disposition and they treated us better, and we considered it certain that we would find the land more populated and with better means of sustenance. Finally, we did this because, by crossing through the land, we would see many of its particularities, because if God our Lord were served by taking some one of us out of there and bringing him to the land of Christians, he could give an account and description of it.

While this passage might seem to convey explicitly the men's resolution to cross overland to the Pacific, in fact it says only that the Narváez survivors elected to follow along the coast but through the interior rather than directly along the coastline. The strand of interpretation that identifies the mountains that the men sighted at this juncture as being located in western Texas (thinking which therefore questions the accuracy or interpretation of Cabeza de Vaca's reference to the North Sea with regard to these mountains), dates back as far as Buckingham Smith (1851) and continues to be repeated by modern editors and translators. We identify these mountains as the Sierra de Pamoranes near the Gulf Coast between the mouths of the Rio Grande to the north and the Río Conchos–San Fernando to the south.

As one of the keenest early readers of Cabeza de Vaca's account, Las Casas (*Apologética* 2:361 [chap. 206])[3] understood the coastal nature of the majority of the Narváez expeditionaries' travels and the subtle difference between the exploration of coastline versus coastal inlands that the men carried out on the Texas-Mexico coast prior to ultimately crossing over from the North Sea to the South Sea: "[f]inally, all these peoples, or the majority of those which Cabeza de Vaca saw and with whom he had contact, and of whom he relates the said customs are the ones near the coast of the North Sea, and those who neighbor them, and not very many leagues inland, since afterward he strayed far from the sea, entering into the land and encountering many other diverse and more organized nations, about whose customs he could learn very little, as he was traveling very rapidly." Writing in the 1550s, Las Casas did not comment on the geographical perplexities of the Cabeza de Vaca account. He neither marveled at how far from their intended destination the Narváez expeditionaries had landed, nor commented on the incredible distance through completely uncharted lands that the four Narváez expedition survivors had almost miraculously traveled. Perhaps in an era of radically changing geographic perceptions, events such as those that Cabeza de Vaca experienced seemed far more comprehensible and far less remarkable than they do today. In contrast to this notion, however, stands Cabeza de Vaca's own comment in the proem to the 1555 edition on the delights of contemplating the twists of fate he had experienced.

The closest Cabeza de Vaca ever comes to commenting directly on his overland journey's scope is to say that he understood that "from one coast to the other at its widest point, the distance may be two hundred leagues" (f63r). He is silent on the fact that he and the other three survivors of the Narváez expedition apparently narrowly missed their goal of reaching Santisteban del Puerto as they traveled along the coast before embarking in the summer of 1535 on their trek across northern Mexico. Had they traveled south along the western coast of the Gulf of Mexico even as far as the Río de las Palmas they might have discovered remnants there of Nuño de Guzmán's

3. Las Casas, Bartolomé de. *Apologética historia sumaria* (1555–59), ed. Edmundo O'Gorman, 2 vols. Mexico: Instituto de Investigaciones Históricas, Universidad Nacional Autónoma de México, 1967.

1527 explorations to that river. Likewise, Cabeza de Vaca does not observe the fact that it was sheer luck on the survivors' part that by the time they reached the area that is today the southern portion of the Mexican state of Sonora in the spring of 1536, they found Spaniards there; Nuño de Guzmán had extended the frontier of New Spain (as Cabeza de Vaca would have known it in 1528) northward along the coast of the South Sea all the way to the Río Yaqui between 1531 and 1533, naming the newly organized province Nueva Galicia. Upon reentry into the sphere of Spanish-dominated lands, the surviving Narváez expeditionaries must have undergone substantial debriefing, in which they would have opened their countrymen's eyes onto the vast territories of North America to the north of New Spain. Likewise, their compatriots would have related to them the monumental developments of Spanish exploration in the Americas that they had missed in their absence between 1528 and 1536. Among the most spectacular of these was the Spanish search for, and invasion of, the Inca empire in Peru in 1530–32.

PAUL SCHNEIDER

From Brutal Journey[†]

15. *The Isle of Bad Fortune*

Narváez was dead, along with his dream of a North American empire. But some 250 of the men and boys who had followed him to La Florida were still alive, spread out in various states of desperation along the coast of Texas.

While still at sea a few weeks before, when Cabeza de Vaca concluded that his own crew of rowers could not keep up with Narváez's and ordered them to rest at their oars, they had waited for the third boat, which they could still see far behind them. It was the one commanded by Captains Téllez and Peñalosa, and after discussing Narváez's shocking assertion that it was henceforth every boat for itself, the two crews decided to try to stay close together.

Given the moral reprobation heaped on Narváez for abandoning his subordinates by writers beginning in his own time and continuing to the present day, it's interesting to note that Pantoja's predictions of doom for any boat that tarried at sea came very close to coming true. For five days the boats of Cabeza de Vaca and Téllez and Peñalosa struggled against the winds and currents, losing

† From *Brutal Journey* by Paul Schneider (New York: Henry Holt, 2006), pp. 198–212. Reprinted by permission.

strength and unable to get ashore. What's more, despite their best efforts to hang together, they were once again separated by a night storm, this time permanently. Between the cold from the repeated drenching by November waves and the lack of drinking water, many of the passengers slipped into a senseless stupor. Late on the fifth day after parting from Narváez, there were only five people in Cabeza de Vaca's boat who could still row. The rest, he remembered, "were fallen on top of one another in it, so close to death that few were conscious."

By dark of that same day, there were only two left who were strong enough to operate the tiller: Cabeza de Vaca and the helmsman. They were now entirely reliant on their makeshift sails to move them toward shore. A few more cold hours passed, and even the unnamed helmsman asked Cabeza de Vaca to take over from him. He was certain that he was about to die any moment, he explained apologetically, and then lay down and closed his eyes. For hours in the dark after that, Cabeza de Vaca leaned against the tiller, the only conscious being in a boat full of bodies.

But the helmsman didn't perish. When Cabeza de Vaca checked at midnight, "to see if he was dead," he found him revived enough to take another watch. Fatigued now himself, Cabeza de Vaca tried to sleep, but found he couldn't. He lay there, listening to the sea, thinking his own morbid thoughts. "Certainly, at that hour I would have willingly chosen to die rather than to see so many people before me in that condition," he remembered.

In the darkest hour, right before the dawn, the sound of the sea changed. In his semiconscious state, it took a while for Cabeza de Vaca to comprehend what he was hearing. But suddenly, it clicked, and both he and the helmsman realized almost simultaneously that they were listening to the thunder of waves crashing on a beach. In the blackness they groped for the anchor, found it, and threw the line over the stern. Only a few dozen feet paid out before the bundle of rocks hit bottom. The waves were louder now, nearer.

As anxious to be ashore as they both were, neither was desperate enough to want to land the ungainly boat in the dark. They prayed the anchor would hold, checked it constantly, listened—is the wind coming up? And though the waves always did sound as if they were getting louder, they managed to keep behind the surf line until the eastern sky lightened.

The jolt of the great wave that pitched the forty-foot boat up onto the beach shocked most, but not all, of the near-dead passengers out of their lethargy. As soon as the long, low beach appeared like a line of white against a grey background, Cabeza de Vaca had taken an oar, and with the helmsman at the tiller, the two pointed the bow toward shore. Their hope for a smooth surf in to the beach didn't quite work out, however. Just as they approached the shore an immense set of waves roared in. The last one lifted the stern precariously high, leaving the man at the back looking down at the boat below him and leaning with all his pathetic weight against the tiller in an effort to keep the clunky thing from broadsiding and broaching. In the benches, men who hadn't moved in half a day or more began to come to as the cold November brine poured over them.

For once, the worst didn't happen and the boat stayed reasonably straight. The wave heaved them up onto the sand about as far, Cabeza de Vaca thought, as a horseshoe pitch. There, the semi-revived passengers tumbled out into the surf, "half walking, half crawling" their way to slightly higher ground at the back of the beach. There were more than a few, however, who didn't revive and had to be hauled out of the boat by the others.

According to Cabeza de Vaca, the date was November 6, 1528, but the elapsed time since leaving Apalachee suggests it was more like the second half of that month. At any rate it was bitterly cold. Someone cobbled together a fire. Someone else found some water, and the men crowded around, slurping up what they could, attempting to fill the few jars they still had. Rations had been strictly adhered to at sea, and there was still a little corn in the boat, which they began to toast and eat. With the heat and the food, and the adrenaline, strength temporarily flowed back into many limbs. Just the change of being on land was tonic to some.

One who was particularly revived was Lope de Oviedo (not to be confused with the historian of the same surname). From the top of the dunes he and Cabeza de Vaca looked over the pancake-flat land they had worked so hard to get to. There wasn't much to see, just an expanse of tough grasses stretching away indefinitely, cut through here and there with glinting water. But in the distance in a few places they could see higher hummocks of trees. They weren't much more than low mounds breaking the line of the horizon, but Cabeza de Vaca thought if Oviedo could make his way to the closest one and climb a tree, he might be able to get a wider view.

It was a copse of oak trees, great thousand-year-old behemoths with spreading branches that sagged all the way to the ground so that even a weakened man like Oviedo could virtually walk right up one to get a view of the surroundings. From the treetop he could tell immediately that they were on an island, most likely either Galveston or its neighbor to the west, the Oyster Bay Peninsula, which at that time may have been disconnected from the coast. More exciting to Oviedo though were the ruts and trails he'd followed through the underbrush to get through the trees. They could only have been made by cattle, he thought, and where there were cattle there must also be Europeans. He rushed back to tell Cabeza de Vaca.

This was titillating news, but by no means conclusive, and Cabeza de Vaca told him to go back and take a closer look for a road that might lead somewhere. Oviedo took the widest path he could find, but found neither cattle nor Europeans. He came instead to a deserted Indian village, from which he stole a few things including some dried fish and "a small dog." Or at least he thought the village was deserted: by the time he got back to the beach with his loot, two hundred armed Indians were following him.

They weren't in hot pursuit, or even showing signs of animosity, which was a good thing since there was nothing that the cold, wet, would-be conquerors of North America could do but hope for mercy. One or two Spaniards stood on wobbly legs and attempted to look ready to put up a defense, but most just slouched where they were and peered up like wounded skunks, waiting to see what would happen to them next.

"It was out of the question for us to think that anyone could defend himself," Cabeza de Vaca recalled, "since it was difficult to find even six who could raise themselves from the ground."

All that was left in the great arsenal of conquest were a few cheap manufactured trinkets. Cabeza de Vaca dug into the gear for the usual "beads and bells," which he and Solís then carried solicitously up the beach and presented to the assembled archers. By now they had seated themselves on a nearby bank of grass where they could see both the boat wreck and its victims, and be seen by them. They were large men, nearly naked, with pierced nipples and ears through which they had pushed inch-thick reeds of varying lengths. "Our fear made them seem like giants," Cabeza de Vaca remembered.

The baubles did their work. The bells in particular were of interest; in addition to the usual assortment of shell beads and pottery shards, archeologists on the Texas coast have found tiny bells called "tinklers" that the precontact coastal Indians manufactured from small olive-shaped shells using coyote teeth for clappers. Solís and Cabeza de Vaca presented the gifts like penitents seeking salvation, and after a moment's consideration, the giants accepted their offerings. As a sign of friendship, each took an arrow from his quiver and presented it to Cabeza de Vaca. Tomorrow morning, their hand gestures seemed to suggest, they would bring the hungry foreigners food.

At dawn, as promised, a contingent arrived with fish for the castaways to eat. The leeward shore of Galveston Island is laced with inlets, bays, and tidal streams that in fall and early winter are choked with spawning black drum, redfish, sea trout, croaker, and sea catfish. The islanders caught them in great numbers in weirs and traps, and were experts as well at shooting fish with arrows from their dugout canoes. They also brought roots to eat, dug with great effort from immense stands of cattail.

The locals returned the next day as well, bringing with them not only more food but also the women and children of the village, that they too might see the strangers who had washed up. The adult women wore Spanish moss, and the young, Cabeza de Vaca noticed, "cover[ed] themselves with deerskins." It was another good day of trading, "and thus they went home rich in the bells and beads that we gave them," he said.

For virtually the first time in the history of the expedition, good relations with the local Indians did not immediately deteriorate. For a week, the islanders brought supplies of cattail roots and dried fish to the castaways on the beach. There was plenty of driftwood for fires, and slowly, with sleep and warmth, strength crept back into Cabeza de Vaca and his crew. It was as good a situation as they had had since leaving Boca Ciega Bay, but who knew how long it could last? Days were notably short now, and the beach was not a place to spend the oncoming winter, counting on the continued hospitality of strangers.

One morning after the Indians had delivered some breakfast and then gone on their way, Cabeza de Vaca gave the order to relaunch the boat. The waves by now had half-buried the hull in the sand, so they stripped off their clothes to keep them dry while they worked to free it. It took the better part of the morning on their knees scooping away at the sand with bare hands, sticks, and shells just to dig it out. Eventually, though, they got the hull loose and righted it. Everything they still possessed was put back aboard, and they stood naked, at the water's edge, waiting for Cabeza de Vaca's signal to shove off.

It was exhausting, he recalled later, "because we were in such a condition that other much less strenuous tasks would have sufficed to place us in difficulty." Men groaned, shouted, heaved. And slowly, slowly, the gawky craft inched toward the surf. Once the bow was floating in the water, those at the front clambered on board and took up the oars. Others continued to shout and push from behind, climbing in only as the boat made its way into deep enough water to support their weight without grounding. All who could lift an oar now pulled with all they could.

But they didn't make it.

Cabeza de Vaca figured they were "at a distance of two crossbow shots out to sea" when the first big wave washed over them. This is a tricky distance to translate: tests done in the 1940s with reproductions of period weapons have shown that sixteenth-century crossbows could fire a bolt nearly four hundred yards, but that the practical range for aiming was more like fifty to seventy-five yards. Given that the first wave struck while some of the men were still outside the boat pushing, and that waves large enough to break eight hundred yards offshore would have convinced even desperate men to wait for calmer seas, the boat was most likely a hundred yards from the beach when trouble began.

The wave was so suddenly cold and powerful against their naked bodies as it poured over the bow that almost everybody simply let go of the oars. Out of control now, the boat lurched immediately broadside, and the next wave simply rolled it over. Most of the men jumped or tumbled free and managed to thrash their way back to the beach, but three, including Cabeza de Vaca's fellow commander, Solís, held onto the swamped boat. When it rolled they were trapped underneath, and when it sank they drowned.

These are the first three deaths that are specifically accounted for out of the forty-nine persons who began the voyage in Cabeza de Vaca's boat. There were surely others, however. Some of the five who had died of thirst off the coast of Alabama; some who gave out during the days at sea when Cabeza de Vaca says everyone but himself and the pilot were unconscious. But several dozen—maybe even forty—members of his original complement were still alive and managed to wade ashore. "The sea, with a single thrust, threw all the others, who were in the waves and half drowned, onto the coast," he recalled. From this point in the story onward, however, the numbers dwindle, often without explanation.

Everything was lost, including the clothes they had carefully taken off and stowed in the boats to keep dry. They had long ago given up their hope of conquering great lands and spreading news of the One True God to the heathens. They had eaten their beloved horses, fled from the Apalachee Indians, and been deserted by their governor. But the Spaniards among them were still, up to that moment, in some measure conquistadors; they had their steel swords even if they were too weak to wield them. They had a boat and a place to go. Some still had their helmets and their beads and bells to trade. They had porters and slaves. They had clothes.

But now, whether slave or conquistador, hidalgo or commoner, they were alike: forty naked, drenched human bodies, shivering uncontrollably in a cold north wind on a Texas beach in late fall coming onto early winter. Even to themselves, now fairly used to seeing each other in states of near starvation, they looked beyond hope. The ribs of every one of them were visible, remembered Cabeza de Vaca. Some wept openly. Others gave up, sat with their arms wrapped around their knees, blue lips and skin, waiting for death. A few who were not ready to face eternal judgment, however, fanned the embers in the campfires. And when "God granted" that a flame was found, they piled on driftwood from as far as they could drag it until they had built several roaring bonfires.

Nakedness wasn't just a practical issue. It was also a symbolic turning point, after which the Spaniards could no longer differentiate themselves from those whom they had come to conquer. As the historian Felipe Fernández-Armesto has pointed out, "clothes were the standard by which a people's level of civilization was judged in Medieval Latin Christendom." The Spanish obsession with clothing was so deep that Cervantes later parodied it: when all else has failed, Don Quixote decides the only way to prove that his love for Dulcinea has driven him truly out of his mind is to get naked. "For the love of God, my master," his trusty sidekick Sancho begs, "let me not see your Grace stripped, for I'd feel so sorry that I'd never stop weeping. . . . If your Grace wants me to witness some of your insane actions, please perform them with your clothes on and be brief about it and to the point."

Ironically, their nakedness doubtless saved more than a few from drowning. But once back on shore they looked at each other's shivering flesh and were confronted with the awful possibility that what they had always believed was Spanish cultural and moral superiority over the rest of the world was, in the end, just material superiority. Their "civilization" of tools, trinkets, and clothing had washed away. They named the island Malhado, or "bad fortune," and began to pray.

"And thus we were beseeching our Lord for mercy and the pardon of our sins, shedding many tears, each one having pity not only for himself but for all the others whom they saw in the same state," said Cabeza de Vaca.

Out of fear that the islanders might try to prevent their escape, the Spaniards hadn't told their hosts of their plans to relaunch the boat and leave. At sunset, therefore, as they had done every day, the Malhado islanders came back to the beach with food. But after one look at the situation they turned and began to leave, lest whatever bad thing had happened to their new friends might somehow happen to them. Only after Cabeza de Vaca chased them down and explained the situation—the boat had turned over, three men had drowned, the two bodies lying there not far from the huddled mass of naked sufferers were in fact dead—did the islanders come close. When they fully understood what had happened, they sat down with the men and began to cry.

The Indians of Malhado Island turned out to be fantastic weepers. They positively howled for more than half an hour and carried on "so sincerely that they could be heard a great distance away." Some of the Narváez survivors later figured out that these people always cried long and hard for the dead, and often for the living as well. But under the current circumstances, their sympathy was less comforting than it might have been, for it just rubbed in to the Spaniards how far they had fallen. In the imperial mind, you had to be pretty badly off indeed if even the Indians were feeling sorry for you.

"To see that these men, so lacking in reason and so crude in the manner of brutes, grieved so much for us increased in me and in others of our company even more the magnitude of our suffering and the estimation of our misfortune," remembered Cabeza de Vaca. The curious tone of surprise at the thought that Indians might be capable of empathy is even clearer in the survivors' joint account of their ordeal: "They began to cry with the Christians *as if* they sorrowed over the happening" (italics added).

It's a telling moment, in which the would-be conquerors are at last forced to look their would-be victims in the eye. Here begin the "novel things" Cabeza de Vaca had predicted for his readers: the weak are now strong and sympathetic, and the strong are now pathetic and meek. Spanish imperial reality, as more than one literary scholar has noted, is hereafter inverted in Cabeza de Vaca's memoir.

Who these Malhado islanders were is not a simple thing to deduce. Unlike the Apalachee and Safety Harbor peoples that the expedition had encountered in Florida, the coastal Indians of Texas were seasonally migratory hunter-gatherers who left little or nothing in the way of architectural remains. What's more, after the Narváez survivors passed through, no European is known to have interacted with the coastal Texans until the hapless French explorer La Salle briefly arrived in Matagorda Bay nearly a century and a half later.

By that time, waves of disease and displacement were emanating into the region from the Spanish to the south and west, and to a lesser extent from the French and English to the east and north. Native life was in flux, with collapsing local populations and immigrant groups like the Apache, Comanche, and others pushing in from the European frontiers. The result was an impenetrable tangle of ethnic identities: there are more than a thousand "tribes" mentioned in the documentary sources for the region. The first twenty-three of those are in Cabeza de Vaca's narrative, including the Hans and Capoques he said lived on Malhado Island.

The safest approach to their identity would be to leave it there without attempting to elaborate. That said, the Hans and Capoques were probably related either to people later known as the Akokisa or to those now referred to by archeologists as the Karankawa. Or both: the Hans and Capoques spoke different languages, and Galveston Island was near a transition zone between Akokisa and Karankawa. Whoever they were, in the wake of the boat wreck Cabeza de Vaca thought they represented his company's only hope for survival through the upcoming winter. When the weeping subsided, therefore, he suggested to his men that they try to convince the Indians to take them home with them to their village.

It was another inversion of expectations: instead of bringing civilization to grateful heathens, the leader of the conquerors now begged to be given the privilege to learn to live like the locals. Not everyone in his company agreed with the plan, however. A faction among the naked and shivering were downright terrified by the prospect of moving into an Indian village. The main dissenters were those who had previously been to Mexico, either with Cortés or with Narváez, and were certain that once in the heathen's lair they would become human sacrifices to some devilish idols. They remembered Cempoallan, where every day, according to Bernal Díaz's recollections, there were "sacrificed before us three, four, or five Indians whose hearts were offered to the idols and their blood plastered on the walls, and the feet, arms, and legs of the victims were cut off and eaten, just as in our country we eat beef brought from the butchers." Or they remembered the rack at Tenochtitlan that supposedly held 136,000 skulls.

"We should not even speak of it," they said of Cabeza de Vaca's plan.

But he was now in sole command of this particular remnant of the expedition, and he overrode their concerns. Not that he thought their fears unjustified; he later confessed that he, too, worried they would be killed in the village. But there was no other choice, he told his fellow sufferers. Staying on the beach for the coming winter with no tools, no boat, and no clothes was certain to kill them all, probably sooner rather than later. He cut off discussion, turned again to the islanders, and begged as best he could with hand gestures and signs for them to take in and care for him and his motley crew.

Even though they had been feeding the castaways now for a week or more, this was a lot to ask. The appearance of two hundred warriors on the day the Spaniards first landed suggests the nearby village or villages supported a population of at least four or five hundred persons. But unlike the corn-growing cultures to the east, the Texas coastal peoples were not likely to have on hand the sort of surplus necessary to support the sudden addition of forty starving and sick individuals. Nonetheless, the islanders "took great pleasure" in the prospect of aiding the strangers and told the castaways to wait there on the beach for them to return. They then collected huge loads of driftwood from the beach and hurried off in the direction of their town.

This was strange and worrisome: the firewood was something new. Throughout the rest of that cold day, the forty naked conquistadors huddled by their fires and wondered about the arrangements. Why couldn't they have simply gone to the village immediately? What was all the wood for? Those among them who were opposed to the plan from the beginning grumbled aloud that it could not be good. The fires were for roasting men, they thought.

At dusk, the islanders returned and announced it was time to leave. A few of Cabeza de Vaca's men had revived a bit, but most were still so weakened from exposure that they were incapable of walking far or fast. The islanders urged them on, and when that failed they simply picked them up and carried them. Into the darkening night the survivors were hustled along on strong shoulders, and after a short while the warmth from the fire on the beach was only a memory. The cold and uncontrollable shivering set in anew. But just when the castaways began to fade they arrived at a roaring fire of driftwood that had been built not for roasting, but for reviving.

"Fearing that on the road some one of us might fall unconscious or die, they made provision for four or five very great bonfires placed at intervals, and at each one they warmed us," recalled Cabeza de Vaca. "And when they saw that we had regained some strength and warmth, they carried us to the next one, so rapidly that they almost did not let our feet touch the ground."

Finally the village itself appeared out of the dark, and the survivors were deposited in a shelter that had been specially prepared for them. It was almost certainly constructed in the traditional Karankawa way: a frame of long willow poles, sharpened and driven into the ground at both ends, and covered with mats and skins. Often, only the windward side of the frame was covered leaving one side open to the air. At the back would be platforms to sleep on, as well as more skins and mats. But the only detail Cabeza de Vaca remembered was that there were "many fires" in the house, around which he and his comrades heaped themselves in their desperate attempts to get warm, to get rest, and in many cases simply to stay alive another day.

With their patients attended to, the rescuers began to make music. All through the night the Malhado islanders sang and danced in the village center. Cabeza de Vaca and the others had no way of knowing the significance, religious or otherwise, of the goings on, but it didn't sound overtly mournful or solemn. It sounded rather like a "great celebration."

In their convalescents' hut, the half-dead foreigners listened and wondered. "There was neither rejoicing nor sleep," said Cabeza de Vaca, "as we were awaiting the moment when they would sacrifice us."

Only in the morning, when their hosts arrived with a healthy breakfast of roots and fish did the terror begin to subside.

ANDRÉS RESÉNDEZ

From A Land So Strange[†]

* * *

What had begun as a guest-host relationship between the natives and the Spaniards eventually degenerated into a relationship between masters and slaves. The transition was gradual but unmistakable. No doubt, the castaways did not take long to outlive their initial welcome. The Capoques and Hans had been extraordinarily generous to the marooned explorers, but with the onset of winter, the strangers must have been expected to pull their own weight. The Indians were surely shocked at how useless the foreigners were. The castaways must have been laughably incapable of hunting with bows and arrows, and their fishing skills could not have been much better, as their knowledge of local traps, weirs, and edible fish was minimal. Since the strangers could not be entrusted with manly occupations, they were given women's work. They had to dig for roots, carry firewood, and fetch water.

One incident in particular strained their relationship. Not all of the Spaniards had taken up residence with the Indians. Five raftsmen had chosen to spend the winter by the beach; their fear of being sacrificed and eaten by the natives must have been overpowering. It had been a grave mistake. And the very thing that they dreaded the most—cannibalism—came to pass, albeit not in the way that they had expected it. Finding themselves without any food and in great necessity, they ate one another. And as Cabeza de Vaca notes with disarming logic, "Only one remained because he was alone and had no one to eat him."

When the Indians learned what had happened, they became very upset. "The scandal among them was such that they would have killed the men had they seen them at the start; and all of us would have been in grave danger." Ironically, in later centuries Europeans accused the native peoples of coastal Texas of cannibalism. Little did they know that in the sixteenth century the Europeans themselves had been the cannibals, and the Indians the ones appalled by such behavior.

The castaways' situation became even more precarious when the native islanders began dying from an "illness of the bowels," perhaps dysentery spread by the decomposing bodies of the Europeans. About *half* of all the Indians on the island died. It was an astonish-

† From *A Land So Strange: The Epic Journey of Cabeza de Vaca* by Andrés Reséndez, (New York: Basic Books, 2007), pp. 143–48. Reprinted by permission.

ing calamity and a terrible foreboding of the demographic disaster that would soon engulf the entire continent due to the introduction of new pathogens to the New World. Perhaps with good reason, the strangers were held responsible. "And taking this to be very true," Cabeza de Vaca writes, "the Indians agreed among themselves to kill those of us who remained."

As the natives prepared to carry out their intentions, the Indian man who had come to own Cabeza de Vaca intervened. He forcefully defended the castaways by reasoning that if they had the power to cause illness among the natives, then they surely would have prevented the deaths of so many of their own kind. This Indian man, who must have been sufficiently influential to hold slaves and go against general opinion, noted that none of the foreigners did any harm or ill and concluded that the best thing to do was to let them be. Somehow his point of view carried the day, and the lives of the strangers were spared.

The men would remain on the island as slaves to the natives. Life became so harsh for the survivors that they took the habit of calling the island *Malhado*, the "Isle of Ill fate." For the next six years or so the castaways' lives revolved around unceasing work. Their chores were deceptively trivial: carrying wood, digging for roots, or fetching water. There was nothing insidious or cruel about these activities, but they were constant as well as physically challenging and often painful. The heavy stumps chafed directly against their bare backs, and the bearers' feet were hurt from walking over summer-hot sand and amidst fierce spiny plants. Cabeza de Vaca's fingers bled constantly from digging roots; and he was forced to venture completely naked through thickets of cattails and other plants.

By this time, the survivors were entirely at the mercy of their masters. The native children mocked the Christians almost daily. According to Cabeza de Vaca, "Any child would give them a good hair pulling, and for them this was great fun, the greatest pleasure in the world." That was merely juvenile humor; the adults did not hesitate to use violence to obtain compliance. The captives reported being beaten with sticks, slapped in the face, and having their thick beards jerked out. A minor omission, delay, or infraction could bring about severe punishment, even death. Cabeza de Vaca recounts how three Christians were killed "only for daring to go from one house to another . . . and another three who remained alive expected to meet the same end." The castaways' daily anxiety over being punished or killed must have taken a dramatic toll. None of them could depend on staying alive from one day to the next. One Spaniard who had committed no infraction at all was killed simply because one Indian woman had a dream "of I don't know what nonsense," the castaways recall, "because in those parts they believe in dreams and kill their own children because of dreams."

Undoubtedly, the castaways had become slaves. Yet it is also important to note that societies like the Capoques and Hans were not "slaving societies," in the sense that they did not actively procure and exploit slave labor. They certainly possessed slaves, which were a byproduct of their continuous warfare with neighboring groups or came about when wandering strangers like the castaways "joined" these bands to escape starvation. However, this system was a far cry from that employed by more centralized and hierarchical societies like Portugal and Spain, for instance, or other indigenous societies in the American continent. For the coastal peoples of Texas, slaves were decidedly marginal to their survival and well-being. For one thing, a slave may have represented one more pair of arms but also an additional mouth to feed. Rather than systematically procuring and exploiting slaves, they were tolerated like stray dogs and permitted to stay as long as they made themselves useful. Indeed, as the castaways would discover, some of the natives of Texas flatly refused to take them, even as slaves. But once the castaways had gained admittance, their lives depended entirely on the will of their masters. This peculiar context did not lessen the sufferings of Cabeza de Vaca and his companions. But it helps us understand why the castaways were enslaved only gradually, why they had to seek out unwilling masters who often abused them, and why during their six-year stay along the Texas coast they were able to flee from one indigenous clan to another.

The once-mighty conquistadors had endured a precipitous fall. Life as an abused slave must have been indescribably bitter for the likes of Cabeza de Vaca and Captains Dorantes and Castillo. Castillo could have enjoyed the life of a judge or a municipal officer, had he only chosen to stay in Europe. What foolish impulse had compelled him to join the Narváez expedition and forsake a lifetime of comfort and happiness? Captain Dorantes may have been more of a man of action, perhaps more accepting of reversals of fortune and violence. After all, he already bore a scar on his face from military action. But surely he never imagined spending his last days on earth enslaved by a bizarre, naked people halfway around the world.

And what to say of the Royal Treasurer? Generations of Cabeza de Vacas had worked to further the imperial aims of Spain. His grandfather had been the famous captain who had conquered Gran Canaria. With the history of his ancestors in mind, Álvar Núñez Cabeza de Vaca must have also dreamed of great acts of conquest and bravery when the Florida expedition got underway. Yet his ambitions had been shattered in the whirlwind of a hurricane, a colossal navigational mistake, a difficult march through Florida, a harrowing

raft passage, and a sordid enslavement. Surely this nobleman suffered greatly as he tried to reconcile himself to spending the balance
of his life digging for roots until his fingers bled and stoically with-
standing beatings at the hands of natives who would never understand what he was meant to be.

The man best able to cope psychologically with the adverse con-
ditions was in all likelihood the African Estebanico. He was no
stranger to the life of bondage, as he had already once been captured, taken away from his homeland, and sold in Europe. His sufferings certainly increased in the New World as the expedition
foundered, but his social standing had changed but little. He had
been Dorantes's slave; but now his master had himself become
enslaved, an odd twist of fate that probably gave Estebanico a certain
unspeakable satisfaction. Although it is possible that his subordina-
tion to Dorantes and the other Spaniards persisted in some fashion,
the fact that the white Europeans were also enslaved must have
reduced the disparities. Indians, not Spaniards, exercised the ultimate authority now, a fact that must have complicated immensely
Dorantes's ability to enforce his authority over the African. With the
passing of time, Estebanico became just another slave largely undis-
tinguishable from his former masters.

Estebanico's sheer survival is miraculous. All the other castaways
were elite Spaniards who were likely to outlast Africans, simply
because they were better nourished and their bodies had been less
exposed to the ravages of punishing physical labor. Moreover, Europeans in commanding positions were able to use their authority in
ways that shielded them from danger and maximized their chances
of survival. And yet, Estebanico managed to outlive dozens of Spaniards who could have reasonably expected to be among the last men
standing. By all accounts, he was the ultimate survivor. He had experienced the life of bondage on three different continents and had
been forced to face incredible perils and adventures. Against astonishing odds, he had survived through it all.

* * *

BEATRÍZ RIVERA-BARNES

Is There Such a Thing as Too Much Water?[†]

The Hurricanes That Foundered and the Swamps That Hindered Álvar Núñez Cabeza de Vaca

This ecocritical approach to Álvar Núñez Cabeza de Vaca begins with a squall line in the near distance and ends in the coastal lowlands of the Florida panhandle. The horse has ceased to reify the conquistador and has become a hindrance. Water, too much water, gales from the north colliding with warm water expanding, the shifty nature of the Canarreos shoals between Cuba and the Isle of Pines, the Gulf Stream, the rough seas of the Yucatan channel, all elements of the inconstant weather, idiosyncratic Caribbean weather that carried the unfortunate Narváez expedition to the inhospitable Florida coast. A one-legged god sealed their fate, and his name is *hurakan*.

It was *hurakan* who killed men and precious horses, destroyed ships, spilled wine, and did not even spare the trees, towns, houses, and churches. It was *hurakan* who propelled the Narváez expedition east when they were trying to go west, and landed them in what Cabeza de Vaca calls a land so strange and so evil and so hopeless that it seemed impossible either to stay in it or to escape from it (102). This was a land inhabited by poor and wretched people, a land where the earth is drenched with water, where thirst always increases, and where water kills you.

Although more than just a regionally specific name for a strong cyclone, the triadic *hurakan* does remain regionally specific, for the Caribbean and the Gulf will always be *hurakan*'s domain, from Cuba to Florida to Texas to Mexico to Puerto Rico. Climates and landscapes change, species become extinct, and water may soon become scarce, but *hurakan* and the swamps remain (110).

For the Quiché Maya, *hurakan* is the god who causes rain and flood and whose epithet in the *Popol Vuh* is *Heart of Sky, Heart of Earth*. In the beginning there was the Sovereign Plumed Serpent and the sky over pooled water, a god whose name was Heart of Sky. Then came *his* word. Heart of Sky spoke to the Plumed Serpent, the manifold begetter-knower-thinker. They talked, they thought, they worried, they agreed with each other, joined their thoughts, and the dawn of life was conceived (73). For the forming of the earth, they simply said, "Earth."

† From *Reading and Writing the Latin American Landscape* by Beatríz Rivera-Barnes and Jerry Hoeg (New York: Palgrave Macmillan, 2009), pp. 25–38. Reprinted by permission.

The Heart of Sky trinity (Hurricane, Newborn Thunderbolt, Raw Thunderbolt) was therefore present at the origins of creation. After the earth was created, the mountains were created, followed by the trees, rivers, animals, and finally man, an experiment.

This reading of the stormy beginnings of the Narváez expedition is about the encounter of a one-legged god (*hurakan*) with an unlucky chronicler named Álvar Núñez Cabeza de Vaca on November 9, 1527, off the coast of Trinidad, Cuba, an encounter that would ultimately produce what the critic Beatríz Pastor describes as a narrative discourse of failure (*discurso narrativo del fracaso*).

Such is Cabeza de Vaca's *Naufragios*, a rendering of the hapless Narváez expedition that turned conquerors into mere survivors. Unlucky from the start, the Narváez expedition was a license to conquer the entire Gulf Coast of what would one day become the United States, and the forty-year-old Cabeza de Vaca went along as the treasurer, to ensure that Charles V got his 5 percent of anything precious that Narváez came across along the way. But there would be no 5 percent, only shipwrecks, suffering, death, and perhaps too much water.

Pastor writes that in a narrative of failure, the landscape as an aesthetic concept disappears and is supplanted by an ever hostile and threatening natural environment (204). Although the expedition went from the Gulf Coast of Florida all the way to the Pacific Coast of Mexico, this study will focus on Cabeza de Vaca's very negative rendering of Florida's Gulf Coast, the place where they arrived after all those storms.

On the ninth of November or thereabouts, Cabeza de Vaca and an officer named Pantoja arrived at the port of Trinidad with two ships. Their intention was merely to get a certain number of supplies that a gentleman named Vasco Porcalle had promised Narváez and to leave Trinidad as soon as possible because they had been told that this was a very bad port and that many ships had been lost in the vicinity. Andrés Reséndez writes that unbeknown to the would-be conquistadors on this expedition, somewhere in the Caribbean or the Gulf, "billowing clouds and localized thunderstorms began to clash and combine with each other, and this mass of clouds, rain, and wind started to rotate around a low pressure center due to the earth's spinning motion" (65). What Reséndez is describing is a hurricane that was drifting toward Cuba.

Since *hurakan* is so regionally specific, Spanish explorers had never experienced hurricanes before reaching the American side of the world. Columbus was lucky enough to have enjoyed relatively good weather throughout most of the first voyage and was the first to describe a hurricane during his second voyage. Although quite astonished by the force and brutality of the wind and the water, Cabeza de

Vaca remained unaware of what was happening. Initially, *hurakan* was too much and too foreign for Cabeza de Vaca's pen. Cabeza de Vaca simply states that the weather showed signs of becoming ominous as it started to rain and the sea became turbulent (79).

In spite of the numerous letters delivered to Cabeza de Vaca by messengers on canoes, Cabeza de Vaca insisted on staying with the ships while Porcalle and Pantoja were ashore (78). But the next day it rained even harder and the strong north wind was making the sea rough and perilous. As the storm strengthened, the sailors began to fear that they would lose everything if they remained anchored in this shallow port, and they were so insistent that Cabeza de Vaca finally ceded and took a canoe to the town in order to speed the business transactions.

Before leaving, Cabeza de Vaca warned the sailors, "que si el sur, con que allí suelen perderse muchas veces los navíos, ventase y se viesen en mucho peligro, diesen con los navíos al través y en parte que se salvase la gente y los caballos" (79).

In spite of Cabeza de Vaca's warnings about the south wind and his exhortation to scuttle the ships in a place where the men and the horses would be safe if the storm strengthened, three days later, the two ships were lost and sixty men and twenty horses had perished. Cabeza de Vaca described how seven or eight men, including him, held on to each other for dear life so as not to be carried away by the wind. "Andando entre los árboles, no menos temor teníamos de ellos que de las casas, porque como ellos también caían, no nos matasen debajo. En esta tempestad y peligro anduvimos toda la noche" (79–80).

This November hurricane is only the beginning of Cabeza de Vaca's narrative, Chapter 1 of a thirty-eight-chapter-long narrative of failure. The misadventures begin with too much water and soon transform water into a hostile element. Cabeza de Vaca's experience with Cuban waters differs greatly from Columbus's. In the October 28, 1492, entry, Las Casas mentions that the admiral had not experienced rough seas in the islands up until then. Where Cabeza de Vaca sees bad harbors where many ships are lost, Columbus sees a most beautiful island, "full of good harbors and deep rivers, and the sea appears as if it must never rise, because the growth of the beach reaches almost to the water, which it usually does not when the sea is rough" (119). It is almost difficult to believe that Columbus and Cabeza de Vaca are practically in the same waters!

Even in doubt, when the currents were against his ships, or when crossing the Sargasso Sea, Columbus never wavered. The eerie Sargasso Sea had to be a good sign; there were birds and there were crabs, so land had to be nearby! The result is that throughout the first voyage, the natural environment is always beautiful beyond description and welcoming enough to make a man wish to remain there forever (119). Far from being a narrative of failure, Columbus's journal of the first voyage was a discovery of nature, as well as a business plan, an effort to sell the Indies to the Spanish sovereigns, a 1492 version of venture capitalists who had to be convinced that they had spent their money wisely.

Naufragios differs from Cortés's first four letters from Mexico as well, in spite of the fact that the Narváez expedition was a green vengeance. Indeed, this was Narváez's feeble attempt to get back at Cortés for the loss of an eye as well as other humiliations, and also to quell the envy that the man who conquered the Aztec empire inspired in many other aspiring *Conquistadores*.

In the beginning of their respective enterprises, both Columbus and Cortés are boastful of their accomplishments and of everything they are seeing, discovering, and conquering. Obviously, failure ultimately awaits Columbus and Cortés. It appears that luck only accompanied Columbus on his first voyage and the various renditions of the second, third, and fourth voyages (whether they be Michele de Cuneo's, Dr. Chanca's of Columbus's, or others) could very well be considered narratives of failure. As to Cortés's Honduras expedition, it resembles Cabeza de Vaca's experiences in Florida. However, if in Greek tragedy heroes must fall from high, then both Columbus's and Cortés's narratives are tragic, as opposed to Cabeza de Vaca's *Naufragios*, which was a failure from the very beginning. If the treasurer Cabeza de Vaca wrote his narrative, it was to seek repair for eight years and five thousand miles worth of suffering. Only four out of four hundred were spared in this brutal misadventure.

Chapter 2 of *Naufragios* is short and terse. There seem to be few words to describe the weather. The heading of the chapter is Como el gobernador vino al Puerto de Xagua y trajo consigo un piloto. But the chapter is not just about how the governor came to the Port of Xagua and brought a pilot along.

On February 20, 1528, Narváez arrived in Xagua (Cienfuegos) after having spent the winter trying to recover the men, horses, morale, and ships lost to the November storms. Cabeza de Vaca, who had been in Xagua all this time, was expecting his arrival and therefore preparing the ships so the expedition could get on its way again after a three month hiatus. With him, Narváez brought a pilot named Miruelo because, as Cabeza de Vaca explains, he had been to the Río de las Palmas (that was in northern Mexico) and knew the north coast well (82).

Two days after Narváez arrived, the fleet was ready. It consisted of four hundred men, eighty horses, four ships, and a brigantine that Narváez had recently purchased in Trinidad. Another ship with forty men and twelve hoses awaited them in Havana. From the port of

Xagua, they sailed west along the southern coast of Cuba for what was supposed to be a weeklong cruise. Unfortunately, they sailed straight into the sandy shallows of the Canarreos shoals, between the island of Cuba and the Isle of Pines, where they remained stuck for a fortnight.

Cabeza de Vaca does not go into details, nor does he describe the shoals; he simply mentions that they sailed into the shoals and ran aground. It is in the October 19 entry of the journal that Columbus first mentions shoals. "I tried to go there to anchor in it so as to go ashore and see so much beauty; but the bottom was shoal and I could not anchor except far from land" (101). The next day, anchored at another port he has christened Cabo Hermono, Columbus almost sails into shoals but avoids them: "and I found all of the bottom so shallow that I could not enter or steer for the settlement" (103).

It would appear that Columbus is more adept in these uncharted waters than Narváez's entire fleet. While Narváez sails right into the sandbars, Columbus immediately realizes that it is dangerous to anchor in these islands, "except during the day, when one can see with one's own eyes where the anchor is dropped, because the bottom is all varied, one part clear and the next not so, I stood off and on at the alert all this Sunday night" (105).

In the October 24 entry, Columbus demonstrates his awareness of these waters and his ability to read them: "This bottom is all spotty, one part rocky and another sandy, because of which one cannot anchor safely except by sight" (113).

The Narváez expedition, on the other hand, remained stuck in the sandy mire until another type of bad luck came along, in the shape of a storm: "al cabo de los cuales, una tormenta del sur metió tanta agua en los bajíos, que pudimos salir, aunque no sin mucho peligro" (82). Free at last, they arrived in Guaniguanico where another storm awaited them and carried them to Cabo de Corrientes where they ran into a third storm.

In an article titled "Circulation of the Caribbean Sea," A. L. Gordon explains that water flows into the Caribbean Sea from the southeast and continues westward as the Caribbean current before turning sharply eastward and entering the Gulf of Mexico as a narrow current known as the Yucatan Current. It is in the Gulf of Mexico that a river of seawater whose discovery dates back to the Ponce de Leon expedition of 1513 originates. Dallas Murphy remarks that the exact site where Ponce de León actually landed is of no importance compared to what Ponce de León found when he turned around and tried to sail back south down the Florida coast: "The ships were making bow waves and leaving foaming wakes, but getting nowhere. In fact, they were going backwards" (22). Murphy then points out that this was the first ever record of the Gulf Stream.

According to Paul Schneider, this river of seawater known as the Gulf Stream is formed by the warming and expanding of water bottled up in the Caribbean behind the chain of the Greater Antilles Islands and that this warm water spills through the Yucatan channel where it expands and is ejected around the tip of Florida and up past the Bahamas. Consequently, "Gales from the north in late winter or early spring colliding with the current from the south can pile up enormous seas in the Yucatan Channel" (63).

After Guaniguanico and Cabo de Corrientes, the Narváez fleet reached Cabo de San Anton and sailed, always with the weather against them, until they were twelve leagues away from Havana. But they never made it to Havana because another storm blew them into the middle of the Gulf of Mexico and they remained at the mercy of these waters for over a month until they finally spotted land one month later, on April 12, 1528.

Cortés had a similar experience in these waters in February of 1519, when he set sail from Punta de San Antón, the last point of Cuba, to Cape Catoche in the Yucatan. Gómara, Cortés's secretary, writes that "after Cortés had begun the passage of the strait that lies between Cuba and Yucatan, a matter of 60 leagues, a violent northwester came up and blew the fleet off its course; the ships were scattered" (26). The difference between Cortés's experience and that of the Narváez fleet is that all of Cortés's ships save one found their way to the island of Cozumel, whereas the Narváez fleet remained at the mercy of the Gulf waters and weather for an entire month and never reached Mexico.

Schneider points out that some scholars have recently suggested that the Narváez expedition believed for that entire month that they were progressing toward Mexico and that this theory is not impossible to defend because in spite of their skills at dead reckoning, the currents off Cuba could confound even the best of navigators.

In other words, instead of reaching Mexico, they reached Florida on April 12, 1528. Cabeza de Vaca writes that they crossed, "por la costa de la Florida y llegamos a la tierra martes 12 días del mes de abril, y fuimos costeando la vía de la Florida" (82–83). This would seem to imply that they knew they had sailed east and reached the Florida coast.

However, in Chapter 4 of his narrative, Cabeza de Vaca clearly states that the pilot did not know where they were and that he was still hoping to find the Río de las Palmas in northern Mexico. "El gobernador mandó que el bergantín fuese costeando la vía de la Florida y buscase el puerto que Miruelo el piloto había dicho que sabía; más ya él lo había errado, y no sabía en que parte estábamos" (86).

Perhaps Narváez should have been better able to read these waters since he had already sailed from Cuba to the Yucatan in pursuit of Hernan Cortés eight years earlier. "To go from Havana to the Río de las Palmas, all Miruelo had to do was follow a rutter and estimate his speed, plotting all of this information on a chart to keep track of his progress across the Gulf of Mexico" (Reséndez 80). Now the question is, should Narváez and his pilot have known this much? This is followed by another question: should readers of this chronicle become overly judgmental armchair navigators and fail to take into consideration that these waters, these depths and shallows, and these weather patterns remain treacherous to this day of laptop computer navigation?

In *Admiral of the Ocean Sea*, Samuel Eliot Morison describes what must have been Columbus's experience when he navigated these exact waters on the second voyage. "Columbus, with all his good luck, missed the two greatest harbors in Cuba . . . Nipe Bay on his first voyage and Jagua Bay on the Second" (459).

It was from the port of Jagua that the Narváez expedition sailed west along the southern coast of Cuba on February 22, 1528, until they reached the Canarreos shoals where they remained stuck for a fortnight. Although Morison makes no mention of the Canarreos shoals, there is a description of the next important bay Columbus's fleet encountered after missing Jagua, the Gulf of Cochinos (Bay of Pigs) whose northeastern shore "is noted for the subterranean streams that flow down though the limestone and break out under the sea not far from the shore" (459). Morison then adds that the most trying part of this voyage was ahead after the fleet crossed the Gulf of Cazones and left the deep water for a shallow bank and encountered a white, thick, shallow sea where they could not anchor their ships.

"No wonder the men were dismayed," Morison writes. "The Admiral had boldly sailed into a tangled archipelago . . . which are difficult enough to navigate today with chart and beacons. Moreover, the people were baffled by the different colors of the water. As they came upon the shoals . . . the water at first was clear as crystal, but suddenly turned an opaque green; then after a few miles went milk white, and finally turned black as ink" (460).

Had Columbus sailed onward instead of turning around and heading back to Hispaniola, perhaps those aboard the *Capitana* would have sighted the coast of Florida as well and been the first to experience the Gulf Stream. But although Columbus's luck was starting to show signs of failing him, he was not yet that unlucky.

Reséndez writes that the pilot Miruelo could only have had a limited understanding of the Gulf Stream and its impact on the passage he was contemplating (from Havana to northern Mexico). "Because the Gulf Stream runs in a northwest to southeast direction as it exits the Gulf of Mexico, Narváez's ships would have run almost perfectly against it" (81). This is far from following the water! But Dallas Murphy points out that following the water is easier said than done (1). After having traveled for nearly two months, Reséndez is of the opinion that the Narváez and Miruelo could only be certain of direction and distance, the two most important elements of dead reckoning navigation. "They had traveled long enough to cross the Gulf of Mexico, and in the right direction. The Río de las Palmas had to be farther up along the coast" (82). Little did it matter if the sun was setting on the sea rather than on land!

Cabeza de Vaca does mention Florida several times, and there is much debate and disagreement among the members of the expedition. This could have had to do with differing opinions as to their whereabouts and to decisions as to who would explore this inhospitable land. They found a shallow bay that Narváez ordered the ships to enter when the tide was rising. Today, some scholars consider this narrow cut to be John's Pass and Boca Ciega to be the bay. Translated from the Spanish, Boca Ciega is Blind Mouth. Other scholars believe that the bay could very well have been Charlotte Harbor or Tampa Bay, an area that Juan Ponce de León had explored in June 1513.

In his description of Ponce's voyage to Florida, Herrera mentions several islets in the open sea with an entrance between them where Ponce's fleet stopped for water and firewood and had a skirmish with members of the local population. Robert Fuson, who states that these were the Gulf of Mexico islands facing Charlotte and Lee Counties in Florida, believes that Narváez made a terrible decision when he elected to leave the fleet and march inland (183). The plan was to rendezvous with the ships somewhere north of Tampa Bay.

Cabeza de Vaca writes that forty men were sent inland, six on horseback: "de los cuales poco nos podíamos aprovechar" (86). Horses were of little or no use, more of a hindrance than a help in these sandy flatlands, soggy *terra firma*. The inland expedition went north until they reached what Cabeza de Vaca described as a very large bay that seemed to go far inland and that Rolena Adorno believes to be Old Tampa Bay that the Spaniards named Bahía de la Cruz.

It was the next day, after Cabeza de Vaca and the other men returned to where the ships were stationed, that Narváez made his fateful decision to send more explorers inland while Miruelo went up the coast in search of a port that he said he knew. Although Rolena Adorno and Patrick Charles Pautz believe this port to be the Río de las Palmas, on the opposite side of the Gulf of Mexico, it could very well be that Miruelo was looking for a port on the Florida coast since he had been blown by a storm to the Florida coast sometime between 1521 and 1524. "Unfortunately, he did not bother to record the latitude nor did he even make a sketch map of the location. In other words, Miruelo did not know where he had been, and he might not have been in Florida at all" (Fuson 178).

I quote Fuson in an effort to point out how difficult, if not impossible, it is to determine where exactly Miruelo and Narváez thought they were. Perhaps the only answer is in Cabeza de Vaca's text: "y no sabía en que parte estábamos, ni adónde era el Puerto" (86). In other words, they had no idea as to where they were.

After the fleet departed, the expedition went inland, four leagues along the coast until they encountered four Indians who lead them to their village where corn could be found. But instead of corn, what they found were crates belonging to Castilian merchants and dead bodies covered with painted deer hides in each of these crates (87). "Hallamos también muestras de oro" (87). So they asked the natives in sign language where the gold came from, and the natives gestured that it was far away, in a province called Apalache.

There is no beauty and little or no efforts to describe this land. It was on the first of May 1528 that Narváez decided that three hundred explorers should walk inland and that the ships should travel along the coast in the direction of the Río de las Palmas until they found it. Cabeza de Vaca urged Narváez not to leave the ships unless they were in a secure and populated port and argued that not only did the pilots not know where they were, that the horses were of no use and that they were traveling mute, but also that they knew nothing about this land and were ill prepared for this expedition (88). "Mi parecer era que de debía embarcar y ir a buscar Puerto y tierra que fuese mejor para poblar, pues la que habíamos visto, en sí era tan despoblada y tan pobre, cuanto nunca en aquellas partes se había hallado" (88).

From this point on, Cabeza de Vaca constantly uses the adjective *pobre* to describe this land, without explaining how or why he considers it to be poor. The reader of the *Naufragios* could surmise that this land so strange is *poor* in terms of agriculture, since the explorers find very little corn or, for that matter, anything else growing in the marshes. It is also poor in terms of cities, since they have not come across anything vaguely resembling Cortés's Mexico-Tenochtitlán. Often, Cabeza de Vaca alludes to this land being underpopulated, so it could be poor in terms of souls. But Cabeza de Vaca also calls this land *mala*, bad, evil, and the people wretched, an impossible land, impossible to dwell in it, and impossible to escape from it (103, 110)

Reséndez writes that the verdant expanse of the Florida interior "must have appeared to them like yet another kind of sea; the terrain was flat, endless, and, except occasional rivers and marshes, mostly featureless" (91).

Immediately, Cabeza de Vaca fears the inland expedition, but he went on this expedition all the same, preferring to risk his life than to put his honor in jeopardy (90). Very soon, Cabeza de Vaca's misgivings prove to be correct: this is a bad place.

May 1, no food, no souls, no houses, no populated areas, and at the same time this land so strange is so far away from what William Rueckert describes as an ecological nightmare "of a monstrously overpopulated, almost completely polluted, all but totally humanized planet" (Rutherford, 113). A nightmare all the same, if there are rivers, for Cabeza de Vaca, they are hurdles: "lo pasamos con muy gran trabajo a nado y en balsas: detuvimos un día en pasarlo, que traía muy gran corriente" (91).

After having spent a day fighting against the great currents of this river, the exhausted and hungry expedition finally comes across as many as two hundred natives who informed them that they were not too far away from the sea. So Narváez sent Cabeza and forty other men on foot to search for the port, and by noon of that same day they had set out, they came across sandbars that seemed to go far inland, and they followed them, up to their knees in water, constantly stepping on oyster shells that cut their feet. John Hoffmeister writes that the Ten Thousand Islands on Florida's West Coast geologically began from offshore mounds of quartz sand deposited by a longshore current from the north. "Upon these mounds, extensive oyster beds were formed in favorable places. When the mounds were built up to the intertidal zone, mangroves established themselves and islands were formed" (120).

When the explorers returned to the same river they had crossed with so much difficulty a few days before, they found themselves too ill equipped to cross it again. Adorno and Pautz are of the opinion that the Spaniards believed that this river was the Río de las Palmas or the Río Pánuco (61). Reséndez adds that the sight of this body of water must have been as beautiful as it was disorienting, for no European map showed a bay close to the Río de las Palmas (85). Disorienting perhaps, but nowhere does Cabeza de Vaca mention beauty, and if every place has a story to tell, this place seems to be misleading and betraying the intruders who return to where they had crossed the river beforehand and followed it downstream in search of a port that, alas, could not be found: only knee-deep water awaited them.

On June 17, the Spaniards were still walking either in search of Apalache or of the evasive port in Northern Mexico. Again, they came across natives who offered to direct them to Apalache, and again, a river is but an obstacle: it is either too deep, too wide, or too fast. "Aquella noche llegamos a un río, y la corriente muy recia" (93). They did not dare cross it on foot and proceeded to build a canoe instead. The crossing took an entire day and also a life. The current swept Juan Velásquez off his horse, and the two vanished in the waters. Many scholars believe this river to be the Suwanee River.

Reséndez writes that the terrain began to change after a month and a half of nothing but marshes. Suddenly, the trees were taller, the air cooler, and the climate more temperate (95). Cabeza de Vaca described this as "tierra muy trabajosa de andar y maravillosa de ver, porque en ella hay muy grandes montes y los árboles a maravilla altos, y son tantos los que están caídos en el suelo, que nos embaraz-aban el camino" (94). Twice in the same sentence, Cabeza de Vaca uses either the word *marvel* or a derivative of *marvel*. The land, in the north central portion of present-day Florida, between the Aucilla and Apalachicola Rivers, is marvelous to behold and the trees are marvelously tall. It is difficult to determine if Cabeza de Vaca is experiencing awe at the sight of this strange land, for in the same sentence he immediately mentions how their progress is hindered by the great number of the marvelously tall trees that have fallen to the ground. Many of the trees still standing had been severed in two by lightning from the great storms and tempests. Even this land so unloved by Cabeza de Vaca and his companions seems to suffer from too much water, and the Spaniards, instead of awe, only appear to be experiencing fatigue, thirst, and hunger.

By the end of Chapter 6, this place has definitely become a bad place, in the sense that it always seems to be preventing the expedi-tion from making headway. Cabeza de Vaca writes that there are thick woods and great groves and lagoons where there are fallen trees that cause obstructions (96).

Chapter 7 begins with a description of the land as being flat and composed of sand and *tierra firme* (firm earth, solid ground). In the open woods, there are large trees such as walnut trees, laurels, liq-uidambars, cedars, savins, evergreen oaks, pines, oaks, and palmet-tos. It is interesting to note that at this moment in time, in 1528, explorers and conquerors are no longer at a loss for words when describing the American landscape. Columbus expressed his sorrow at not knowing, whereas Cabeza de Vaca seems to know what every tree is called. The trees are no longer very green, or very tall, or either like or unlike those of Castile in the springtime; now the trees all have names.

As to the water, it is ever present and always impossible. The lagoons are deep, they have sandy bottoms, and they are difficult to cross, "parte por tantos árboles como por ellas están caídos" (97).

There are also fields of maize and pastures for cattle. And the region is cold. One year after the expedition had departed from Spain, they reached Apalache, an area in the Florida panhandle between the Wakulla and Apalachicola Rivers. Between 1000 AD and 1600 AD, this region was inhabited by what present-day scholars refer to as Mississippian societies who had left small, powerful chiefdoms behind after their decline (Reséndez 98–99). It was at an Apalache chiefdom that the explorers stayed from June 25 to July 19 or 20, 1528, at which time they decided to depart because the Indians were continually attacking them wherever they went to get water. "Y esto desde las lagunas, y tan a salvo, que no los podíamos ofender, porque metidos en ellas nos flechaban" (99). Here, Cabeza de Vaca is making the natives go through a process of *naturalization*, for they have become as treacherous, as inhospitable, and as impossible as their natural environment.

Fleeing the wrath of the natives, the explorers crossed the same lagoons where they had been attacked on the day of their departure, and by the end of the second day they came to a lagoon that was very difficult to cross because the water was chest-high and the presence of many fallen trees (99). Again, the natives become one with the environment, for they choose to attack the explorers just when they are chest-deep in the lagoon and unable to defend themselves. The natives and their environment seem to be working together to repel the intruder.

After a few men and horses succumbed to the natives' arrows, the governor ordered the horsemen to dismount because the horses had become such a hindrance. Even the good weapons they carried were of no use compared to the arrows that could pierce oaks as thick as a man's lower leg through and through. Cabeza de Vaca used the word marvel to express the natives' skill at shooting arrows after having seen an arrow that had pierced the base of a poplar tree the depth of two or three inches (100). A few sentences later Cabeza de Vaca uses the word *maravilla* to describe the strength and the height of the natives who have become one with this inhospitable land. Paul Schneider points out that with their weak language skills, the explorers asked captive Apalaches where they should go to find food and gold. The Apalaches pointed to the sea, to a town called Aute. The problem was that there was no getting to Aute without crossing a vast swamp (153).

After nine days of travel under constant attack by the native population, the explorers found an empty village where they rested for two days before setting out to look for the sea again and discovering a great river that they named Río de la Magdalena, which could very well be the Aucilla, the Saint Marks, or the Ochlockonee, according to Adorno and Pautz (69).

The following day, they reached what seemed a bay or the entrance to the sea where they found many oysters. For the first and perhaps only time, Cabeza de Vaca mentions pleasure as well as gratitude for having found a place such as this: "con que la gente holgó; y dimos

muchas gracias a Dios por habernos traídos allí" (102). But this happiness and gratitude are short lived, for the men sent to reconnoiter
the coast return with news that the bays go too far inland for passage
and that the sea is very far. At this point, many of the explorers are ill,
including Narváez. Schneider describes them as being in a soggy
nowhere, chest-high in hell (154). Even when the wounded, hungry,
thirsty, feverish expedition finally finds salt water, they are still "in
this cursed place, there was nothing but shallows and mudflats" (161).

Being in Aute, or in hell, seems about as difficult as leaving Aute,
or hell. Paul Schneider points out that Aute was not a single town,
but rather a collection of villages on the Wakulla River, south of Tallahassee, in what is now the St. Mark's National Wildlife Refuge
(159). The expedition was faced with the impossibility of being there
and the impossibility of getting away from there. The journey was
difficult to the extreme, many of the men, including Narváez, were
suffering from an unnamed illness.

There was no going forward, no going back. Cabeza de Vaca writes
that anyone could guess what could happen in a land so strange, and
so evil, and so lacking in everything (103). Aware that some of the
explorers were considering abandoning the expedition, Narváez seeks
their opinion about "tan mala tierra, para poder salir de ella" (104).
Cabeza de Vaca describes the ailing explorers' desperate attempts to
leave this bad place where their sins had taken them (105). Instead of
reifying or mystifying the explorers, the horses have begun to serve
other purposes. In their desperate attempt to leave this bad place, the
horses' hides are cured in order to make vessels for water (105–6). By
September 22, all the horses had been eaten (106).

Beatríz Pastor writes that in a narrative discourse of failure such
as this one, the American natural environment is always hostile
and threatening. It is the most formidable enemy. Nature becomes
extreme and excessive, and the European explorer feels alienated in
this destructive place that he knows nothing about (204). Consequently, the question is, does biophobia have a place in environ-
mental writing or in a corpus of ecocriticism?

The answer is yes. By taking the reader through brackish inlets in
chest-deep water and into shallow and dangerous inlets that extend
very far inland, Cabeza de Vaca reanimates a nature that has long
ceased to exist. Ironically, there is always water, too much water, and
yet the more water there is, the more their thirst increases. So much
so that they are finally obliged to drink salt water: "la sed crecía y el
agua nos mataba" (108). They were thirsty, and at the same time
water was killing them. But the reader is as thirsty for a time when
nature was still so formidable.

WORKS CITED

Adorno, Rolena, with Patrick Charles Pautz. *Álvar Núñez Cabeza de Vaca: His Account, His Life, and the Expedition of Panfilo de Narváez*. Lincoln: University of Nebraska Press, 1999.

Cabeza de Vaca, Álvar Núñez. *Naufragios*. Ed. Juan Francisco Maura. Madrid: Cátedra, 2005.

Cortés, Hernán. *Letters from Mexico*. Trans. Anthony Pagden. New Haven: Yale University Press, 1986.

Fuson, Robert H. *Juan Ponce de León and the Spanish Discovery of Puerto Rico and Florida*. Blacksburg, VA: McDonald & Woodward, 2000.

Hoffmeister, John Edward. *Land from the Sea: The Geologic Story of South Florida*. Coral Gables: University of Miami, 1974.

Morison, Samuel Eliot. *Admiral of the Ocean Sea: A Life of Christopher Columbus*. Boston: Little, Brown, 1942.

Murphy, Dallas. *To Follow the Water*. New York: Perseus Books, 2007.

Pastor, Beatríz. *Discursos narrativos de la conquista: Mistificación y emergencia*. Hanover, NH: Ediciones del Norte, 1988.

Popul Vuh. Trans. Dennis Tedlock. New York: Simon and Schuster, 1985.

Reséndez, Andrés. *A Land So Strange: The Epic Journey of Cabeza de Vaca*. New York: Perseus Books, 2007.

Rutherford, John. *Breve historia del pícaro preliterato*. Vigo, Spain: Universidad de Vigo, 2001.

Schneider, Paul. *Brutal Journey: Cabeza de Vaca and the First Epic Crossing of North America*. New York: Henry Holt, 2007.

Álvar Núñez Cabeza de Vaca:
A Chronology

1485–92   Álvar Núñez Cabeza de Vaca is born in Jerez de las Fron-
           tera, Spain. This is a period of intense transformation in
           the newly forming Spanish nation: the Jews are expelled
           from the Iberian Peninsula by the Catholic royalty, Isa-
           bella of Castille and Ferdinand of Aragón; Granada, the
           last Muslim caliphate in Iberia, is conquered by Spain;
           Christopher Columbus sails across the Atlantic to land in
           the New World; and Antonio de Nebrija, a Salamanca
           philologist, publishes the first grammar of the Spanish
           language.
1503–27   Cabeza de Vaca works for four different dukes of Medina
           Sidonia. The scattered biographical records of this period
           show him as loyal and perspicacious and offer a glimpse
           of his voyeurism. He fights in Bologna and Ravena in
           1512, on the side of the Catholic royalty, and in support
           of Pope Julius II. Finally, the chronicler participates
           in the repression of the *comunero* movement. Probably
           around 1520, Cabeza de Vaca marries María Marmolejo,
           a descendant of a *converso* family.
1527–36   The *Adelantado* Pánfilo de Narváez embarks on an
           expedition to Florida. Cabeza de Vaca serves as treasurer.
           After a power struggle, Cabeza de Vaca takes his own
           route. He survives shipwrecks and other natural and
           human disasters and, along with three other Spaniards—
           the Moroccan slave Estevanico as well as Andrés Doran-
           tes and Alonso de Castillo Maldonado—he wanders from
           Florida to Texas, New Mexico, Arizona, and finally to
           northern Mexico. A mix of travelog and ethnographic
           reflection, the journey places him in landscapes previ-
           ously unseen by any European and exposes him to
           numerous native tribes, which he describes in his chron-
           icle drafted in 1538 and popularly known in Spanish as
           La relación or *Naufragios*, and in English as the *Chronicle*

of the Narváez Expedition. Two other accounts of Cabeza de Vaca's serendipitous travels are available, one by Gonzalo Fernando de Oviedo y Ortiz, the other by Fray Marcos de Niza.

1537–40   Cabeza de Vaca returns to Spain. Soon after, the first version of *La relación* circulates in manuscript, generating much interest among readers and especially explorers. He is named *Adelantado* to the River Plate, located today between Argentina and Uruguay. On November 2, he sails to South America.

1541–45   He exercises his duties as *Adelantado* in the River Plate. Eventually, though, his compatriots plot to bring him down and Cabeza de Vaca is arrested on charges of corruption and is in jail for more than a year. He is returned to the Iberian Peninsula in chains on March 7, 1545.

1542   The first version of *La relación*, printed in Zamora while Cabeza de Vaca is in Paraguay, circulates, generating much interest among readers and especially explorers.

1545   A legal case against Cabeza de Vaca takes place. According to his secretary, Pero Hernández, Cabeza de Vaca is imprisoned and on trial by the Corte for eight years. Eventually he is released and his reputation is restored. He revises from memory the *Comentarios*, a chronicle of his years as *Adelantado* in South America thought to have been written by Pero Hernández.

1555   A joint edition of *La relación* and *Comentarios*, with the former slightly amended and retitled *Naufragios* (Shipwrecks), appears in Valladolid, Spain. It is believed that Cabeza de Vaca lived in Spain at the time.

1559   Probable date of Cabeza de Vaca's death. He appears to be buried in Jerez de la Frontera, in the same monastery where some of his ancestors were laid to rest. Shortly before, England and Spain became allies in the war against France.

Selected Bibliography

• indicates works included or excerpted in this Norton Critical Edition

Original Editions, Spanish Editions, and English Translations

• Adorno, Rolena, with Patrick Charles Pautz, eds. *Álvar Núñez Cabeza de Vaca: His Account, His Life, and the Expedition of Pánfilo de Narváez*. 3 vols. Lincoln: University of Nebraska Press, 1999.

Augenbraum, Harold, revised and annotated, based on the Fanny Bandelier translation. *Chronicle of the Narváez Expedition*. Introd. by Ilan Stavans. New York and London: Penguin Classics, 2002.

• Bandelier, Fanny, trans. *The Journey of Álvar Núñez Cabeza de Vaca, and His Companions from Florida to the Pacific, 1528–36*. New York: Barnes, 1904. [Includes the report of Father Marcos de Niza and the letter from the Viceroy Mendoza].

———. *The Narrative of Álvar Núñez Cabeza de Vaca*. Trans. Gerald Theisen. Barre, MA: Imprint Society, 1972. [With Oviedo's version of the lost Joint Report presented to the Audiencia de Santo Domingo.]

Barreda, Trinidad, ed. *Naufragios*. Madrid: Alianza Editorial, 1985.

Cabeza de Vaca, Álvar Núñez. *Relación que dio Álvar Núñez Cabeza de Vaca a lo acaesido en las Indias en la armada donde iva por governador Pánfilo de Narváez . . .* Zamora, Spain: Agustín de Paz y Juan Picador, 1542.

———. *La relación y comentarios del gobernador Álvar Núñez Cabeça de Vaca de lo acaescido en las dos jornadas que hizo a las Indias*. Valladolid, Spain, 1555.

Covey, Cyclone, trans. *Adventures in the Unknown Interior of America*. Albuquerque: University of New Mexico Press, 1984.

———. *Cabeza de Vaca's Adventures in the Unknown Interior of America*. New York: Collier Books, 1961.

Favata, Martin A., with José B. Fernández, eds. *The Account: Álvar Núñez Cabeza de Vaca's Relación*. Houston: Arte Público Press, 1993.

———. eds. *La relación: o, Naufragios*. Potomac, MD: Scripta Humanistica, 1986.

Ferrando, Roberto, ed. *Naufragios y Comentarios*. Madrid: Historia 16, 1984.

Hakluyt Society, trans. *The Conquest of the River Plate: 1535–1555*. Vol. 2: *The Commentaries of Álvar Núñez Cabeza de Vaca*. London: Hakluyt Society, 1891.

Hallenbeck, Cleve, trans. *Álvar Núñez Cabeza de Vaca: The Journey and Route of the First European to Cross the Continent of North America, 1534–1536*. Glendale, CA: Arthur H. Clark, 1940.

Hodge, Frederick, with Theodore H. Lewis. "The Narrative of Álvar Núñez Cabeza de Vaca." In *Spanish Explorers in the Southern United States, 1528–1543: The Narrative of Álvar Núñez Cabeza de Vaca*. Trans. Thomas Buckingham Smith. New York: Charles Scribner's Sons, 1907.

Maura, Juan Francisco, ed. *Naufragios*. Madrid: Cátedra, 1998.

Peña, Enrique, ed. *Relación de Álvar Núñez Cabeza de Vaca*. Buenos Aires: Jacobo Pauser, 1907.

Pupo-Walker, Enrique, ed. *Castaways*. Trans. Frances M. López-Morillas. Berkeley: University of California Press, 1993.
————. *Los naufragios*. Madrid: Editorial Castalia, 1992.
Sánchez, Luis Alberto, ed. *Naufragios y Comentarios*. Mexico: Premiá Editores, 1969.
Smith, Thomas Buckingham, trans. *The Narrative of Álvar Núñez Cabeza de Vaca*. Washington, DC, 1851.
————. *Relación de Álvar Núñez Cabeza de Vaca*. New York: J. Munsell, 1871.
Vedia, Enrique, ed. *Naufragios de Álvar Núñez Cabeza de Vaca y relación de la jornada que hizo a la Florida con el adelantado Pánfilo de Narváez*. Madrid: Imprenta y Estereotipia de M. Rivadeneyra, 1852.

Criticism

Adorno, Rolena. "The Discursive Encounter of Spain and America: The Authority of Eyewitness Testimony in Writing History." *William and Mary Quarterly* 49 (Apr. 1992): 210–28.
————. "The Negotiation of Fear in Cabeza de Vaca's *Naufragios*," *Representations* 33 (1991): 1963–99. [Reprinted in *New World Encounters*. Ed. Stephen Greenblatt (48–84). Berkeley: University of California Press, 1993.]
————. "Peaceful Conquest and Law in the *Relación* (Account) of Álvar Núñez Cabeza de Vaca." In *Coded Encounters: Writing, Gender, and Ethnicity in Colonial Latin America*. Ed. Francisco Javier Cevallos-Candau et al. (75–86). Amherst: University of Massachusetts Press, 1994.
Ahren, Maureen. "The Cross and the Gourd: The Appropriation of Ritual Signs in the *Relación* of Álvar Núñez Cabeza de Vaca and Fray Marcos de Niza." In *Early Images of the Americas*. Ed. Jerry M. Williams and Robert E. Lewis (215–44). Tucson: University of Arizona Press, 1993.
Belloguín, Andrés García. *Vida y hazañas de Álvar Núñez Cabeza de Vaca*. Madrid: Editorial Voluntad, 1928.
Bannon, John Francis. *The Spanish Borderland Frontiers, 1513–1821*. Albuquerque: University of New Mexico Press, 1974.
• Bishop, Morris. *The Odyssey of Cabeza de Vaca*. New York: Century, 1933.
Carreño, Antonio. "*Naufragios* de Álvar Núñez Cabeza de Vaca: Una retórica de la crónica colonia." *Revista Iberoamericana* 53 (July–Sept. 1987): 499–516.
Chipman, Donald E. "In Search of Cabeza de Vaca's Route across Texas: An Historiographical Survey." *Southwestern Historical Quarterly* 91 (1987): 127–48.
Coopwood, Bethel. "The Route of Cabeza de Vaca." *Texas State Historical Association Quarterly* 3 (1899–1990): 108–40, 177–208, 229–64; 4 (1900 01): 1–32.
Davenport, Harbert, with Joseph K. Wells. "The First Europeans in Texas, 1526–36." *Southwestern Historical Quarterly* Oct 2 XXII (1918–19), 111–42, 205, 259.
Delgado-Gómez, Angel. *Spanish Historical Writing about the New World*. Providence, RI: John Carter Brown, 1992.
Fernández, José. *Álvar Núñez Cabeza de Vaca: The Forgotten Chronicler*. Miami: Ediciones Universal, 1975.
————. "Opposing Views of La Florida: Álvar Núñez Cabeza de Vaca and El Inca Garcilaso de la Vega." *The Florida Historical Quarterly* 59 (1976): 170–80.
González, Alejandro Acosta. "Álvar Núñez Cabeza de Vaca: Náufrago y huérfano." *Cuadernos Americanos* 9, no. 1 (1995): 165–99.
Hanke, Lewis. *Aristotle and the American Indians*. Bloomington and London: Indiana University Press, 1975.
Howard, David. *Conquistador in Chains: Cabeza de Vaca and the Indians of the Americas*. Tuscaloosa; University of Alabama Press, 1997.

• Krieger, Alex D. *We Came Naked and Barefoot: The Journey of Cabeza de Vaca across North America.* Ed. Margaret H. Krieger. Austin: University of Texas Press, 2002.

Lacalle, Carlos. *Noticia sobre Álvar Núñez Cabeza de Vaca: Hazañas americanas de un caballero andaluz.* Madrid: Instituto de Cultura Hispánica, 1961.

Lafayete, Jacques. "Los milagros de Álvar Núñez Cabeza de Vaca (1527–1536)." In *Mesías, cruzadas y utopías: El judeo-cristianismo en las sociedades hispánicas* (65–84). Mexico: Fondo de Cultura Económica, 1984.

Lewis, Robert E. "Los *Naufragios* de Álvar Núñez: Historia y ficción." *Revista Iberoamericana* 48, nos. 120–21 (July–Dec. 1982): 681–94.

Long, Daniel. *Interlinear to Cabeza de Vaca: His Relations from Florida to the Pacific, 1528–1536.* Santa Fe, NM: Writers' Editions, 1939.

McGann, Thomas. "The Ordeal of Cabeza de Vaca," *American Heritage* 12, 1 (December 1960): 32–7, 78–82.

de Madariaga, Salvador. *The Rise of the Spanish Empire.* New York: Free Press, 1947.

Maura, Juan Francisco. "Veracidad en los *Naufragios*: La técnica narrativa de Álvar Núñez Cabeza de Vaca." *Revista Iberoamericana* 61 (1965): 187–95.

Milanich, Jerald T., with Susan Milbrath, eds. *First Encounters: Spanish Explorers in the Caribbean and the United States, 1492–1570.* Gainsville: University Press of Florida, 1989.

Molloy, Sylvia. "Alternidad y reconocimiento en los *Naufragios* de Álvar Núñez Cabeza de Vaca." *Nueva Revista de Filología Hispánica* 35 (1987): 425–49.

Morison, Samuel Eliot. *The European Discovery of America: The Southern Voyages, 1492–1616.* Oxford: Oxford University Press, 1974.

Niza, Fray Marcos, "Relación on the Pánfilo de Narváez Expedition." In *The Journey of Álvar Núñez Cabeza de Vaca, and His Companions from Florida to the Pacific, 1528–36.* Trans. Fanny Bandelier. New York: A. S. Barnes, 1904. [Includes the report of Father Marcos de Niza and the letter from the Viceroy Mendoza.] 203–31

• Oviedo y Valdéz, Gonzalo Fernández. *The Journey of the Vaca Party: The Account of the Narváez Expedition, 1528–1536, as Related by Gonzalo Fernández de Oviedo y Valdés.* Trans. Basil Hedrick and Carroll L. Riley. Carbondale: University Museum, Southern Illinois University, 1974. [The Joint Report.]

Pastor, Beatriz. *Discursos narrativos de la conquista: Mitificación y emergencia.* Hanover, NH: Ediciones del Norte, 1988.

Ponton, Brownie, with Bates H. McFarland. "Álvar Núñez Cabeza de Vaca: A Preliminary Report on His Wanderings in Texas." *Quarterly at the Texas state Historical Association* 1.3 (1898): 166–86.

Pupo-Walker, Enrique. "Pesquisas para una nueva lectura de los *Naufragios* de Álvar Núñez Cabeza de Vaca." *Revista Iberoamericana* 53 (July–Sept. 1987): 517–39.

Spitta, Silvia. "Chamanismo y cristianidad: Una lectura lógica intercultural de los *Naufragios* de Cabeza de Vaca." *Revista de Crítica Literaria Latinoamericana* 19. no. 38 (1993): 317–30.

Stavans, Ilan, ed. *Becoming Americans: Four Centuries of Immigrant Writing.* New York: Library of America, 2010.

———. *The Hispanic Condition.* New York: HarperCollins, 1996, 2001.

———. *Imagining Columbus: The Literary Voyage:* New York: Palgrave, 1992, 2001.

———, "1536, July 24: Álvar Núñez Cabeza de Vaca," *A New Literary History of America.* eds. Greil Marcus and Werner Sollars. Cambridge, MA and London: Harvard University Press, 2009: 11–15.

———, general ed. *The Norton Anthology of Latino Literature.* New York: Norton, 2011.

———, ed. *The Oxford Book of Latin American Essays.* New York and London: Oxford University Press, 1997.

Swan, Gladys. "Do You Believe in Cabeza de Vaca?" *Kenyon Review* 12 (1990): 151–59.

Wagner, Henry R. *The Spanish Southwest, 1542–1794*. Albuquerque, NM: Quivira Society, 1937.

Weber, David J. *The Spanish Frontier in North America*. New Haven, CT: Yale University Press, 1992.

———. "Sobre el legado histórico de los *Naufragios* de Álvar Núñez Cabeza de Vaca." *Revista de Estudios Hispánicos* (1992): 75–78.

Rabasa, José. *Writing Violence on the Northern Frontier: the Historiography of Sixteenth Century New Mexico and Florida and the Legacy of the Conquest*. Durham, NC: Duke University Press, 2000.

• Reséndez, Andrés. *A Land So Strange: The Epic Journey of Cabeza de Vaca*. New York: Basic Books, 2007.

• Rivera-Barnes, Beatríz, with Jerry Hoeg, eds. *Reading and Writing the Latin American Landscape*. New York: Palgrave Macmillan, 2009.

Rodman, Maia. *Odyssey of Courage: The Story of Álvar Núñez Cabeza de Vaca*. New York: Atheneum, 1965.

• Schneider, Paul. *Brutal Journey: The Epic Story of the First Crossing of North America*. New York: Henry Holt, 2006.

de Sopranis, Hipólito Sando. "Datos para el estudio de Álvar Núñez Cabeza de Vaca." *Revista de Indias* 27 (1947): 69–102.